The rough guide to

AMSTERDAM & HOLLAND

WITH A CHAPTER ON LUXEMBOURG AND SELECTED BELGIAN CITIES

Researched by

MARTIN DUNFORD, JACK HOLLAND, EVE HASLETT AND CHRIS RICKETTS

With additional accounts by
Sue Weightman, John Rudge,
Abi Daruvalla and Mark Fuller

Written and edited by

MARTIN DUNFORD AND JACK HOLLAND

Routledge & Kegan Paul
London, Boston, Melbourne and Henley

Thanks to: Mark Ellingham, Sue and Andy, Arnold
Petie, Caroline Simcoe-Gerson (NNTO London),
Odette Taminau (VVV Amsterdam)

First published in 1984
by Routledge & Kegan Paul plc
14 Leicester Square, London WC2H 7PH, England
9 Park Street, Boston, Mass. 02108, USA
464 St Kilda Road, Melbourne,
Victoria 3004, Australia and
Broadway House, Newtown Road,
Henley-on-Thames, Oxon RG9 1EN, England

Phototypeset in Linotron Sabon and Helvetica
by Input Typesetting Ltd, London
Printed in Great Britain
by Cox & Wyman Ltd
Reading, Berks

Library of Congress Cataloging in Publication Data

Dunford, Martin.
   The rough guide to Amsterdam and Holland,
with Belgian cities and Luxembourg.
   (The Rough guides)
   Includes index.
   1. Amsterdam (Netherlands)—Description—Guide-books.
2. Benelux countries—Description and travel—Guide-books.
I. Holland, Jack, 1959–   . II. Title.   III. Series.
DJ411.A53D86   1984   914.92'3   84–6842

British Library CIP Data available

ISBN 0–7102–0158–3

The Rough Guide to
AMSTERDAM
& HOLLAND

WITH A CHAPTER ON LUXEMBOURG AND SELECTED BELGIAN CITIES

MARTIN DUNFORD, JACK HOLLAND,
EVE HASLETT AND CHRIS RICKETTS

Other available rough guides include
**SPAIN, PORTUGAL, MOROCCO, TUNISIA,
GREECE, MEXICO** and **PERU.**

Forthcoming:
**ITALY, FRANCE, EASTERN EUROPE,
ISRAEL** and **YUGOSLAVIA.**

Series Editor
MARK ELLINGHAM

FREE MAPS AND INFORMATION

It's a good idea to pick up what free information you can either in advance from the **Netherlands National Tourist Office (NNTO)** or, once you're in the country, from the VVV (**Tourist Information Centres**). NNTO offices, in most major capitals; including

BRITAIN   143, New Bond Street, London W1.
AUSTRALIA   Suite 302, 5 Elizabeth Street, Sydney NSW 20000.
CANADA   327 Bay Street, Toronto, Ontario.
USA   576, Fifth Avenue, New York NY 10036.

As well as the usual glossy bumf they do a good free map of Holland and adequate plans of Amsterdam, Rotterdam and The Hague; their *Just for You* pamphlet has some useful tips for young people on a budget.

The best **large-scale maps** of particular areas are those produced by the **ANWB** (a sort of equivalent to our own AA): available from McCarta Ltd (122 Kings Cross Road, London WC1 price £2.35) though you pay less if you buy them in Holland, where you can get them at most bookshops. You should find everything you need on our **town plans**, but in case you want a really detailed map the **Falk** ones are the best – £1.30 from the NNTO but again cheaper if you wait until you arrive.

The **VVV** have offices all over the country and are there to provide local tourist info, book hotels, etc. Unlike the NNTO, with whom they have a certain rivalry, they are a private organisation and so charge for just about everything, sometimes giving the impression they're more out to make a profit than actually to help people. Earnest advice should often be treated with a certain amount of scepticism – the VVV cater for people with money and sometimes find it hard to conceive of anyone travelling on a shoestring – however, they can be useful for lists of rooms, walking tours and rough town plans.

Both the **Belgium** and **Luxembourg** tourist people have offices in London, and can provide you with invaluable maps and much other information.
Belgian National Tourist Office   38, Dover Street, London W1.
Luxembourg Tourist Office   36/37, Piccadilly, London, W1.

CONTENTS

Part one BASICS
1

Costs and where to go / Getting there / Red tape / Sleeping / Eating and drinking / Getting around / Health and insurance / Cash and communications / Galleries, museums and churches / Public holidays / Festivals / Finding work and a roof / Books / Other things / Dutch terms: a glossary

Part two THE GUIDE
17

Part three CONTEXTS
175

for Margaret and Ann

Part one
BASICS

COSTS AND WHERE TO GO

There's no escaping the fact that Holland is expensive: even staying in the cheapest rooms and living frugally you'll have to watch your budget closely. But it can be done – follow our guidelines and you can take in Amsterdam and elsewhere without spending a fortune.

If money's tight, £2 is about rock bottom price for a **room** in Amsterdam. Out of the capital it's going to cost from £1.50 for a Sleep-In, £5–£7 each for a pension. Budget **eating** is best done in the *Mensa* restaurants of university towns, but ubiquitous fast food places and pizza parlours provide reliable stand-bys – expect to pay around £2. **Drinking** can be expensive in bars, but works out absurdly cheap if you buy from supermarkets – Dutch beer costs as little as 50p a litre. **Getting around** is easiest by train, cheaper by bus and cheapest by hitching, but given the short distances nothing should leave you too much out of pocket. A train ticket from Vlissingen to Amsterdam, perhaps the longest single journey you'll make, costs less than £8. Add this all together and you can get by on £6–£7 a day.

All this makes it silly to just stick to the capital – get out and see the rest of the country. Perhaps nowhere as much as Holland are so many vividly distinct towns squeezed into so small a space, and great galleries and museums punctuate travel everywhere – by buying a **museumcard** you'll get into most of them free. The **Randstad** towns, within easiest reach of Amsterdam, are the obvious target, but if you're after a bit of peace, make for the **northern islands** – bleak, desolate and still very largely untouched. Heading south, **Limburg** is the place to stop: green and wooded, its gently rolling hills form a world apart from the bulb fields and windmills of the north. Remember, the VVV only plug the popular places, and it's a good idea to take time discovering the towns off the well-trodden tourist path – **Leeuwarden** and **Groningen** are excellent examples. Each of Holland's provinces has an historic and subtly different character, which we've summarised in the respective chapters. But it's **Amsterdam** that's the great pull: it could take you weeks to discover all its facets and peculiarities – hopefully the pointers we've given will help. . . .

GETTING THERE

Train, coach and boat
Four companies **sail** to Holland: *Sealink* have morning and evening sailings between Harwich and the Hook of Holland, *Olau Lines* at similar times from Sheerness to Vlissingen – on the bottom prong of Zeeland and more convenient if you're heading for the south of the country. Whichever you choose, prices are fairly standard – around £16 single and double that for an ordinary return. Both routes take about eight hours, though in winter the North Sea is unpredictable and it can take longer. Rates for motor vehicles vary with the time of day and the seasons: with *Sealink*, prices for cars range from £16 off-season to £40 in the busier months (plus a charge per passenger), and morning sailings are always quite a bit cheaper than evening ones. Five-day excursions are available for between £75 and £140, which covers a car and four people. Motorbikes travel

for a flat rate of £8 all year round. Ferries also run from Hull to Rotterdam (Europort) and Great Yarmouth to Scheveningen, both of which, if you live in the north of England, could work out a better deal. *North Sea Ferries'* nightly Rotterdam service takes fourteen hours and costs around £30 single, which includes breakfast and an evening meal. *Norfolk Line* runs four services a day to Scheveningen and it takes about eight hours. Prices are similarly dear but again include meals.

Whatever way you go, *hitching* won't save as much money as it used to. No longer can you ride across gratis in a lorry driver's cab as the authorities on both sides of the water have cracked down, making drivers pay for any unauthorised passengers.

If you're not driving or hitching, an all-in London-Amsterdam **train** or coach ticket is better. Those under 26 can get a *Transalpino* rail ticket for a mere £15 single, £30 return – on sale at most major travel agents; if you're older, ordinary British Rail fares from London's Victoria Station (via Harwich) vary from £27 single (£54 return) to £19 single (£38 return) if you travel during the day. **Coaches** are a slightly cheaper alternative: *Grey-Green, Miracle Bus* and *Supabus* all do London-Amsterdam tickets at £19 single and £34 return, once again it's less expensive if you're under 26. These often go via Belgium and are much the best bet if you want to spend as little time on a boat as possible.

For a **short break**, *Sealink* do a five-day return fare for £31 (on a day sailing) or a 52-hour excursion ticket to the Hook for just £18. Numerous holiday packages are available, and for full details you should apply to the NNTO, but to give you some idea of prices: Sealink's Mini-Break costs £45 and includes one night's B&B.

By plane
If you shop around a bit and are flexible on dates, it's possible to get return **flights from London** for as little as £60 – check the London magazines *Time Out* and *LAM* and the back pages of the Sunday newspapers. For little more than the price of a standard British Rail return, it can be well worth the extra hassle. Otherwise, scheduled Pex/Superpex returns with *British Airways* or *KLM* can be had as cheaply as £82, again depending how adaptable you can be – the usual demand is that you spend Saturday night abroad.

For **Americans** the best option for this part of Europe continues to be *Icelandair* to Luxembourg: just a few hours from Amsterdam and as good a place as any to start a tour of the Low Countries. **Australians**, on the other hand, are more likely to want to stop off on the way, and there are frequent and affordable flights from the ex-Dutch islands of Indonesia – KLM fly something like twice a day between Jakarta and Amsterdam.

RED TAPE

If you're a citizen of Britain, the Irish Republic, Australia, New Zealand, Canada or the United States you need only a valid passport to stay three months. For longer than this you'll need an extension visa, either from the Dutch embassy in your own country or via the Dutch police. In practice, passports are not always date stamped as you enter the country, and restrictions are fairly loose. Be careful though, about having enough money to stay alive – officials have taken to checking poorer visitors on arrival, and if you can't flash a few travellers' cheques or notes you may not be allowed in.

SLEEPING

Hotels, hostels and rooms
Whichever way you look at it, accommodation in Holland is expensive, and unless you have unlimited supplies of cash you're going to have to give some serious thought to where your bed is to be for the night. **Hotels** can cost you anything from f25 upwards, and prices are calculated per person rather than per room, making it no more economic for couples. VVVs always have lists with prices, which they will normally hand out free. Classification is done on a purely voluntary basis but is fairly reliable, though the prices themselves are probably the best guide to standards. **Pensions** are slightly cheaper (f20–25) and amount to much the same thing,

though with a more intimate atmosphere.

If you're counting the pennies, **hostels** are a better idea and there are a number of options. Some of the larger and more popular Dutch towns have a **Sleep-In**: dormitory accommodation heavily subsidised by local councils and very cheap at between f6 and f10 a head – sometimes even cheaper than camping. Rooms are comfortable but spartan, and you can add on a couple of guilders for sheets if you don't have a sleeping-bag. Lockers are provided for your gear and the only drawback is that many Sleep-Ins are only open in July and August. You'll find them in Amsterdam, Alkmaar, Rotterdam, Breda, Rosendaal, Arnhem, Zwolle and Groningen. The only other dormitory-type accommodation is **Youth or Student Hotels**, where you can have a bed from about f15, with a choice ranging from bunk-bedded dorms right up to triples, doubles and singles, depending on how much you can afford. Again, you can normally lock away your stuff if you wish. There are a number of these in Amsterdam, but outside of there you'll be hard pushed to find them in all but the really major cities.

There are some fifty official **Youth Hostels** in Holland, though to use them you need to be a member of the **YHA** (membership (age 16–21 £3, 21 and over £5) from the YHA shop, Southampton Street, London WC1); if you don't have a card you can sometimes pay extra and join for one night. Prices are around f15 a night including breakfast but minus sheets. Living is communal and the atmosphere hearty, though one major disadvantage is the unreasonably early curfew that's imposed at night.

A final alternative, and a viable one, is rooms in **private houses**, which tend to work out at around f20 a head. If there are any at all in the town you happen to be staying in, the VVV will have a list; the best thing to do is to get hold of that and follow them up yourself. Sometimes, though, they will try to sell you the list at a vastly inflated price or, still worse, guard it fiercely, insisting that they book the room by telephone and you hand over a f3.50 booking fee; wherever this is local VVV policy we've included addresses you can chase up yourself. Even more irritating: sometimes they withhold their lists until all the hotels in town are full, putting you in the anomalous position of not being able to afford a room at the half-empty Hilton while the VVV hang on to their stock of cheap rooms. Once again, we've printed addresses where this seems liable to happen.

Camping
Camping is illegal anywhere but on **official sites**. These are plentiful, well-equipped and generally quite reasonable: standards and prices are controlled by local and provincial by-laws. Expect to pay around f5 a head per night, though it can work out dearer than that if you're alone, as you pay per person plus a standard charge for the tent. Municipal sites come a lot cheaper than private ones, but watch out for peculiar institutions known as *Recreatiecentrums*, which masquerade as campsites but are more like holiday-camps, with a lot more on offer, including higher prices. These, almost without exception, are best avoided – unless you have a perverse urge to witness their nightly cabaret or latest camp beauty contest.

Every place of any size has at least one campsite, though they're normally in the outermost outskirts of town; don't forget to add on the cost of bus fares to any economies you think you're making by camping. If we don't mention a site in the guide, the VVV can always direct you to the nearest one. Hot showers are usually available but you nearly always pay extra for the luxury; plus, particularly in the more isolated spots, there's often a camp shop which, while convenient, frequently takes advantage of its monopoly and charges over the odds. Finally, don't forget to take a stout sleeping-bag – Holland's climate is much the same as England's and even summer nights can be extremely chilly – and watch out for mosquitoes which, due to the amount of water around, are rife.

EATING AND DRINKING

Eating cheaply and well can be a problem – at the bottom end of the scale you're often dependent on snack-bars and take-aways, of which there are no shortage. **Dutch fast food** has its peculiarities. Chips are commonly rendered unrecognisable by lashings of mayonnaise (synthetic tasting curry sauce, goulash sauce or tomato sauce are alternatives), and invariably complemented by *kroketten* – spiced and frequently inedible meat covered with bread-crumbs and deep fried. You'll see these things sitting solitarily in heated glass compartments outside take-aways, fast food at its most literal for which you put a guilder in the slot. Often cheaper and certainly the more tasty snack, are salted raw herrings (what we would call roll-mop), eel and other delicious fishy things – always available from street stalls. Tip your head back and dangle the herring into your mouth, Dutch style. Sandwiches are 'open', and can vary from a slice of tired cheese on old bread to something so garnished that it's almost a complete meal. Waffles and *poffertjes* are also popular – small fritters sold on the street and served with butter and a light dusting of sugar.

Real Dutch food is considerably more edible, if only marginally more imaginative. Where they exist, student restaurants, known as **Mensas**, are always the cheapest possibility, serving a generous and filling meal for around f5. Unfortunately, you'll only be able to find these in the larger university towns. Elsewhere it's best to stick to **eetcafes** – bars that sell food – rather than orthodox restaurants; they tend to be cheaper and often a lot better. Best value item on the menu is the ubiquitous *uitsmijter* – ham, cheese or beef on bread and topped with two fried eggs, normally around f6. In winter most bars serve *erwtensoep*, an extra thick and immensely filling pea soup with chunks of bacon or sausage. Both of the above are really classed as snacks, though you can easily make them do as a main meal. Other options are *dagschotels* (dish of the day): a meat and two veg combination with a selection of pickles and *appelmoes*, a kind of puréed apple that gets served up with almost everything. This sort of meal will rarely cost less than about f10, but portions tend to be enormous. Some restaurants do something called the **Tourist Menu** – at f16.25 a three-course meal that is seldom very good value.

You can get a much better 3-course affair at a **vegetarian restaurant**. These vary little over the country, nearly always doing a set meal for around f8. Another cheap standby are **pizzerias**, where you can buy a large pizza or pasta dish for about f7. Legacies from Holland's adventurous imperial past are the **Indonesian** ('Indeesch' or 'Chinees-Indeesch') restaurants you find on every corner. Keep these for a real binge: Indonesian food is like highly spiced Chinese – lots of meat and fish with rice and noodles liberally piled on. *Nasi Goreng* and *Bami Goreng* are spicey meat dishes, one with rice and the other with noodles. *Rijstaffel* is terrific value

for money and makes for a real feast: countless different rice dishes that can easily feed two. **Mexican** restaurants are also very common – lots of bean-based stodge, hot and very filling, and nearly always wrapped in little potato pancakes known as *tortilladas*.

Beer is the most commonly consumed beverage. Ask for *een pils* and you get a tiny (0.25 cl) glass, much of which will be frothing head. Requests to have it poured 'English style' meet with a variety of responses, but it's worth trying. One glass will cost you f1.75 on average, though prices can fluctuate alarmingly, depending on where you are. The best places to drink are **brown cafés**, most plentiful in Amsterdam and so called because of the dingy colour of the walls, tinted brown by decades of tobacco smoke. Rare places do large beers, for which you pay proportionately less. **Jenever**, or Dutch gin, is not unlike English, but a little oilier and traditionally drunk straight; it's served in minuscule glasses and knocked back in one go. Of the two varieties, *Oud* is mellower and smoother, while *Jong* packs more of a punch. Ask for a *borreltje* (straight jenever) or a *bittertje* (with angostura). Beer and jenever are both dirt cheap and if you buy them by the bottle from the supermarket – Grolsch or Heineken cost about f1 for half a litre while a bottle of jenever sells at around f15.

Dutch **coffee** is the espresso kind, black and strong and often served with *koffiemelk* – evaporated milk; ordinary milk is never used in coffee. **Breakfast** is not the spartan snack you get in the rest of Europe but a fully-fledged meal of ham, cheese, eggs and bread, with coffee ad-lib. Department-store restaurants are the best places to start the day like this.

Holland is famous for its **cheeses**, though don't go expecting hundreds of different varieties – you'll be disappointed. Most are variations on soft, creamy **Gouda** and **Edam**, with taste depending on stages of maturity. *Jong* is mild and inoffensive, *Belegen* medium-mature and quite flavoursome while *Oud* can sometimes be fairly pungent. *Leidse* is Gouda with cumin seeds, *Maasdam* is strong and creamy and full of holes.

Basics

Brood	Bread	Sla	Salad
Boter	Butter	Broodje	Sandwich/roll
Kaas	Cheese	Dranken	Drinks
Vlees	Meat	Nagerechten	Desserts
Vis	Fish	Stokbrood	French bread
Eieren	Eggs	Suiker	Sugar
Groenten	Vegetables	Zout	Salt
Vruchten	Fruit	Peper	Pepper

Starters and snacks

Haringsla	Herring salad	Koffietafel	a light midday meal
Huzarensalade	Egg salad		of cold meats,
Voorgerechten	Hors d'oeuvres		cheese, bread and
Soep	Soup		perhaps soup
Erwtensoep	Pea soup with	Pindakaas	Peanut butter
	bacon or sausage	Honig	Honey
Patates/Frites	Chips	Smeerkaas	Cheese spread
Uitsmijter	Ham or cheese with		
	eggs on bread		

Meat

Biefstuk (hollandse)	Steak	Fricandeau	Roast pork
Biefstuk (duits)	Hamburger	Spek	Bacon
Worst	Sausage	Kalfvlees	Veal
Kroket	Spiced, minced	Lever	Liver
	meat in	Lam	Lamb
	breadcrumbs	Kip	Chicken
Fricandel	A kind of frankfurter	Kalkoen	Turkey
	sausage	Eend	Duck
Ham	Ham	Hutspot	Beef stew
Karbonade	Chop		
Gehakt	Minced meat		

Fish

Haring	Herring	Garnalen	Prawns
Paling	Eel	Schol	Plaice
Spiering	Whitebait	Schelvis	Haddock
Mackreel	Mackerel	Kabeljauw	Cod
Zalm	Salmon	Tong	Sole
Mosselen	Mussels		

Vegetables

Aardappelen	Potatoes	Wortelen	Carrots
Champignons	Mushrooms	Bloemkool	Cauliflower
Erwten	Peas	Knoflook	Garlic
Rijst	Rice	Prei	Leek
Uien	Onions	Stoofsla	Lettuce
Zuurkool	Sauerkraut	Komkommer	Cucumber
Bonen	Beans		

Terms

Gebakken	Baked	Gestoofd	Stewed
Gekookt	Boiled	Rood	Rare
Geraspt	Grated	Half doorbakken	Medium
Gegrilld	Grilled	Doorbakken	Well-done
Gebraden	Roast	Hollandse saus	A milk and egg
Gerookt	Smoked		sauce

Desserts

Gebak	Pastry	*Wafels*	Waffles
Flensjes	Thin pancakes, crèpes	*Vla*	Milk pudding
		Koekjes	Biscuits
Pannekoeken	Pancakes	*Ijs*	Ice-cream
Poffertjes	Small pancakes, fritters	*(Slag) room*	(Whipped) cream

Fruit and nuts

Appel	Apple	*Peer*	Pear
Aardbei	Strawberry	*Perzik*	Peach
Citron	Lemon	*Pruim*	Plum/Prune
Druif	Grape	*Appelmoes*	Apple purée
Kers	Cherry	*Pinda*	Peanut
Framboos	Raspberry		

Drinks

Pils	Dutch beer	*Frisdranken*	Soft drinks
Jenever	Dutch gin	*Koffie*	Coffee
Wijn	Wine	*Melk*	Milk
(wit/rood/rose)	(white/red/rosé)	*Karnemelk*	Buttermilk
Droog	Dry	*Proost*	Cheers!
Zoet	Sweet		
Vruchtensap	Fruit juice		

GETTING AROUND

In a country as compact as Holland, getting from one place to the next is rarely a problem. Bus and train networks cover similar routes, bus journeys taking longer but working out cheaper. It's easy to transfer from one to the other – most train and bus stations are found more or less adjacent near the centre of town. You'll find approximate frequencies of buses and trains in the **Travel Details** section at the end of each chapter, and any local difficulties are indicated in the text.

Train services (*Nederlandse Spoorwegen* or *NS*) are punctual, fast and frequent. The Intercity and slower *Stoptrein* services operate on one of the densest rail systems in Europe, and you seldom have to wait more than a few minutes for a connection. There are a variety of tickets that'll save you money: a **Dagretour** is the simplest – a cheap day return; a **weekend return** leaving on Saturday, returning Sunday, is the price of a Dagretour + f2.50; an **evening return**, valid for travel after 6pm, costs the single fare + f3. Worth considering if you're touring around are **Rover Tickets**, which give unlimited travel on the NS network: a three-day Rover costs f72, seven days f99. Buy either of these tickets and you can also get a reduced pass for unlimited travel on the country's bus, tram and metro lines: this costs f8 with the three-day Rover, f16 with the seven-day; you have to buy both tickets together and will need to show your passport. If you want to widen your explorations a **Benelux Tourrail** ticket enables you to travel on all Dutch, Belgian and Luxembourg railways for eight out of a specified sixteen days. It costs f162 (f115 if you're under 26) and is available from any rail station from April to October.

Bus services aren't as fast or frequent as trains and only operate regionally: travel any distance and you'll find yourself making time-consuming changes. Bus services can, however, save up to 40 per cent on a medium-distance journey. To use them you'll need to tangle with the **Strippenkaart** system, a card of numbered strips, which is also used on the tram and metro systems of Amsterdam and major cities. On most buses the driver cancels the requisite amount of strips, though on city transport it's up to your honesty to stamp it on entry. The best value Strippenkart is a **15-strip** (f7.40), which you can buy from bus and train stations or post offices; bought on the bus they work out 50 per cent more expensive. If you're intending going on a long journey find out from the bus station how many strips you'll use before you start – there comes a level when it's best to pay twice the price of a 15-strip and get a **Dagkaart**, which gives a day's unlimited bus travel. Where there's no train link, bus services are included under Travel Details.

In a country where no form of transport comes cheap, **hitching** can work out the best way of getting around – distances are short and the Dutch remarkably willing to give lifts: I rarely waited longer than fifteen minutes, but if you're heading to or from a city always use a sign showing where you want to go – single exit roads usually lead to a variety of destinations.

Using your **own transport** presents no difficulties: motorways link the main cities and on the whole are free from jams and delays. Speed limits are 100kph on motorways, 80kph on other roads and 50kph in built-up areas. Seat belts are compulsory for driver and front passenger, and the Dutch police are particularly heavy on drinking and driving. To take your car over you'll need an International Driving Licence, though British and Irish motorists no longer need a **Green card** – third party cover on your own policy is automatic in EEC countries. If you're a member of the AA or RAC the Dutch **ANWB** organisation offers reciprocal breakdown facilities. **Car hire** is available from the well-known firms like *Avis* and *Hertz*; prices start at f25 a day plus a charge per kilometre. **Taxis** are prohibitively expensive – only really worth considering if you're in a group and it's late.

If you're not pushed for time **cycling** is *the* great way of getting about and seeing the country. In Holland's flat polder landscape it's a particularly natural way of travelling and there's an extensive system of cycle paths, often diverted away from the main roads into the countryside. The ANWB maps show all the cycle paths and are a great help if you're thinking of touring. **Bikes** can be hired from all main train stations for f6 a day + f50 deposit (f200 in large towns), and if you have a valid train ticket it's cheaper still at f4. In addition, most bike shops will hire you a machine, usually for a little more but with the advantage that they'll often take your passport in lieu of a deposit. There's a rule for Amsterdam that you should remember wherever you are: if a bike is unlocked, even for a minute, no one is going to have any scruples about stealing it. A market in ripped-off bikes flourishes, so lock your machine and chain it to something really unmoveable, preferably in an open space. Should you be riding around on something that would be a real prize to a thief, park it at a railway station (f1 a day). Seeing two men attacking a beautiful racing bike with bolt cutters, in full view of passers-by, is one of my sadder memories of Amsterdam.

HEALTH AND INSURANCE

Britain and Ireland have reciprocal **health agreements** with Holland that provide free medical advice and treatment. To get this you need to take certificate E 111, obtained by completing the application form SA 28 from the DHSS. You won't be turned away from a doctor or hospital without it but may have to contribute towards treatment, so if you don't have an E 111 **travel insurance** is a good idea: policies cost around £10 a month and cover your cash and possessions too. You'll need to keep all medical bills to reclaim costs and must get a written statement from the police should you have something stolen.

Chemists or **Drogists** (open Mondays to Fridays) supply non-prescription drugs, Tampax and other essentials. Minor **accidents** can be treated at the first-aid centre of most hospitals (the local VVV will advise on out-patient treatment) and you'll find the numbers of **doctors** under D or M (*medecins*) in the yellow pages. In **emergencies**, dial the ambulance number in the nearest phone box.

CASH AND COMMUNICATIONS

Dutch **currency** is *guilders*, available in advance from any British bank. The guilder, indicated by an 'f' (confusingly; stands for 'florin', its alternative name), is divided into 100 cents, the 25c piece commonly called a *kwartje*. Current exchange rates are around f4.3 to the £, f3 to the $, and there are no restrictions on bringing currency into the country. The best way of carrying the bulk of your money is in **travellers' cheques**, available from any British bank (whether or not you have an account) and cashable in almost all Dutch banks and many hotels and pensions. If you do have a bank account and a **Eurocheque card** you can use them to get cash in the majority of banks, something you can also do with major **credit cards** – but not *Visa*.

There's no shortage of places to **change money**: banks, usually open from 0900–1600, have standard rates and commissions, as do the VVVs. The latter give a lower rate but charge less commission – better for small amounts if you can stand the queuing. Larger railway stations also offer facilities, and though rates here too are low they stay open late – worth remembering if you've missed the banks. Many hotels, pensions and campsites will also change money – at a price.

Post offices open 0900–1700, often later in big cities. They're efficient too, but make sure you join the right queue – *Postzegelen* for stamps. You can have letters sent **post-restante** to any post office in Holland by addressing them 'Post-Restante' (*Postliggend* in Dutch) followed by the name of the town. You'll need your passport to collect any post.

Phone boxes are similar to the push-button British kiosks. They take 25c, f1 and f2½ coins; only whole unused coins are returned. Cheap rate on the international service is between 8pm and 8am; to dial a number first use the international number, then the STD (area) code without the first 0. Some main international codes: Australia 0961, Great Britain and Northern Ireland 0944, Irish Republic 09353, United States/Canada 091.

GALLERIES, MUSEUMS AND CHURCHES

If you intend to visit more than a couple of Holland's museums, it's *essential* to buy a **museumcard**. Available from the VVV (f7.50 if you're under 25, f20 otherwise) they are valid for a year and give free entry to all state and municipally run museums, not only in Amsterdam but throughout the country. When you consider it costs f4.50 to visit Amsterdam's Rijksmuseum alone, this is pretty evidently a bargain. Where museumcards aren't accepted, we've said so in the text. Another good buy is the **Cultureel Jongeren Paspoort** or **CJP**, which for f8.50 gets you a museumcard, free membership of the Melkweg and a discount on theatre and concert tickets. Only available to those under 25, it can be bought from the *Uit Buro* near the Stadsschouwburg in Amsterdam.

Throughout Holland you'll come across two main groups of museums: a **Rijksmuseum** is a state museum, housing a national collection on a specific theme; **Gemeente** and **Stedelijk** museums are run by the municipality and vary in nature from place to place. In all three the term 'museum' is used to include art gallery, and you'll often see the word *tentoonselling* used to indicate a temporary exhibition. Generally, the opening times of Rijks, Gemeente and Stedelijk museums follow a pattern: closed on Mondays, open from 1000–1700 Tuesdays to Saturdays and 1300–1700 on Sundays. We've included the spring and summer opening times of all museums in the text but remember that non-state museums may vary considerably out of season.

Though not all Holland's **churches** have the bare austerity of Saenredam's famous paintings, the Calvinist Dutch carried to a fine point the art of reducing the sense of religious mystery to a minimum. During the Reformation iconoclasts destroyed the rich decoration and Catholic images that had covered the Gothic churches and the lavish wall paintings were plastered over. A despairing E. V. Lucas commented 'Place even the cathedral of Chartres in a Dutch market-place and it would be a white-washed desert in a week.' In North Brabant and Limburg, however, parts of Holland where Catholicism has survived, churches have been restored with varying degrees of success to their original condition. And, elsewhere, later decorators have made a virtue of the white walls, allowing their brilliance to emphasise the soaring Gothic lines.

As in most matters the Dutch have taken a practical attitude to the problem of churches and their falling attend-

ances. No one seems to have any scruples about turning the buildings into coffee houses, meeting places or even shops, though sometimes this secularisation has had unfortunate results. You'll occasionally have to pay to get into a church, but a greater problem is restoration: several of Holland's major churches are closed for essential repairs, though most remain partially open to give you some idea of their glory.

PUBLIC HOLIDAYS

You'll find almost all shops and banks closed on the following days, and state-run museums adopt Sunday opening times – apart from Christmas, Boxing and New Year's days when they're all closed: New Year's Day, Good Friday

(many shops open), Easter Sunday and Monday, 30 April (many shops open), Ascension Day, Whit Sunday and Monday, Christmas and Boxing Days, Liberation Day (5 May, 1985 only).

FESTIVALS

Many of Holland's festivals, like the flower shows of Keukenhof in the spring, are specifically tourist orientated (and well publicised by the VVV), but other cultural events are well worth looking out for. The **Holland Festival** is the largest, with theatre, opera and concerts in Amsterdam, Rotterdam and The Hague – a national affair celebrating mainly Dutch artists and performers. In June-July Amsterdam hosts the **Zomerfestijn** (Summer Festival) of theatre and music, co-ordinated by the Shaffy theatre (see p. 55) this usually has one play in English on at any one time. The Hague's **North Sea Jazz Festival** (early June) is the

largest of many musical events, a well organised programme of the world's best jazz musicians. Cheap accommodation is available, and various operators do 'all-in' trips from London. Elsewhere there's the **Camel Jazz Festival** (Amsterdam, July and August), **Jazz in the Woods** (Apeldoorn, June), the avant-garde **Jazz Marathon** (Groningen, May) and the **Pink Pop Festival** (Geleen, late May). Classical events include a performance of Bach's **St Matthew Passion** in Naarden's beautiful Grote Kerk (the week before Easter) and a series of summer evening concerts at the **Concertgebouw** in Amsterdam.

FINDING WORK AND A ROOF

In order to **work** legally in Holland it's necessary to get a work stamp from the police: all EEC nationals are entitled to a three-month stamp on arriving, but it's only possible to renew it if you're in work. As for actually finding a job there's not much to say except that it's difficult. Temporary job agencies or *uitzendburos* provide the main source of casual labour, and during the summer it's often possible to get work from them though, due to the worsening unemployment situation, it becomes harder every year. There's still hotel work in the tourist

season but little else, especially for people over the age of 22 who get paid more and consequently find it much more difficult to get any sort of job. To find something in Amsterdam can take weeks of tramping around agencies. The newspapers aren't much use, but *uitzendburos* and cleaning agencies sometimes advertise so it's worth keeping an eye on them. The *Arbeidsburo* (labour exchange) has been known to find work for non-Dutch speakers, particularly skilled manual workers, but recently seems to have dried up considerably.

Summer jobs in the glasshouses can sometimes be picked up and much the best way of finding them is by taking a trip down to Aalsmeer and other bulb areas for a hunt around yourself.

All in all, the present job situation in Holland is dire and doesn't seem likely to improve in the near future. Cuts in social welfare payments and youth unemployment schemes are pushing more Dutch people into the low-paid temporary work market previously the preserve of foreigners, and the hey-day of casual jobs for wandering travellers seems to be over.

Though it's applicable to most other parts of the country, for simplicity, we've confined our **housing** information to Amsterdam where, as in most major cities, cheap rented accommodation is in short supply, and flat hunting requires a determined effort. Much of the housing is controlled by the council and the only people eligible for a council flat are those holding an *urgentie bewijs* – an urgent need certificate that you can get if you've been living here for two years but still don't have a suitable home. Anyone who thinks they may stay for a while would be well advised to register at the *Bevolkings Register* at Herengracht 535 as soon as they arrive, as the *urgentie bewijs* is a useful piece of paper to have.

Most newcomers are, however, forced to seek accommodation in the private sector, which can prove expensive. The newspapers *De Telegraaf* and *De Volks- krant* have large 'to let' sections, particu- larly on Fridays and Saturdays, though it's well worth buying them every morning. Obviously, if you've plenty of money you shouldn't have too many problems, otherwise there's little chance of finding anything for much less than f500 a month. Very often an *overname* is charged: illegal money paid to the previous tenant to cover furniture and fittings left behind. This varies enorm- ously and can be extortionate, but it's usually unavoidable and can only be regained by charging it to the next tenant when you move out. Landlords sometimes ask for a *bergsom*, which is a deposit to cover the contents of the flat and reclaimable when you leave.

Flat-finding agencies advertise regu- larly in newspapers: these are worth investigating, though of course they charge a fee – normally one or two months' rent on finding you a place.

Beware of agencies which ask for money before they hand out an address – cowboys are common.

When all's said and done, a lot of housing is acquired by word of mouth. A remarkable grapevine springs up in the summer amongst the travelling community; people are constantly coming and going, looking for flatmates or just temporary caretakers. Just let everyone you meet know you're home- less. It's also worth keeping an eagle eye on noticeboards everywhere: the main public library on Prinsengracht is a good one, also bars and student eating places like the *Mensas* and *Egg Cream*. Student halls of residence have noticeboards and allow non-students to stay tempor- arily – not a bad option in the short term as the rooms are very cheap. Even tobacconists' windows are worth perusing as the Dutch go in for long summer holidays and often need someone to care for the cats and plants in their absence.

The other way to solve your housing problem is to find a **squat**, or *kraak* as the Dutch say, though it's important to remember that the foreign squatter faces special problems – the main ones being police harassment and deportation. If the police want you out, your rights as an EEC citizen don't count for much and, even though it's not hard to get back, being deported is an unpleasant and expensive experience. It really is important to gain the support and advice of the local squatting group although it must be said that they aren't always very helpful to foreigners. Dutch squatters see their activities as being community orientated and politically motivated, and don't always welcome people they suspect are looking for a short rent-free stay in Holland. Get involved with the local group, get to know the people and keep looking for an empty place yourself – don't expect it all to be done for you.

The short-term squat is probably the best solution for the temporary visitor, i.e. empty flats in blocks due for demoli- tion within about six months. For a variety of reasons, these are likely to dry up in the future but, for the moment at least, they do exist, though you have to be quick and get in before the wreckers, who are sent round by the council to make places uninhabitable. You really need to be tipped off or actually see people moving out and get in that evening – local squatters may be able to provide information. Once you're in the chances are there won't be any trouble but, again, it's worth contacting your local squatting group as they can clarify your legal position. Having established a claim on your property the next problem is lack of furniture, gas and electrical appliances, etc. These are surprisingly easy to pick up – often off the street on rubbish night – and a place can be made habitable in a couple of weeks with next to no outlay.

Long-term squats are much more complicated: they have to be observed for some time and thoroughly investigated before being attempted, and the help of the squatters group is imperative. The main aim of this type of squatting is to get a licence, and the best chance of success is in a place that is already in an unrentable condition.

The big community squats are much more than just a way of alleviating the housing problem: they are definitely political in nature and present a challenge to the establishment by attacking the activities of property developers in a very practical way. Most of the big ones were derelict factories, hotels or warehouses – destined to be demolished and rebuilt as luxury apartments or office blocks, or simply left until land prices rose enabling resale at a profit. Large groups of squatters moved in and set about creating a complete environment from nothing, building living spaces, workshops, studios, print shops, cheap cafés, crèches, etc. These communities house hundreds of people and try to provide services which are lacking in inner city areas. Living in one means quite a commitment: you have to be prepared to participate fully in the community and spend a lot of time and energy on the squat. Because of this they can't really be seen as a solution to the short-term housing problem of someone just passing through.

Addresses

Bevolkings Register, Herengracht 535 (Monday-Friday 0830–1500).
Bureau voor Rechtshulp (free legal advice centre), Spuistraat 10.
Openbare Bibliotheek (public library), Prinsengracht 585.
Arbeidsbureau, Singel 202.
Student Housing Office, Oude Turfmarkt 139.
Individual student halls listed under Studenthuis in the telephone book.

BOOKS

When Voltaire left Holland with the resounding 'Adieu! canaux, canards, canaille', he was perhaps echoing the feelings of most writers: over the years very few have got around to writing anything on the country, and it's often derisively dismissed in passing. Most books of any relevance at all confine themselves to particular aspects of Holland – art, for example – rather than simple description. There are one or two interesting 19th-century works but you'll have to trust to luck and hope you can pick them up second-hand somewhere, as they're very much out of print now: try **The Travel Bookshop** (13 Blenheim Crescent, London W11) or **Piccadilly Rare Books** (30 Sackville Street, London W1).

Best of the bunch is **E.V. Lucas**, *A Wanderer in Holland* – a witty and readable account of the country before the ravages of the last war. **Henry Havard**, 19th-century French traveller and bon viveur, has two books in translation – *The Heart of Holland* and *Picturesque Holland* – and **William Temple**, a 17th century English diplomat, gives a comprehensive picture of life in the Golden Age in *Observations upon the United Provinces of The Netherlands*. Much more recent, and a good buy if your journey is taking in other parts of Europe, is **Patrick Leigh Fermor**'s *A Time of Gifts* (Penguin £2.95), which includes a beautifully written and evocative chapter at the beginning of his tramp from the Hook of Holland to Constantinople.

Art

R.H. Fuchs, *Dutch Painting* (Thames & Hudson £3.95) is as complete an introduction to the subject as you could wish for. **Friedlander**'s *Van Eyck to Bruegel* (Phaidon £6.50) fulfils the same function for the Flemish painters, while **Fromentin**'s *Masters of Past Time* (Phaidon £6.50) takes in the major figures of both fields – expertly and entertainingly. A more specific introduction is *The Pelican History of Art – Dutch Art and Architecture 1600–1800* (Penguin £10).

History

J.L. Motley's *Rise of the Dutch Republic* is the definitive work, but suffers from being eighty years old and in several cumbersome volumes. **Geoffrey Cotterell**'s *Amsterdam* gives a more concise, up-to-date and offbeat view, with special regard to the capital, and for an accurate and intelligent account of the Golden Age you should see **J.L. Price**, *Culture and Society in the Dutch Republic in the 17th Century*. The Diary of Anne Frank (Pan £1.75) remains one of the best things you can read on the war years.

Literature

Because of the nature of the language, Dutch literature has been much neglected and there's virtually nothing in translation apart from *Max Havelaar* by **Multatuli**: published by Quartet at £6.95 and an illuminating, eloquent and sometimes very funny 19th-century classic that is on all Dutch school syllabuses.

Land reclamation

Pieter Spier in *Of Dikes and Windmills* makes something that could be very dull into a light-hearted and informative book, with a mixture of amusing anecdote and historical fact.

OTHER THINGS

BIKE-HIRE see p. 9.
BOOKS *De Slegte* is a chain of second-hand bookshops with branches in most of the larger Dutch cities – good for cheap English paperbacks.
CONTRACEPTIVES Durex-type contraceptives are available from chemists, but to get the pill you need a doctor's prescription.
DRUGS Since the permissiveness of the late 1960s, Amsterdam has had a social and sensible attitude to **cannabis** – the city imports and sells it through two outlets, the *Melkweg* and *Paradiso*. Buy dope elsewhere and you're likely to be ripped off. Though there's little chance of actually being busted, you're only allowed to have 28 grams in your possession – which, given the strength and quality of the dope here, is more than enough. It's acceptable to smoke in some bars, but as a few are strongly anti, don't make any automatic assumptions. Outside Amsterdam, attitudes change radically, and though certain provincial bars permit smoking, common sense and circumspection should be the order of the day. Wherever you are, you may be offered other drugs, all of which are, of course, illegal.
GAY LIFE In keeping with the Dutch reputation for tolerance, no other country in the world accepts homosexuals so easily. The age of consent is 16, and Amsterdam is a magnet for the international gay community – a city with a suitably dense sprinkling of bars, saunas, discos and advice-centres, staffed by activists committed to preserving rights that have been hard-won. Additionally, several towns have thriving scenes of their own: Rotterdam, Breda, Nijmegen and Groningen all display a liberality unheard of even in most other European capitals. *COC* is a nationwide gay organisation with branches in most major towns: they offer help, information, and usually a coffee-bar.
MEDIA British newspapers are on sale just about everywhere, normally the same day as they come out. For those wanting to practise their Dutch, *De Volkskrant* is the progressive liberal, leftish daily, while *De Telegraaf* is a right-wing scandal sheet reminiscent of *The Sun*. The fashionable *Het Parool* and news magazine *Vrij Nederland* are the successors of underground printing during the Nazi occupation. Best of the English language publications is *The Paper*, an excellent independent monthly magazine which has news, articles, listings and translated Dutch fictional extracts; available from bookshops all over Holland, but principally in Amsterdam – price f2.95. Others include *Holland Herald* – a glossy monthly produced by KLM for their business travellers and by no stretch of the imagination worth f3.60 – and *Holland Tribune*, a bi-weekly newspaper that costs f2.50 and again caters mostly for Amsterdam business people.

As far as **radio** goes, you can pick up BBC Radio 4 and the World Service, as well as BBC 2 most of the time on the

TV. In addition, the official Dutch and cable channels show masses of British and American programmes with Dutch subtitles.

MOSQUITOES thrive in Holland's watery environment, and you can get quite badly bitten if you don't take precautions. An antihistamine cream like *Phenergan* is the best antidote.

STUDENT TRAVEL *NBBS* have offices in most Dutch cities and are listed throughout the guide. For young people, rather than just students, they can help with Transalpino tickets and cheap flights to most parts of the world.

SHOPPING Holland's weekend fades painlessly into the working week and most shops remain closed on Monday morning. Other days, hours are 0900–1800 apart from Saturday, when most things start to shut slightly earlier. Chemists follow the same pattern, but in most towns you can always find at least one open at night or at weekends. *HEMA* and *Vroom and Dreesman* (V&D) are the big department store names you find everywhere. HEMA is the cheaper of the two – a sort of Dutch version of Woolworth's, good for toiletries and odds and ends. Both usually have an upstairs restaurant and can be reasonable places to have lunch. Every town has a market at least once a week, and the more interesting ones are listed in the text.

TAMPAX on sale at all chemists.

TIME Central European time, i.e. one hour ahead of GMT. Clocks are put forward between early April and the end of September, making it two hours ahead of GMT and one in front of BST.

WINDMILLS Only about 1,000 remain out of 10,000, of which some 300 are still in regular use. Now classed as national monuments, the government gives a grant to people who are prepared to live in and look after them. If you're into it, the best place to see windmills is Kinderdijk, near Rotterdam, though they're still very much part of the landscape in the polderlands north of Amsterdam. Some have been moved and reassembled out of harm's way in the open-air museums at Zaanse Schans (Zaandam) and Arnhem.

WOENSDRECHT A small town near Bergen-op-Zoom, Woensdrecht was named last year as the site for 48 American cruise missiles. Reaction to the announcement was swift – the IKV (the Dutch equivalent of CND) organised a demo at the airbase, and a small peace camp has been set up. No decision has yet been made as to whether the missiles will actually be deployed, but if the worst happens, cruise will be here in 1986.

WOMEN'S MOVEMENT A number of well-organised feminist groups exist throughout Holland. The main women's centre in most towns is called the *Vrouwenhuis,* and deals with women's problems from a feminist perspective, often offering a café as a meeting place. For addresses of *Vrouwenhuizen* and the main women's cafés and restaurants, see town listings.

DUTCH TERMS: A GLOSSARY

ABDIJ abbey or group of monasterial buildings.

AMBULATORY covered passage around the outer edge of the choir of a church.

APSE semi-circular termination at the east end of a church.

BEGIJNHOF similar to a *hofje* but occupied by Catholic women (*Begijns*) who led a semi-religious life without taking full vows.

BURGHER member of the upper or mercantile classes of a town, usually with certain civic powers.

CARILLON a set of tuned church bells, operated either by an automatic mechanism or played by a keyboard.

CLERESTORY arcade of windows in the upper storey of a church.

CABINET-PIECE small, well-finished painting of a domestic scene.

GASTHUIS hospice for the sick or infirm.

GEMEENTE municipal; e.g. *Gemeentehuis* – town hall.

GEVEL gable. The only decoration practical on the narrow-fronted canalhouse was on its gables: initially fairly simple, they developed into an ostentatious riot of individualism in the late 17th century, before turning to a more restrained classicism in the 18th and 19th.

HALL-CHURCH church where the outer aisles are the same height as the central one – common in Holland.

HIJSTBALK pulley beam, often decorated, fixed at the top of a gable to lift goods, furniture, etc.

HOF courtyard.

HOFJE almshouse, usually for elderly women who could look after themselves but needed small charities like food and fuel; usually a number of buildings centred around a small, peaceful courtyard.

KERK church; e.g. *Grote Kerk* – the principal church of the town. **Onze Lieve Vrouwe Kerk** – church dedicated to the Virgin Mary.

LAKENHAL found in old weaving towns – the main building where cloth would be produced, graded and sold.

MARKT central town square and the heart of most Dutch communities – normally still the scene of at least once-weekly markets.

MISERICORDE ledge on choir stall on which occupant can support himself while standing; often carved.

POLDER an area of land reclaimed from the sea.

PLEIN Dutch word for a square or open space.

RAADHUIS town hall.

RIJKS state.

SPIONNETJE small mirror on canal house enabling occupant to see who is at door without descending stairs.

STADHUIS most commonly used word for a town hall.

STEDELIJK civic, municipal.

WAAG old public weigh-house, a common feature of most towns – usually found on the *markt*.

Part two
THE GUIDE

THE NORTH AND
THE FRISIAN
ISLANDS

NORTH HOLLAND
AND TEXEL

AMSTERDAM

GELDERLAND
AND
OVERIJSSEL

SOUTH
HOLLAND AND
UTRECHT

THE SOUTH

BELGIUM AND LUXEMBOURG

Chapter one
AMSTERDAM

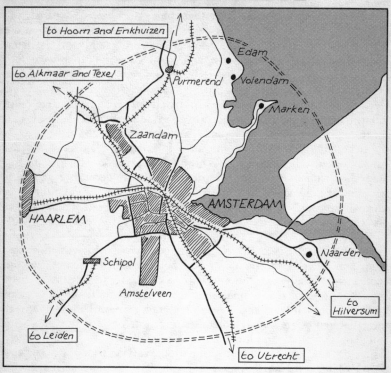

Gezillig. The word is literally untranslatable but it sums up **AMSTERDAM**. The nearest thing to it in English is 'laid-back'; the 'relax, take-it-easy' attitude of the Dutch which has its roots in a glorious liberal past and its proof in a city that has an unmistakably youthful stamp – a free and easy atmosphere you'd be hard pushed to find anywhere else in Europe. That's not to say it's the same as it was in the hedonistic 1960s – it's dirtier than when I first visited, the red-light district seedier, the drugs industry more discredited – but the fact remains that the counter-culture label is a hard one to shrug off, however many of its wrecked victims wander the crowded streets.

Though a slow starter, by 1600 Amsterdam had a population of 50,000 plus, fuelled by its growing commercial success and refugees from the religious strife of Antwerp, who had swelled the city's pool of wealth, skill and resources. As William Temple noted, Amsterdam triumphed 'in the spoils of Lisbon and Antwerp', stealing their trade and monopolising world shipping – the flag-bearer of the emergent Dutch nation, founded on principles of tolerance, humanity and, above all, financial gain. With all this sudden prosperity apparently forced upon them, people found themselves squashed into an area that had changed little through the middle ages, and it became clear that some sort of city extension was needed. A plan was drawn up for three new concentric canals to girdle the bulbous thumb of medieval Amsterdam, providing valuable living and working space for the surplus population. Once the canals were dug, the council would lease the land to buyers on very strict conditions: the three main waterways, Herengracht, Keizersgracht and Prinsengracht, were set aside for the residences and offices of the richer and more influential Amsterdam merchants, while the radial canals were designated for more modest craftsmen's homes. Stylistic controls also existed: even the richest burgher had to conform to rules already laid down by the council when he built his house. This produced the loose uniformity you see today, with individualism restricted to heavily decorative gables. It was almost the end of the century before the scheme was finished – a time when, ironically, the demise of great Amsterdam had already begun – but it remains to the burghers' credit that their plan was executed with such success.

This century Amsterdam's elegant terraces have seen German occupation and Jewish deportation, radical outbursts in the sixties and the encroaching apathy of the seventies, but the city remains a tight communal web of shady canals and calm enclaves, in its more tranquil parts seemingly little changed since Rembrandt's day. Though many of the canal houses are now the premises of private business, lots more are still people's homes, and it continues to be a relatively small and largely residential city; one that's best seen on foot, varying from the peace and charm of the **Jordaan** – Amsterdam's working-class turned bohemian quarter – to the neon-lit night life of **Leidseplein**, just spitting distance down the road.

Dam Square is the place to start, centre of the city and within easy reach of just about everywhere you might want to go. Museums are the big pull: a huge range, from the Dutch paintings of the **Rijksmuseum** and superlative **Van Gogh Museum**, to the all-too-easily missed and little-visited **Amstelkring**. But really, just exploring the magnificent canals and their patrician houses can be enough of a reward in itself. **Nightlife** too is varied, vibrant and above all youthful: it's important to remember that one third of Amsterdam's population these days is aged between 18 and 30, and first and foremost it's a young people's town, with diversions geared accordingly. All this may sound expensive, and Amsterdam is by no means cheap, but you can live quite reasonably if you know how – eating in student restaurants, sleeping in hostels – and with careful planning can get by on relatively little.

Finally, don't fall into the trap, like most people, of coming to Holland and only seeing Amsterdam. Most of the country is quick and painless to reach, and it would be a big mistake to leave without seeing at least a couple of other Dutch cities. Your shortlist of the nearest places should include Haarlem, Leiden, Alkmaar, Hoorn and Naarden – for accounts of which (as well as everywhere else) see the appropriate chapters.

GETTING AROUND THE CITY

As Amsterdam's centre is relatively small, apart from walking by far the most efficient and enjoyable way to get around is by **bicycle**. You'll end up seeing more, getting places quicker and possibly paying less. There are several places to hire bikes: *Centraal Station* is not such a good idea in Amsterdam as although it's only f5.75 and you get a decent machine, you have to pay f200 deposit. If you don't carry that kind of small change around, and you're camping, you can often hire one from the *campsite*. If not try *Heja,* past the Oud West at Bestevaerstraat 39 (f6 + f50 deposit), *Koenders,* Utrechtstraat 105 (f6 + f100 deposit) or *Vullings,* Vossiusstraat 1 (f7.50 + f100 deposit).

Getting around on **public transport** can be a complicated business, due to the plethora of different tickets available. It can take you most of your stay just to find out the cheapest way of doing things, so we've included a brief résumé of the alternatives. For further info, pick up a tram/bus/metro map from the GVB (the Amsterdam transport service) outside the Centraal Station.

The current system has been running for about four years and is still largely in its experimental stages. Like that of many other European capitals, it manages on the basis of trust – no one checks your ticket, no one makes you buy one. People who don't pay are popularly known as 'black riders'; abuse seems rife and the number of inspectors to deter it has in effect decreased in recent years, as they now need to travel in groups of three or four to protect themselves from irate and aggressive 'black riders'. Assuming you wish to pay your way the alternatives listed below can all be used on trams, buses, the metro and surburban trains. Prices will probably have changed a little by now, but the principles should have remained the same.

The **Strippenkaart** can be used all over Holland, and the same rules apply to it on all forms of transport in Amsterdam. Don't pay over the odds for it when you get on, you can get one cheaper at the usual places (see p. 9). As almost all of Amsterdam you're likely to want to visit is contained in one zone, it can often work out the cheapest option. Alternatively, you can buy a **pass** that is valid for the whole of the city and lasts anything from 1 to 4 days, from the GVB. 1-day pass – f7.40, 2-day – f10, 3-day – f12.25, 4-day – f14.50. In certain circumstances

HET IJ

POST OFFICE

ÉPVAARTHUIS

PRINS HENDRIK KADE

NOORDZEE KANAAL

KATTENBURGER STR.

MARITIME MUSEUM

ONTELBAANSTOREN

LENBURGER

S GRACHT

ALKENBURGER STR.

WITTENBURGER

HOOGTE KADIJK

ARON KERK

LAAN

VROUWENHUIS

MUIDER STR.

PLANTAGE PARK

PLANTAGE

TUS PLANS

MIDDEN

ZOO

LAAN

NIEUWE KEIZERS GRACHT

KERK STR.

PRINSEN GRACHT

STRAAT

MUIDERPOORT

SARPHATI STR.

TROPEN MUSEUM

SINGEL GRACHT KADE

MAURITS

TI STR.

WIBAUT STR.

OOSTER PARK

RUYSCH STR.

this can work out cheaper than the Strippenkaart, depending on how long you're staying, where you want to go, etc. It's really up to you to weigh up the pros and cons. **Sterabonnementen** (star season tickets) are worthwhile if you're going to be in Amsterdam for any length of time. A 1-star ticket is valid for one zone, and a 2-star for all 7 Amsterdam zones. Prices: 1-star: week – f10.75, month – f33, year – f330; 2-star: week – f14, month – f48, year – f480. These are available from the post office (you'll need your passport) and you can also get them for any number of zones outside Amsterdam, though you'd probably be better off paying a little more for a train season ticket if you want to go further.

If you're feeling especially rich, **taxis** are plentiful and expensive – around f2 per kilometre – but they don't cruise the streets, instead hanging around in long lines outside the Centraal Station and on the main city square. If by any chance you can't find one, phone 77 77 77.

THE CITY

THE STATION AND DOWN DAMRAK

You arrive at Cuypers's **Centraal Station**, finished in 1889 and an imposing neo-Renaissance building with a poky labyrinthine interior totally at odds with the grandeur of its façade. The inside never seems to be finished and it's a series of temporary passages with directions given by sets of meaningless but supposedly international symbols. Built on three artificial islands, there was considerable controversy when the station was proposed since it obscured the view of Amsterdam's harbour. Still, it went ahead regardless and now the city begins here, fanning out from one point on the Ij. You arrive not in the centre but at the beginning, and Amsterdam lies all before you.

Picking your way through the myriad buskers and street performers and narrowly avoiding the trams that thunder dangerously towards you from both sides, you cross **Stationsplein**, which, like the station, has a permanent unfinished quality, vaguely resembling a building site as they reclaim parts from water and construct the concrete burrows that lead down into Amsterdam's sparkling new metro. The view from here is a strange mixture of the small and the monumental – the spidery spire of the Oude Kerk and the looming dome of St Nicolaas help form the faintly oriental Amsterdam skyline; what Charles Tennant called 'a thick crowd of towers, cupolas and spires', high above the roofs and gables of the rest of the city.

Don't be deceived by the rather grubby exterior of the **St Nicolaas Kerk** (Wednesday/Friday 1100–1500), the entrance, sandwiched between two run-down buildings and just yards away from the notorious Zeedijk, belies the richness and peace of the inside. It has been the foremost Catholic church of Amsterdam since it was finished in 1887, taking over from the clandestine Amstelkring which had served the purpose since the Reformation. Dedicated to the patron saint of the city and fronted by two Baroque towers, it's unfortunately the worse these days for lack of funds, and the windows of its gloomy dome have been bricked up until money is forthcoming for repairs. The crown of Kaiser Maximilian is on the high altar, presented to the city and adopted in its coat of arms after he was cured of an illness during a pilgrimage here. Amsterdam was a centre of great medieval pilgrimages due to a supposed miracle in 1345, when a man who was about to die received communion and instead of dying simply vomited and lived. What he vomited had been thrown into the fire, only to reappear as the Holy Host – in the same form as it had been given to the man. It was later placed in a shrine, attributed with powers of healing and a chapel was built on the site of the house where it had all happened. This became the target of an annual pilgrimage, still commemorated every year by the *Still Omgang* – a night-time procession through the streets of the city.

Damrak leads straight ahead with a sense of real promise, blazing a trail to the heart of it all: the cafés and restaurants that line its right-hand side are best avoided as they're mostly over-priced tourist traps, and, on the left, glass-roofed river boats herd together, lying in wait for prospective victims. Beyond them are the triangles and towers of the **Beurs** – the Amsterdam Stock Exchange, built between 1898 and 1903 by Berlage, and a seminal architectural work. It's a squat, heavy-looking red-brick building with a minimum of ornamentation, apart from the crude stone trimmings. An eclectic blend of styles from Romanesque to Renaissance, the emphasis is on simplicity and the functional – no better demonstrated than inside (entry at Damrak 62) where the ironwork is exposed and even glorified in the main hall which, combined with the shallow-arched arcades, give a real sense of space. What decoration there is pronounces structural detail, usually with brief but regular flashes of stone where iron meets brick.

Turn left off Damrak and you're in the notorious **red-light district**, bordered by the oldest street in the city, Warmeosstraat, and stretching across two canals that marked the edge of medieval Amsterdam. One of the most ancient parts of town, today's dubious trafficking hasn't always gone on here, and the rich façades of **Oudezijds Voorburgwal** point to a more venerable past – it was once known as the 'Velvet canal' because so many wealthy people lived on it. That was in the 16th century, and the continued prosperity of Amsterdam as a port brought sailors flooding into the nearest streets in search of women. Market forces obliged, and now **Oudezijds Achterburgwal** and the narrow connecting passages between the canals are thick with people most evenings of the year, thronging here to discover just how shocking it all is. The saddest thing is that this is one of the real sights of the city: the atmosphere is festive and entertainment for whole families that giggle and blush at the signs that invite them in for various kinds of naughty titillation. Men line the streets hawking their goods within, while the women sit and ply their trade behind glass – shop windows that take their place among the other high street businesses. A woman sitting in a window next door to the wholesome fare of a butcher's shop is one of the most bizarre sights I remember.

This area is bounded to the north by **Zeedijk**, where you must run the gauntlet of clutches of Surinam heroin dealers who will try to fast-talk you into a quick sale while idling groups of policemen look on. They claim to have the area under control but there's little evidence of it, and the best thing you can do is hurry on and ignore the whole business. Zeedijk comes out at Nieuwemarkt and the old St Antoniespoort (now the Jewish museum), which is at the end of Kloveniersburgwal, the outer of the three canals of 16th-century Amsterdam. Halfway up is the **Trippenhuis**, a great overblown brag of a house built for the Trips in 1662 and a suitable reflection of the importance of the Amsterdam *Magnificat*. This was the name given to the cliquey group of families who shared out power between them for about two centuries – Six, Trip, Hooft, Pauw – the names recur throughout the history of the city. This building was actually large enough to house the Rijksmuseum collection for most of the 19th century, until Cuypers's purpose-built version was ready.

The **Oude Kerk** stands between Warmeosstraat and Oudezijds, its precincts offering a reverential peace after the excesses of the red-light area; though you can't entirely escape it and the houses around have the familiar *Kamer te huur* (Room to let) sign and window seat. There's been a church here since the late 13th century, even before the Dam was built, but most of the present building dates from the 14th century onwards. Ransacked in the religious uprising of 1566, stripped bare after the Reformation and having recently undergone a very thorough restoration, the Oude Kerk is a survivor rather than any architectural masterpiece. Its vault paintings are the faded remnants of what was Amsterdam's principal medieval church and the rest a mixed account of the troubled years that followed. It'll cost you a guilder to get in and another to ascend the tower (May-October Monday-Saturday 1000–1600).

There was always a great rivalry between the Oude and **Nieuwe Kerk** (daily 1100–1600, Sunday 1200–1400/1600–1700) – despite its name a 15th-century structure several times rebuilt after fire. This centred on the question of a tower: the Oude Kerk acquired one in 1565, making the Nieuwe Kerk very jealous indeed and it retaliated by planning one of immense height, only to be thwarted by the upheaval of the Reformation.

In the 17th century another was designed, but it was decided that the new town hall could not be overshadowed by anything, not even a church tower – such was the true power of religion when pitted against Amsterdam's mercantile greatness – and the church lost out again. The chances of it getting one now are pretty slim, as it has been desanctified and is now only used as a museum, for organ concerts and for state occasions – Queen Beatrix was crowned here. The inside is neat, orderly and white, with fixtures, such as the massive pulpit and organ, which date from a prestige reconstruction after a mid-17th-century fire. A wealth of household names from Dutch history lie here. Most significant, if only because of its size, is the tomb of Admiral de Ruyter in the choir, carved by Verhulst in 1681, lest anyone should forget Holland's most valiant naval hero. The poet Vondel is here too, remembered by a small urn near the entrance.

DAM SQUARE AND THE ROYAL PALACE

Dam Square gives the city its name: in the 13th century the river Amstel was dammed here, and the small fishing village that grew around it became known as Amstelredam. In the middle ages boats could sail right into the square from the Ij and unload their imported grain in the middle of the rapidly growing town, and the later building of the Nieuwe Kerk and Royal Palace formally marked Dam Square as Amsterdam's centre.

Though robbed a little of its dignity by the trams that scuttle across, the square is still the hub of the city, with all the main streets zeroing in on the maelstrom of buskers, street artists, protesters and dope dealers who find an instant and captive audience in the passers by. Sit on its steps and you're turning your back on the **War Memorial**, an unsightly tusk of ossified stone filled with soil from each of the eleven provinces and Indonesia. It's the gathering place for the square's milling tourists who wonder if, in the musicians and drug pushers, they've really found the heart of liberated Amsterdam.

Across the square the **Royal Palace** (July/August 1230–1600, f1, no museumcards) seems neither Dutch nor palatial – understandably so since it was built from imported stone as the city's town hall. The authorities of Europe's mercantile capital wanted a grandiose declaration of civic power, a building that would push even the Nieuwe Kerk into an ignoble second place. Van Campen's then startlingly progressive design, a Dutch rendering of the classical principles revived in Renaissance Italy, succeeded: at the time it was the largest town hall in Europe, supported by 13,659 wooden piles driven into the Dam's sandy soil. Constantyn Huygens called it 'the world's Eighth Wonder, With so much stone raised high and so much timber under', and the poet Vondel was moved to apostrophise it in a poem that ran to 1,378 lines. It's the magisterial interior that really deserves this praise though: the *Citizen's Hall* screams the pride and confidence of the Golden Age in a disciplined harmony – the enthroned figure of Amsterdam looking down at the world and heavens at her feet, sumptuously inlaid in brass and marble. A good-natured and witty symbolism pervades the building – cocks fight above the entrance to the *Court of Petty Affairs,* and Apollo, god of the sun and music, hopefully brings harmony to the disputes. More soberly, death sentences were pronounced in the High Court of Justice, a small chamber that looks out on to the square. Here, below dramatic reliefs of mercy, sat the town's judges, and it's easy to picture the mob observing the grim proceedings through the grilled windows.

The town hall only received its royal tag in 1808 when Napoleon's brother Louis commandeered it as the one building fit for an installed king. Lonely and isolated, he briefly ruled the country from here, until forced to acquiesce to Napoleon's autocratic demands. On his abdication in 1810 he left behind a sizeable amount of Empire furniture, for the most part still here and exhibited in the rooms he converted. Today the palace is just a backdrop to the square, a neglected token of the past: but if you want some idea of Amsterdam's pride and power in the 17th century, take a look inside.

ROKIN AND SOUTH

Rokin continues the path of Damrak, following the old course of the Amstel. Running parallel, **Kalverstraat** has been a commercial centre since a cattle market started here in the middle ages. Though until recently *the* Amsterdam shopping street, it's declined to the standard European precinct, an unlikeable chain of monotonous clothes shops, differentiated only by the varying strains of disco music they pump out. Kalverstraat comes to an ignoble end in ice cream parlours and fast food take-aways before reaching **Muntplein**. Originally part of the old city walls, the **Muntoren** was topped with a spire by De Keyser in 1620 and it's about the most famous of the towers dotted around the city, a landmark perfectly designed for postcards. From here, Reguliersbreestraat turns left for the gay bars and loud restaurants of Rembrandtsplein, and Vijzelstraat heads straight out to the edge of the Amsterdam crescent. On the right is the heavy uncompromising chocolate cake of the ABN bank, and beyond that another of their buildings – one that caused a huge controversy in the sixties when it became known that it was to fill the empty space between Keizersgracht and Prinsengracht. Like the present threat of the Holiday Inn on Nieuwezijds, it was seen as an encroachment on a city that most people wanted to keep for living, not working in. There was a great uproar – meetings were held, petitions organised – and the most diverse groups of Amsterdammers united in an attempt to keep the bank out: the building is palpable proof that they failed, but the same sort of resistance continues in the squatting groups that still exist today.

At the far end of Vijzelstraat, opposite the Heineken brewery, is an area of green where on 3 April 1945, twenty people were shot by the Germans as an example to anyone who might be considering opposing their authority. An army in the last throes of defeat, they did this kind of thing quite regularly, rounding up as many people to watch as possible. The words on the short section of wall movingly commemorate the incident: attributed to a resistance fighter, they read, 'A nation that succumbs to tyrants gives more than body and possessions, it gives its soul; and the light is forever extinguished.'

Opposite is the **Heineken Brewery**, which made the headlines in 1983 when its chairman, Alfred Heineken, was kidnapped. There's a brewery tour which, for f1, is a must. The only bad thing about it is the ticket queue: there are two tours at 9 and 11 am, and after tickets have been sold for the first they start selling ones for the second. All tickets are usually sold by 9.45 and it's advantageous to be at the front of the queue – you complete the tour sooner and have more time in the hospitality lounge. The tour sensibly confines itself to the interesting parts of the brewing process, best of which is the hot, noisy bottling plant. After watching a Heineken film that looks like an apology for Holland's colonial past you're fed snacks and free beer. The atmosphere is convivial – as you'd imagine when there's two hundred people getting through as much free beer as they can drink. Whether you just have one or drink yourself into a stupor, it's a diverting way of having a lunchtime aperitif.

WEST FROM THE DAM

From behind, the Palace is oversized and drab, a dull grey hunk of stone too large for the space set aside for it. Raadhuisstraat leads west from the post office towards the fashionable Jordaan district. Descartes lived at Westermarkt 6 where, he said, 'everybody except me is in business and so absorbed by profit-making I could spend my entire life here without being noticed by a soul'. Amsterdam, for Descartes, was a frenzied background against which he could work and think. Even so, he must sometimes have been disturbed by what would have been a noisy building-site opposite: De Keyser's **Westerkerk** was being built, as part of the general enlargement of the city. Now the tower soars high above the gables of Prinsengracht, topped with the crown of Maximilian, the constantly recurring symbol for the city and an appropriate finishing touch to what was only its second Protestant church. Completed in 1631, it's not a revolutionary departure from pre-Reformation Gothic forms, while it has the paucity of decoration you'd expect. Though his memorial is in the north aisle, no one knows exactly where Rembrandt is buried:

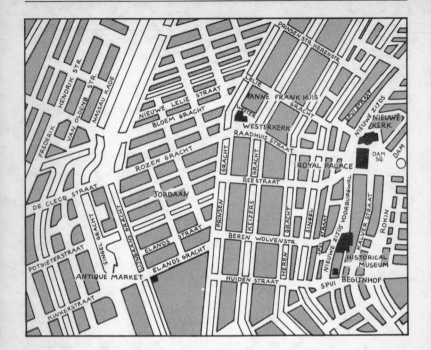

he was destitute when he died which meant he had a pauper's grave that has since been lost. Indeed, there's a chance that he's not here at all since many of the bodies were removed to a cemetery when the underground heating was installed. The memorial was put up in 1906, close to where Rembrandt's son Titus is buried. A delicate child, but the only one from the artist's first marriage to survive for any length of time, he died shortly before his father, delivering a final crushing blow to a life that had become fraught with emotional and financial difficulties.

A little way down the canal at Prinsengracht 263 Anne Frank used to listen to the Westertoren bells, until they were taken away to be melted down for the Nazi war effort. Her family and some friends occupied the tiny annexe of her father's business from July 1942 until their capture in 1944 – Jews, in hiding from what they knew to be the alternative of the concentration camp. The **Anne Frank Foundation** now runs the annexe as a museum (Monday-Saturday 0900–1700, Sunday 1000–1700; f4; no museumcards), and it's one of the most popular tourist targets in town. It's also one of the most worthwhile, though there's little point in telling you much about it here as you get handed an excellent free pamphlet as you go in. As well as the rooms where the Franks lived for two years – left much the same as they were then, even down to Anne's pin-ups on the wall – a number of rooms are given over to small exhibitions. One is a record of the gruesome atrocities of Nazism, another the story of Anne, from her frustrated hopes inside the annexe and the writing of the famous diary, to her eventual death from typhus in Belsen in 1945. The whole thing is a moving experience, a touching testimony to the irrepressible spirit of the young girl and sad reminder of the sort of evil mankind is capable of. The final room houses temporary displays on fascism and racism today, drawing pertinent parallels and with the in-built message that we should learn from what we have seen.

Across the Prinsengracht, on both sides of Rozengracht (most streets here have flower names) is the **Jordaan** (from *jardin*), an area of narrow canals, even narrower streets and simpler, more mixed houses. Outside the concentric-canal plan, this area was not subject to the same 17th-century municipal controls, which led to it becoming the centre of property speculation, developing as a series of canals and streets that followed the original polder ditches and rough paths. Such were the problems when state control was absent and, in contrast to the Baroque splendour of the three *grachts,* the Jordaan became the slum quarter, home of Jewish and Huguenot refugees who had fled here to escape religious persecution at home. Though tolerated, they remained distinct minorities and were treated as such, living here in what was often cramped and insanitary accommodation. Surprisingly, as recently as the 1950s the Jordaan was still more or less a slum, and it's only in the last couple of decades that it's gained the reputation as the home of young 'alternative' Amsterdam. Apart from a few bars and restaurants there's nothing much to see, but it's a great place for idle wanders, a quiet and restful retreat from the nearby turmoil of the city centre.

At Elandsgracht 109 is **De Looier** (Monday-Thursday 1100–1700, Saturday 0900–1700) – an excellent indoor **antique market** where there's an enormous selection from real collectors' items to what is mainly junk, so you feel you can actually *afford* to wander around. A leisurely browse may uncover a real bargain. The **Phonograph Museum** is next door, opened in 1982 and with a collection of old gramophones, all in working order.

Further on, up Kinkerstraat, the **Oud West** has taken on the mantle of the immigrant community and is a noisy congested area of cheap shops and markets, stacked with exotic fruits and spices. It's here that the Turks have made their home – shipped over by a special agreement between the two governments to provide a cheap and servile labour force for the Dutch and vast quantities of cash to prop up their own country's ailing economy.

NIEUWEZIJDS TO LEIDSEPLEIN

Even before Amsterdam's 17th-century expansion, the town could be divided into an old and new side; the outer boundaries were lined by a defensive wall, and it's this that gives **Nieuwezijds Voorburgwaal** (*New Sides Town Wall*) its name. The wall itself disappeared as the town expanded, and in the 19th century the canal that ran through the middle of the street was filled in, leaving the unusually wide swathe that runs from just below Prins Hendrikkade to Spui.

Nieuwezijds begins with a bottleneck of trams swinging down from the Centraal Station. One of the first buildings you see heading into town is **Wyers**, a dilapidated tenement block that is the latest focus of protests over development of the city centre. Plans to build a luxury Holiday Inn on the site have been delayed pending legal action against the squatters who've occupied the building in an attempt to prevent another multinational corporation taking over residential space in what's still a highly residential city. Though the American company exerts a lot of muscle, the squatters have the support of the average Amsterdammer, who doesn't want to see the city transformed into another mess of modern development that would eventually force ordinary people from the centre. Their much publicised battle seems like continuing for some time; we wish them luck.

The trees that fringe Nieuwezijds conceal some good canal houses, and the specialised shops and ludicrously expensive private galleries try hard to preserve some of the refinement the street must have had before the canal traffic gave way to trams. You've only to contrast it with the parallel Nieuwendijk to see how Nieuwezijds has retained some character: Nieuwendijk is a shabby, uninviting pedestrianised stretch of cheap shops and not-so-cheap restaurants, and the dark side streets have a frightening atmosphere of illicit dealings that hurries you back to the main roads. Things only improve as you approach the Nieuwe Kerk: there's a medieval eccentricity to the streets here, and seediness vanishes as upmarket boutiques appear in the old workshops clustered around the church. Walk down the wonderfully-named Zwarte Handsteeg – 'Black Hand Alley' – and you're back on Nieuwezijds. It says much for the Amsterdam school of architecture that their **Post Office** manages to hold its own against the Nieuwe Kerk and Royal Palace: built in 1908, its whimsical embellishments continue the town's tradition of sticking towers on things – here as everywhere, purely for the hell of it.

Nieuwezijds broadens and culminates in **Spui**. A mixture of bookshops and packed cafés, it's a smarter corner of town, though its main attraction is neither obvious nor signposted. Perhaps those who run the **Begijnhof** want it this way: enclosed on three sides, the small court of 17th-century buildings is like a bubble precariously trapped in the rushing modernity outside, a lovely enclave of tranquillity at the same time typically Dutch and totally un-Amsterdam. The *hofjes* or 'little courtyards' are found all over the Low Countries: built by rich individuals or city councils for the poor and elderly, the small houses turn inwards around a small court, their backs to the outside world. This sense of retreat suited women who, without taking full vows, led a religious life in the *hofje,* often having their own chapel. They were known as *Begijns* and Amsterdam's Begijnhof quietly continued its tradition of Catholic worship even after Catholicism was suppressed in 1578. Mass was inconspicuously celebrated in the concealed church here, a dark Italianate building with a breath-holding silence that seems odd after the natural peace outside. There's none of this unhealthy sense of mystery about the **English Reformed Church** that takes up one side of the Begijnhof: plain and unadorned, it was handed over to Amsterdam's English community when the Begijns were deprived of their main place of worship and, like the *hofje* itself, it's almost too charming, a model of prim simplicity. There are several old English memorials here, and the pulpit panels were designed by the young Piet Mondriaan.

Following the tram lines as they swing left towards the Singel takes you to Koningsplein and the beginning of the floating **Bloemenmarkt** that stretches down the canal as far as Muntplein. Open every day except Sunday it sells pots, plants and flowers at seemingly give-away prices. Leidsestraat, where people shop for airline tickets, cuts a narrow path down to Leidseplein – very much the centre of Amsterdam's nightlife, for tourists at least. Things are a little more expensive here and there's probably a greater concentration of bars, restaurants and clubs than anywhere else in the city. *Paradiso* is opposite – a blackened former church that looks as if it should have bats flying around it – and the *Melkweg* skulks around the corner in a converted warehouse. By day, street entertainers are out in force, and on summer evenings Leidseplein can ignite with an almost medieval vibrancy, drinkers spilling out of the cafés to see the sword-swallowers and fire-eaters enthral the milling crowds. The restaurants of Korte Leidsedwarsstraat join in enthusiastically, placing their tables outside so you can eat without missing the fun. On a good night Leidseplein is Amsterdam at its most carefree, exuberant best.

Overlooking the square is the Stadsschouwburg or civic theatre and behind that the **American Hotel**, a brick fairy castle traditionally the meeting place of the intellectuals and media people of Amsterdam, though it's now frequented as much by tourists as anyone else. It retains a beautifully unspoilt Art Nouveau interior that's definitely worth a look, with leaded stained glass, shallow brick arches, chandeliers and furniture that date from the 1920s. Everything is co-ordinated, right down to the smallest detail, in accordance with the complete vision of the movement.

SOUTH OF THE SINGELGRACHT

Amsterdam developed rapidly in the 19th century, spreading out beyond the Singelgracht into sporadic quarters of cluttered housing which were the homes of the new industrial working class. Pass the Heineken Brewery and you're in the solid proletarian area of the **Old South** known as *de pijp* – a series of long, narrow streets lined with forbidding, overcrowded tenements – the bright and noisy heart of working-class Amsterdam. The **Albert Cuyp Market**, on the street of the same name, is the largest in the city and has a massive quantity of just about everything from fruit and veg to cheap clothes. If you're in Amsterdam for any length of time there's no excuse for missing it as it's open every day except Sunday.

Beyond here lies the **New South** – a real contrast to its old neighbour and the first planned extension to the city since the concentric canals of the 17th century. Berlage was commissioned to design it 1915, reviving an idea that had become obscured by the 19th-century sprawl – that it was possible to order cities in precisely the way you wanted them. Like the 17th-century extension, it's all fairly uniform without being planned with robotic adherence to one design – a careful mix of wide curving boulevards and symmetrical blocks of brick apartments designed to general and flexible specifications. These days, it's a spacious green area with plenty of parks and a languorous air that makes it one of the most expensive parts of Amsterdam to live: Apollolaan is probably *the* most desirable of Amsterdam addresses.

A statue of Berlage stands near the RAI exhibition centre, though his plan was actually executed by members of the so-called Amsterdam School, led by Michael de Klerk and Piet Kramer, two architects at their most prolific between 1912 and 1922. Their work can be seen all over the city. De Klerk specialised in low-cost high-density housing and one of his better-known projects is the Eigen Haard estate, west of the station on Zaanstraat and Spaarndammerplantsoen. It's a series of plain brick blocks, characterised by the irregular and eccentric embellishments that were the hallmark of the Amsterdam School – rounded corners, turrets and bulging windows and balconies. Piet Kramer's De Dageraad housing estate, in the south-east of Amsterdam, demonstrates the same clever use of brickwork as decoration, and Van de Meij's Scheepvarthuis, on Prins Hendrik kade, takes the idea to an extreme, adorned with brick flourishes that are entirely fantastic.

THE JODENHOEK

East of the red-light area is the **Jodenhoek**, the old Jewish quarter, though there's little today to remind you of the tragedy of events forty years ago: a small statue and a synagogue are all that's left to mark the place

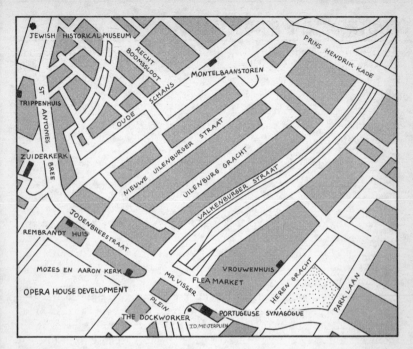

that, from the 16th century onwards, was the home of Jews escaping persecution from all over Europe. Under the terms of the Union of Utrecht they enjoyed a tolerance and religious freedom unknown elsewhere, and quickly became important figures in Amsterdam's rising mercantile society. By the early part of this century more Jewish families in fact lived outside than inside the Jodenhoek, but it was still regarded by most as the centre of Jewish Amsterdam. When in May 1940 the Germans invaded there were 80,000 Jews in Amsterdam, 10 per cent of the city's population. Those that weren't already there were forced into the Jodenhoek in order to create a ghetto where there had never been one, and some 50,000 were subsequently deported to their deaths. Out of a total of 140,000 Jews in the Netherlands, 100,000 were murdered in the concentration camps, and these figures explain why, to some, Amsterdam is still a ghost town.

Nieuwemarkt, today a broad square fringed with untidy development, marks the beginning of what was the Jodenhoek: the Jewish Historical Museum keeps a few poignant photos of the war years, but it's for the Sunday antique market that most people come here. Walk a little further, past the decorative landmark of de Keyser's Zuiderkerk, and you reach the **Rembrandt House** at Jodenbreestraat 6 (Monday-Friday 1000–1700, Sunday 1300–1700; f2) bought by the artist at the height of his fame and popularity. Rembrandt lived here for over twenty years and spent a fortune furnishing it, an expense that was to lead to his bankruptcy. An inventory of the time details a huge collection of paintings, sculptures and art treasures he'd amassed, almost all of which went in the bank-ruptcy hearings, and in 1660 he was forced to move to a smaller house on Rozengracht. The house itself is disappointing – mostly a reconstruc-tion made earlier this century with no artefacts from Rembrandt's life on exhibit. What there are, and in great variety, are his engravings. The Biblical illustrations attract the most hushed attention, but the studies of tramps and vagabonds are more easily accessible.

Much of Jodenbreestraat is 1960s-style redevelopment, complete with dual carriageways, office blocks and pedestrian subways. Modernisation has also struck the old Waterlooplein, currently being redeveloped as a new town hall and opera house. Redeeming feature of this urban mess is the **Waterlooplein Flea Market** (Monday-Saturday) a lively, earthy collection of stalls selling outrageous garments and bric-à-brac, often at outrageously cheap prices. The sooner you arrive the better as things start to wind down early in the afternoon. Watch your bag and change, and don't forget to haggle.

Across from the market the Portuguese Synagogue, built in the 17th century by Sephardic Jews exiled from the Iberian peninsula, is by all accounts very beautiful. However it's also very firmly closed at the moment, and chances of it being opened to visitors seem slim. Just behind the synagogue is J. D. Meijerplein: a small statue marks the spot where in February 1941 400 young Jewish men were rounded up and arrested, loaded on to trucks and taken to their eventual execution at Mauthausen. This was a reprisal for the killing of a German soldier in a street fight between members of the Jewish resistance and the Dutch Nazi party a few days earlier. The arrests sparked off a general strike – the 'February Strike' – in protest at the deportations and treatment of the Jews. Although the strike was broken by mass arrests after only two days, it was a demonstration of solidarity with the Jews unique in occupied Europe. Public transport workers and dockers formed the backbone of the strike, which was led by the outlawed Communist party: Mari Andriesson's statue of *The Docker* on Meijerplein commemorates this event, but a better memorial, tinged with Amsterdam humour, is the legendary slogan 'Keep your filthy hands off our filthy Jews'.

After the war the Jodenhoek lay deserted: those who had lived here were dead or deported and their few possessions were quickly looted. As the need for wood and raw materials grew in post-war shortages, the houses were slowly dismantled and destroyed, a destruction completed in the 1970s with the completion of the little-used metro that links the city centre to the outer suburbs.

Leaving Visserplein via Plantage Middenlaan you pass another sad relic of the war. The **Hollandse Schouwburg**, a predominantly Jewish theatre before 1940, was the main assembly point for Dutch Jews prior to their deportation to Germany. Inside, there was no daylight and families were packed in in conditions that foreshadowed the camps. The house across the street, now a teacher-training college, was used as a crèche. Some, possibly hundreds, managed to escape and there is a plaque outside in memory of those 'who saved the children'.

The Hollandse Schouwburg is little more than a shell now. Its façade is still intact, but the roof has gone and what was the auditorium has become a quiet, grassy courtyard. The memorial – a column of basalt on a base in the form of a Star of David – stands where the stage once was. It seems overblown, another failure to grasp the enormity of the crime. Off the beaten track and with few visitors, it is a temptation to the local kids, whose shouts bring a weary and cautious attendant from his office. A battered slot machine offers a leaflet and photographs. It's almost impossible now to imagine the scenes that went on here, but the sense of emptiness and loss is strong. If sometimes there seems to be a hollow ring to fun-loving Amsterdam, this place is why.

MUSEUMS AND GALLERIES

THE RIJKSMUSEUM

Stadhouderskade 42 (Tuesday-Saturday 1000–1700, Sunday 1300–1700; f4.50).
Don't leave Amsterdam without seeing at least a small piece of the Rijksmuseum, Holland's national museum and containing the finest set of Dutch paintings anywhere. It's a collection which only forms one part of what is a sizeable museum, but it overshadows the voluminous assortments of furniture and ceramics that fill most of the other galleries. You'll find it impossible to see the whole place in one day and it's best not even to attempt it; better to be selective and make several trips.

Top priority for most people will be *The Night Watch*, the most famous and certainly the most valuable of all Rembrandt's pictures. It hangs on the first floor in the central Gallery of Honour, recently restored after it was slashed by a vandal in 1975. The name is an erroneous 19th-century tag, a result of both the romanticism of the age and the fact that it was covered in soot; in fact the scene it depicts takes place in broad daylight. *The Night Watch* shares the Gallery of Honour with a varied selection of non-Dutch painters – there are canvases by Fra Angelico, Bellini,

Tintoretto and Murillo plus works by Van Dyck and Rubens. The rest of the 15th- to 17th-century Dutch works occupy a series of galleries to the right of the information hall. The very best paintings of the Dutch Golden Age are here: portraits by Hals and Rembrandt, landscapes by Van Goyen and the Ruisdaels, the riotous scenes of Jan Steen and peaceful interiors of Vermeer and De Hooch. The gradual movement of each room is vaguely chronological, beginning with Van Scorel and early examples of a more Italian-influenced era in Dutch art.

From the expansive *Isaac Massa and his Wife,* **Hals**'s merry and slightly bloated figures punctuate most of the galleries – though Haarlem is the best place to see his work – leading on to a set of rooms principally, though not exclusively, devoted to **Rembrandt**. The German impressionist painter Max Liebermann remarked that 'when you see Frans Hals you feel like painting, when you see Rembrandt you feel like giving up'. You can see what he meant: if Hals's painterly gusto is delightful, Rembrandt is awe-inspiring. His *Stall Masters* look down at you, captured in mid-sentence and demonstrating Rembrandt's ability to catch a staggering range of subtle expression. *The Jewish Bride* was one of his last works, painted around 1665 and tenderly exuding marital love: the paint is slapped on more freely here except for the hands, which are treated in contrastingly careful and minute detail, all forming what Kenneth Clark called 'a marvellous amalgam of richness, tenderness and trust'.

Rembrandt's more accomplished pupils follow – Dou, Bol and Maes – and finally the beautiful interiors of **Vermeer**: four exquisite paintings which, though unfortunately few, sum up a quiet achievement that, incredibly, only became recognised just over a century ago. The intimacy of *Woman reading a Letter* speaks for itself. Outstanding too are the similar domestic scenes of De Hooch, Metsu and Ter Borch.

Comparatively little happened in Holland in subsequent centuries. The Rijksmuseum doesn't have anything as contemporary as Van Gogh or Mondriaan and the 18th- and 19th-century works on the first floor are a bit of a let-down after all this. The 18th-century collection centres around the work of **Troost,** whose supposedly comic scenes earned him the dubiously deserved title of 'The Dutch Hogarth'. Better is a later painting by **Jan Ekels,** *The Writer,* small, simple and beautifully executed with a lighting and attention to detail imitative of Vermeer. The handy label of the **Hague School** covers a variety of styles and painters who originated from or worked in The Hague in the late 19th century, and there's work here by all of them – Weissenbruch, the Maris brothers, Mauve and Mesdag, along with their contemporaries, Jozef Israels and Jongkind. The **Amsterdam School** were also a mixed bunch, and far and away the best painting from this turn of the century group is **Breitner's** *Singelbrug near Paleisstraat in Amsterdam,* a random moment in the street recorded and framed with photographic dispassion.

The rest of the Rijksmuseum is a mass of fine art, though you'll need to have a keen interest to traipse around a large collection that's not all that fine. Extensive displays of **Delftware** and **Louis XVI furniture** form the highspots; the **medieval collection** may be better – it was closed when I visited. The **historical section** starts promisingly with the 17th-century square showing various aspects of life in the Golden Age, and continues in a series of galleries mostly filled with relics of Holland's naval and colonial past, most conspicuous of which is **Pieneman**'s painting of the *Battle of Waterloo,* a vast canvas that took six years to complete. All the big names of the battle are there, and the artist took two years on the portrait studies alone.

RIJKSMUSEUM VINCENT VAN GOGH

Paulus Potterstraat 7 (Monday-Saturday 1000–1700, Sunday 1300–1700; f4.50)

Van Gogh has proved possibly the most popular, most reprinted and most talked about of all modern artists, and this is his country's shrine to him, comprising the collection of his art-dealer brother Theo and opened to the public in 1973. Paintings, drawings and prints by Van Gogh and his contemporaries are superbly mounted and lit, in a spacious building that is a nostalgic look back at De Stijl. Each floor is one very large room, and you get long views of so many familiar canvases at once that it's hard to take it in, so assimilated is Van Gogh in contemporary consciousness.

Together with the shop, restaurant, reading room and a workshop where you can create your own expressionist masterpiece, are the **early paintings** of 1880–5, in their characteristically sombre tones. *The Potato Eaters* stands out, the culmination of literally hundreds of studies of peasants in North Brabant, where Vincent was born. The bulk of his pictures are on the first floor, beginning with the ones he completed after his move to **Paris** and the subsequent influence of the Impressionists. The following **Arles** paintings depict his new surroundings in rich and uncompromising hues – *Sunflowers* and *The Harvest* are in burning yellows and orange. While in the asylum at **St Remy** he developed a fiercer expressionism, with his colours still as strong but now less varied, for example the almost monotonic *Undergrowth* and *The Reaper*. In **Auvers**, in the last two months of his life, Van Gogh was mainly painting nature, weaving it into almost abstract shapes. *Wheatfield with Crows* shows swirling fields of wheat under black moving skies, painted in clashing colours with a writhing spiralling form. It was only a few weeks later that he shot himself: on him was found his last letter to his brother, in which he wrote – 'my own work, I am risking my life for it, and my reason has half foundered because of it'.

On the second floor is Vincent's large collection of **Japanese prints**, which so influenced him, and an ever-changing selection of his **drawings** – mostly early or from his Paris period. The top floor has a mixture of works by Van Gogh and friends and influences, grouped by subject-matter. There are African women by **Gauguin**, a good group of canvases by **Monticelli** and paintings by **Emile Bernard**, among countless others.

STEDELIJK MUSEUM

Paulus Potterstraat 13 (Tuesday-Saturday 1000–1700, Sunday 1300–1700; f3.50)

Opened in 1895 to house the contemporary overflow from the Rijksmuseum and since 1952 Amsterdam's museum of modern art, the Stedelijk, despite its reputation, is a bit of a disappointment. While their collection is indisputably complete from the mid-19th century onwards, it's difficult to say what you'll see as so much of it is on temporary display; only in July and August does the museum show off the bulk of its paintings and sculpture. Otherwise, the pictures on permanent showing consist of a scant assortment of post-Impressionists, including works by Van Gogh, Jongkind and Cézanne, and a cursory glance at some little-known pieces by Picasso, Braque and Léger. Malevitch and Chagall get a more thorough look-in but most exciting are some of the Stedelijk's more 'eccentric' items. **Jean Dubuffet** has a room to himself, full of crude and challenging paintings that show an uncompromising version of reality that is akin to children's art. He didn't become a full-time painter until he was in his forties, and paintings like *A Walk in the Garden* represent a delightful dig at an art establishment of which he had never been a part.

On the ground floor the philosophy (if there is one) seems to be to integrate the more contemporary painters here with the ordinary life of the museum and the world outside. Galleries are interspersed with cloakrooms, toilets and a large restaurant which you stumble across with some surprise; and the large uncovered windows are a constant reminder of the grey Amsterdam streets outside. Most interesting – down in the bowels of the museum and on permanent display – is **Kienholz's** *Beanery* (1965) – a tableau modelled on his local bar in Los Angeles, and one of the fascinating surprises for which you visit the Stedelijk. The figures have clocks for faces and everything is covered with a thin grime that breathes dissolution and decay. The hum of conversation, the music and the peculiar smell form a constant background to the horror of the newspaper headline in the vending machine – 'Children kill children in Vietnam riots'. This is *real* time, and for Kienholz, inside the bar is 'surrealist time . . . where people waste time, lose time, escape time, ignore time'.

AMSTERDAM'S OTHER MUSEUMS

Amsterdam Historical Museum

Kalverstraat 92 (Tuesday-Saturday 0930–1700, Sunday 1300–1700; f4)
Housed in a converted 17th-century orphanage, this museum attempts to give an account of Amsterdam's historical development, with artefacts and paintings of various periods. What frustrates this is the lack of English info: there's good background stuff on historical and social changes but the items themselves, from medieval tools to 18th-century clocks, remain irritatingly unaccounted for. In 1983 the museum landed itself in a financial crisis, owing the council a cool f3 million. Though it's unlikely to be forced into bankruptcy, one thing that does seem certain is that there'll be no money spent on English translations. The most striking section is the **Civil Guard gallery**, a covered street luring passers-by into the museum by giving glimpses of its large company portraits – there's a selection from the earliest of the 1540s to the lighter affairs of the 17th century. Other than this and a few bits and pieces unearthed when the metro was excavated, the Historical Museum is a bit of a let-down.

House museums

To have a look at one of the patrician houses on the *grachts,* you can visit one of the house museums. Splendidly decorated in mock Rococo style the **Willet-Holthuysen Museum** at Herengracht 605 (Tuesday-Saturday 1000–1700, Sunday 1300–1700; f2) is more museum than house, containing Abraham Willet's collection of glass and ceramics. For me the salons were overly ornate; I felt more at home in the basement kitchen, a well-equipped replica of the 17th century. Less grand though more likeable is the **Van Loon Museum** at Keizersgracht 672: at present it's broke and only open one day a week (Monday 1000–1200/1300–1700; f2; day and times may vary), the lack of funds no doubt accounting for the peeling stucco and shabby paintwork. Built in 1672, the house's first tenant was the artist Ferdinand Bol; fortunately he didn't suffer the fate of many subsequent owners who seemed to have been cursed with a series of bankruptcies and scandals for over two hundred years. The Van Loon family bought the house in 1672, bringing with them a collection of family portaits that now stretches from 1580 to 1949.

Amstelkring Museum

OZ Voorburgwal 40 (Monday-Saturday 1000–1700
Sunday 1300–1700; f3)
Sir William Temple wrote, 'all the violence and sharpness which accompanies the differences of religion in other countries, seems to be appeased or softened here, by the general freedom which all men enjoy, either

by allowance or connivance'. Such was the situation in 17th-century Amsterdam: while most religious freedoms could be bought with hard cash and a proven popularity, Catholics had to confine their worship to the privacy of their own homes. It was a typically civilised and amicable arrangement, and clandestine Catholic churches were common; known as 'Onze Lieve Heer op Solder' (Our Dear Lord in the Attic), the Amstelkring is probably the best preserved of them. The local parish church until 1887, it was replaced by the domed structure opposite the station and is these days only used for weddings and the odd service. It occupies the attic of a wealthy merchant's canal-house, together with those of two smaller houses behind. Galleried, and decorated with 18th-century fittings, the chapel exudes peace and simplicity, retaining the sense of a tranquil retreat from the outside world. The rest of the house is kept in a 17th-century style: reminiscent of interiors by Vermeer and De Hooch, the furnishings never appear false but instead enhance the impression of a house left as it was found.

The Six Collection
Amstel 218

To see the Six collection of 17th-century painting you'll need a note of introduction from the Rijksmuseum – easily available but you need to show your passport. **Rembrandt** was a friend of the burgomaster Jan Six and his *Portrait of Jan Six* is the collection's greatest treasure: painted in 1654, it's a brilliant, informal work, incisively capturing a fleeting insight as Six carelessly removes his gloves. Also here are Rembrandt's painting of Anna Wijmer, Six's mother, and **Hals**'s portrait of another prominent figure in the artist's oeuvre, Dr Tulp. A fine group of works, overlooked by most visitors.

Allard Pierson Museum
Oude Turfmarkt 127 (Tuesday-Friday 1000–1700, Saturday/Sunday 1300–1700; f2.50)

The danger of museums of antiquities is museum fatigue: one 5th-century Athenian vase soon begins to look like the next, with the result that you see everything and nothing. There are two reasons why the Allard Pierson museum doesn't fall into this trap: first, the collection isn't so big that it overpowers; second, the pieces themselves are of a very high quality. All the Greek exhibits are fine, the pottery of the archaic period excellent. The Egyptian collection is similarly good and well explained and, perhaps the highlight of the museum, there's some gorgeous jewellery of gold and precious stones from all the periods. Finally, all this is laid out in intimate galleries that encourage you to explore and make 'finds', and simple background info personalises what might otherwise be meaningless artefacts.

Tropenmuseum

Mauritskade 63 (Monday-Friday 1000–1700, Saturday/Sunday 1200–1700; f3)

As part of the Colonial Institute, this museum used to only display articles brought back from the Dutch colonies. In the 1950s, when imperialism became a dirty word and Indonesia was granted its independence, the Colonial Institute took on the less pejorative title of 'Royal Tropical Institute' and the museum began to collect artefacts from all over the world, eventually deciding, in 1970, to become 'a presentation centre for the third world'. This gives some idea of what it's all about: a mixture of temporary and permanent exhibits, representative of aspects of everyday life and the applied arts in most parts of the undeveloped world, are supplemented by videos, tapes and slides; getting away from old notions of museums being just stuffy, elitist expositions of antiquities. By now, an English booklet should be available (at a price), and labelling and commentary translations are, I am assured, in the pipeline. Even now it's good, but when all that happens this innovative museum will be a must. Downstairs, the Soeterijn Theatre specialises in third world films (many of which are in English), and is one of Amsterdam's main independent cinemas.

Maritime Museum

Kattenburgerplein 1 (Tuesday-Saturday 1000–1700, Sunday 1300–1700; f4.50)

A fortress-like arsenal building houses a well-presented history of the country's maritime past in an endless collection of maps, compasses and weapons. Most impressive are the large and intricate models of sailing ships and men-of-war, dating from the same period as the ships themselves. Loan of an English guide book is available, but only a real passion for ships and sailing will prevent tedium.

Jewish Historical Museum

Waagebouw, Nieuwmarkt (Tuesday-Saturday 1000–1700, Sunday 1300–1700; f2.50)

Though its aims are quite different, the Jewish museum is undoubtedly overshadowed by the Anne Frank house. It gets few visitors, which is a pity, as the main exhibition of the history of Jewish life in the Netherlands is well annotated, and the formation of the state of Israel and the plight of Palestine described with surprising candour. Inevitably, the most poignant part of the museum is the small collection of photos and documents from the Nazi occupation: ID cards carry the condemning J for *Jood*, and terse Red Cross telegrams tell of relatives who have died in the 'hospitals' of Mauthausen and Westerbork. But the main thrust of the display is on less tragic events, and if you are interested in Jewish history you'll probably find it fascinating.

Bijbels Museum
Herengracht 366 (Tuesday-Saturday 1000–1700, Sunday 1300–1700; f3)
Beautifully situated on Herengracht, this is an ecumenical museum that attempts to evaluate the importance of the Bible, chart its history and give an impression of Jewish life. Egyptian archaeological finds and Jewish devotional objects are imaginatively displayed, and a returnable booklet helps keep you informed.

Piggybank Museum
Raadhuisstraat 20 (Monday-Friday 1300–1600; f1; no museumcards)
Anyone who collects 12,000 piggybanks must have a sense of humour, and the Spaarpot museum is a light-hearted collection of the things, from African clay pots to mechanical toys of the 19th century. What can only be described as a remarkable appreciation of kitsch is evident too in the truly horrendous plastic souvenir boxes.

Museum Fodor
Keizersgracht 609 (Tuesday-Saturday 1000–1700; free)
This has no permanent collection and instead shows work by contemporary Amsterdam artists. There's an annual summer exhibition of art bought by the council and it also arranges exchanges of work with other capitals. A small museum, the exhibits change roughly every month, and while there's no information in English, a monthly magazine produced by the gallery should give you some idea of what's going on.

There are quite a few private galleries in Amsterdam – probably about two dozen in all – most of which have regularly changing exhibitions on anything from Russian icons to American Indian arts and crafts. For up-to-date listings check *Amsterdam This Week*.

Canon Photo Gallery
Leidsestraat 79 (Tuesday-Saturday 1100–1800; free)
Best and most central of the galleries devoted to photography, the Canon gallery has two or three exhibitions at any one time, usually by contemporary photographers. Good quality work and not just a plug for Canon.

Multatuli Museum
Korsjepoortsteeg 20 (Tuesday 1000–1700; f2)
In the house where he was born, this museum devotes itself to the life and work of Multatuli (Edouard Douwes Dekker), dissident Dutchman and author of *Max Havelaar* – the classic 19th-century Dutch novel.

The Aviodome
Schipol Airport (April–November Tuesday–Sunday 1000–1700; f4.50; no museumcards)
About twenty tired-looking planes are kept in this geodesic dome, whose slender theme is Dutch involvement in aviation history. All you can do is peer into the cockpits, and even an enthusiast like myself found it an unengaging and expensive day out.

THE FACTS

SLEEPING

Cheap rooms and dorm beds
You can always find room in a dormitory in one of Amsterdam's many youth hotels; in addition most also have a range of cheap **double, triple and quadruple rooms.** For almost all dormitory beds you'll need a sleeping-bag – otherwise you can normally hire sheets. In anything other than dorms sheets are almost always provided.

Sleep-In, Mauritskade 28   The cheapest bed in the city for f9 a night, breakfast on top. It's an enormous place so there's always room, and the many amenities include a bar, free showers, cheap restaurant and films on Sunday evenings. All in all, a convivial atmosphere – run by young people for young people. Open April–October.

Bob's Youth Hostel, NZ Voorburgwal 92   f14 for a bed in a clean bunk-bedded dorm and a rather frugal breakfast.

Kabul, Warmeosstraat 38–42   More plush but also more expensive at f17, without breakfast. Quite a range of other rooms including quads at f20 pp, triples and doubles f25 pp. Late bar next door has regular live bands.

H'88, Herengracht 88   Student building with *Mensa* restaurant downstairs. Main attraction is a bar open until 6 am. f15 including breakfast.

Studentenhotel, Keizersgracht 15   Beautiful location, very neat and clean, and a snip at f10 for a dormitory bed, f19 pp for a quad and f21 for a triple. Bar and cheap restaurant downstairs. Breakfast not included in price.

Hotel Parima, Warmeosstraat 91   One of the more run-down hotels of Amsterdam, but cheap at f12 for a dorm or f17 a double. You won't get much of a welcome, but at prices like these, what can you expect. The **AVC Hotel** next door is similar in price and hospitality.

The Last Waterhole, Armsteeg   Just around the corner from the Kabul and a cheaper alternative at f10. Pretty spartan, live music downstairs every night makes it a dingy, noisy place to stay.

Adam and Eva, Sarphatistraat 105   f15 for a dormitory room including breakfast. Lacks the advantage of being in the centre. Weesperplein metro or tram 6/10.

Shreierstoren Youth Hotel, Gelderskade 10   Cramped, rather gloomy dorms for f15, or f90 a week including sheets.

Magic Inn, NZ Voorburgwal 27   Used to be owned by Magic Bus, which explains the name and logo. Under new management, it offers dorm accommodation at f20 and 2/3/4 bedded rooms at f25. All very clean and very central.

Hans Brinker, Kerkstraat 136   One of the most popular and best-equipped budget hotels in town, it's advisable to book if you want to stay here between June and September. Prices range from f20 for a dorm to f31.50 pp for a double. There are cheaper places.

Cok Budget Hotel, Koninginneweg 34–36   For some reason rooms are always cheaper than advertised – dorms from around f22, doubles at f30 pp should be the minimum you'll pay. And what you pay for are facilities: shops, games room, bar and disco, all efficiently run. Best bet if you want dormitory accommodation without having to rough it.

Adolesce Hotel, Nieuwe Keizersgracht 26   Clean and tidy with a hint of disinfectant. Run by a stern but efficient proprietress. Bar, free showers and usefully near a student *Mensa*. Dorm beds from f20.

More up-market

Hotel Brian, Singel 49   Central and very friendly, you can stay here for f28 pp, which includes an excellent cooked breakfast.

Hotel Galerij, Raadhuisstraat 43   Does singles for f30, doubles f60. **Hotel Ronnie,** next door, is both less expensive and less welcoming at f25 for singles, f50 for doubles. **Clemens,** at number 39, has rooms for between f25–50.

Hotel Silton, Sarphatistraat 66   A little way east of the centre. Plain but comfortable – f35 single, f45 double.

Central Park West Hotel, Romer Visscherstraat 27   If you've money to burn this is the place to do it. Most rooms have all facilities and though expensive – singles from f48, doubles f75, triples f100, quads f125 – it compares favourably with much more costly places.

Camping and youth hostels

Amsterdam has three campsites all within easy reach of the centre and open between March and October.

Camping Vliegenbos, Meeuwenlaan 138   Youth camping north of the city on a 32 bus from Centraal Station (night bus 77). Relaxed and friendly, facilities include shop and bike hire. Maximum stay is three weeks – f3.50 per person, f5 if you're over 30; showers f1.25.

Camping Zeeburg, Zuider Ijdijk 34a   Youth camping to the east, close

to the Ijsselmeer, and larger and better equipped than Vliegenbos. Run
by the same people, prices are the same but it's more difficult to get to
– tram 3/10 to Muiderpoort and a 36 or 38 bus from there. At night
take bus 76. Facilities include a bar, shop, films and playground.

Amsterdamse Bos, Kleine Noorddijk 1   The grown-ups' campsite –
many facilities but a fair way out. Better for those with car or caravan
– otherwise yellow bus 171/172.

There are two **Youth Hostels,** open only to members of the YHA, and
costing around f16 a night.

Vondelpark, Zandpad 5   Main hostel, 300 beds, trams 1, 2 or 5, night
bus 74.

Stadsdoelen, Kloveniersburgwal 97   More central but only open between
March and November.

EATING

Mensas

The *Mensas* are Amsterdam's student restaurants, where anyone can eat
a generous plate of filling canteen stodge for around f5. Without doubt
the cheapest alternative, they're normally open Monday-Friday – lunch-
times and 1700–1900. **De Happetap** is the most central at Damstraat 3
while **H'88,** part of a student complex, is not far away at Herengracht
88. **De Weesper** (Weesperplein metro) is further out and closes during
July and August.

Restaurants

Amsterdam's restaurants cater for all tastes. What follows is a collection
of our favourites – if you want more comprehensive listings see *Use It*
or any number of the other booklets you can pick up all over town.

De Eetuin Eetcafe, Twede Tuindwarsstraat   Fairly standard *Dutch* food
in the heart of the Jordaan. A meal here shouldn't cost you more than
about f15.

Keuken van 1870, Spuistraat 4   Dutch food from f8. Monday-Friday
1100–1900.

Cantharel, Kerkstraat 377   More expensive than the 'Keuken' at around
f10 a head, but it has the advantage of staying open later – Monday-
Saturday 1700–2230.

De Bak, Prinsengracht 193   A good variety of mainly Dutch food – meat
with salad, potatoes, etc. – plus a vegetarian plate. Generous portions
mean you can eat a satisfying meal here for a little under f20. Open till
12 pm. If you're still hungry, the **Pancake Bakery** next door does a good
selection of crèpes, both sweet and savoury.

Sama Sebo, PC Hooftstraat   Just around the corner from the Rijksmuseum, this is one of the most popular *Indonesians* in town. The food

is good – and it's not overpriced. Rijstaffel at around f25 pp. Closed Sundays.

Koh-I-Noor, Westermarkt 29   Though not one of the cheapest, this is probably one of the best *Indians* you'll find. From f20.

Buddah's Belly, Rosenstraat 145   A cheaper Indian/vegetarian altern-ative – from f10.

Kebab House, Gelderskade 23   The name is misleading, this is another Indian restaurant – from around f15. If that's too much, **Orient Fast Food** at Utrechtsestraat 89 is cheaper and more basic and does menus from f10.

Pizzeria Collina, Rozenstraat   Possibly the cheapest *pizza* in Amsterdam – from around f6. On the other side of Rozengracht at Leliedwarsstraat 2, **Mamma Mia** is a little more expensive but very good.

Casa di David, Singel 426   At the bottom of Nieuwezijds. Classier and slightly more expensive.

Doz Santos, Warmoesstraat 24 and Prinsengracht 178 (opposite the Westerkerk)   Friendly service and piles of *Mexican* grub for about f16.

Rose's Cantina, Reguliersdwarsstraat 38   Probably the trendiest restau-rant in Amsterdam, and definitely the most crowded. Be prepared to wait at least half an hour for a table. The food – Mexican – is very good however, but if you want a quiet candlelit dinner, this is not the place. Around f20–25.

Rias Altas, Westermarkt 25   A *Spanish* restaurant, popular, even with Spaniards. You may have to wait for a table, but it's worth it for the superabundance of seafood and rice dishes. Again, at about f20. Rias has a sister restaurant – **Centra** at Lange Niezel 29, behind the Oude Kerk.

Vegetarian restaurants

Meals in vegetarian restaurants proper tend to be a cross-over with macrobiotic food – a blurring that sometimes leads to blandness of flavour. **De Bast,** Huidenstraat 19 (Monday-Saturday 1100–2000) is a case in point: small portions of uninteresting food, pure to the point of tastelessness and expensive at f10–15. Much better is the friendly and popular **Egg Cream,** St Jacobstraat 19, off NZ Voorburgwal (daily, 1700–2000) with filling and tasty meals that *are* meals rather than just lentils and rice. The day's specials are around f10. **De 3 Kruisjes** at OZ Armsteeg 6 (off Warmoesstraat) is smaller, quieter and a little cheaper, the food straightforward and likeable.

There are many more vegetarian places – **De Gouden Eeuw,** Heren-gracht 402 (Tuesday-Sunday 1715–2130) and **Sanitas,** Staalstraat 22 (Monday-Friday 1730–2100) among the best – but remember to go out early as most close by 9 pm. One of the good things about vegetarian eating in Amsterdam is that most half-decent restaurants have a vegeta-rian menu – usually one that's been thought about and not cobbled together from the day's veg. *Indian* restaurants are particularly good for this, and *Pancake* and *Italian* places usually have something free of meat.

BARS AND COFFEE-SHOPS

The traditional drinking-hole is the *brown café* (for a definition of this peculiarly Dutch phenomenon see p. 6), which in many ways you'll find much like the English pub, though not as crowded. Bars rarely have a set clientele and what's going on largely depends on who's there – Amsterdammers tend to flit from one to the other. Follow their example and you'll appreciate bars at their best.

Café Chris, Bloemstraat 42   One of the oldest cafés in the Jordaan, and, legend has it, the first here to accept students.

Cul de Sac, OZ Achterburgwal 99   Down a long alley, this is a welcome and civilised retreat from the red-light district. A restored 17th-century spice warehouse, it's small, quiet and friendly.

De Engelbewaarder, Kloveniersburgwal 59   Once the meeting place of Amsterdam's literati and still known as the 'literary café'. Relaxed and informal, it has *live jazz* on Saturdays and Sundays.

Frascati, Nes 59   Down the murky Nes, just off Rokin. Laid-back, arty clientele – probably due to the theatre attached.

't Gasthuys, Grimburgwal 7   Pleasantly situated opposite the university at the far end of OZ Voorburgwal. Generally lively and convivial, particularly during term-times. Outside seating by the canal.

H'88, Herengracht 88   For die-hard drinkers, this place is open until 6 am every night.

Hoppe, Spui 18   Extraordinarily popular – summer finds people spilling out on to the street about twenty deep, while inside has the atmosphere of a London city pub. Very much the watering-hole of the Amsterdam office-worker.

De Kalkhoven, Prinsengracht 283   On the corner opposite the Westerkerk. Quiet, central bar – a good place to begin the evening's drinking.

Cafe K Appel, Oude Hoogstraat 27   This is the place to go if you like your music amplified to the pain threshold. It's a lively, druggy place – pub entertainments include a dope dealer's alcove at the end of the bar. Formerly known as 'the Café of the Dead'.

De Kroeg, Lijnbaansgracht 163   Noisy and not especially conducive to conversation. Best for the *live jazz* later on – for which see 'Music' listings (p. 52).

Laurier 33, 1e Laurierdwarsstraat 33   Small fashionable bar on the edge of the Jordaan, good for its food and pool table.

Oblomow, Reguliersdwarsstraat 40 In the ultra-chic Reguliersdwarsstraat, this is apparently the haunt of the 'beautiful people' of

Amsterdam, though I suspect they've moved on to pastures new. If the decor doesn't tell you you're supposed to be somewhere exclusive, the prices certainly will.

De Pieter, St Pieterspoortsteeg 29   Calls itself a 'new wave bar' and is consequently about as unbrown as you can get. Mixed crowd – from punks to gays to heavy metal freaks. Very loud, open till 4 am, *live music* on Wednesdays.

De Pieterspoort   In the same street – smaller, quieter, but just as aggressively non-brown.

De Pool, Oude Hoogstraat 8   Quietly sociable – the beaming barman will camply make you welcome.

De Prins, Prinsengracht 124   Popular with students. An astonishing selection of drinks, good food and a generally lively atmosphere make this a great place to drink.

De Puffelen, Prinsengracht 377   While not exceptionally swinging, a genial café with a good choice of beer.

Run-Inn, Keizersgracht 402   On the corner of Runstraat and Keizersgracht. Small piano bar with *blues* and *jazz* most nights. Expect to pay for the music – though not excessively – on your bill at the end of the evening. Intimate atmosphere.

Scheltema, NZ Voorburgwal 242   Formerly a journalists' café – now only frequented by more senior newshounds and their occasionally famous interviewees. Old-fashioned furnishings give it a faded, turn-of-the-century feel.

Schiller, Rembrandtsplein 22   With its beautiful art-deco interior, this used to be the meeting place of Amsterdam's bohemian in-crowd. Currently enjoying a resurge in popularity, it's definitely worth visiting, if only to escape the all-evening cabaret bars that surround it.

De Tuin, 2e Tuindwarsstraat 13   In the heart of Jordaan and a likeably scruffy bar used by the locals.

Twee Heiligen, Prinsengracht 178   Opposite the Westerkerk – a spacious bar with a pool table. Good in summer when the church tower's lit.

English bars
Amsterdam's English community has established itself in a number of bars around the city – these are worth a quick visit to make contacts or if you're feeling homesick. **The Flying Dutchman,** Martelgracht, station end of Nieuwezijds, is *the* English bar – often crowded with regulars, with rarely anywhere to sit its life revolves around the pool table. Slightly less overpoweringly English is **Gary's Place,** across the road at Nieuwendijk 40. You'll find **O'Henry's** at Rokin 89 less patronised by the English fraternity than by tourists seeking English food and beer in an atmosphere 'just like home'.

Coffee-shops

Often very trendy, these places vary from 'smoking bars' which sell tea, coffee, cakes and dope, to hi-tech hang-outs for cool people. **The Bulldog,** OZ Voorburgwal 90, is one of the more legendary of Amsterdam dope bars – small and sleazy, with dealing downstairs. **The Grasshopper,** over at Nieuwezijds 59, is a more restrained and better-decorated smoking bar. **Berlin,** at Van Woustraat 193, is a fair way out but proclaims itself as 'the best in town', and the attractions of **Adam and Eva,** Paardenstraat 11, include videos and 3am closing. Three more: **Biba,** Hazenstraat 15, another dope café; **Haussman,** on the Singel next door to Odeon, white and tubular; **By the Magere Brug,** Kerkstraat 457, a musicians' café.

LIVE MUSIC

The music scene

While the top Dutch pop combos continue to croon away in English, many young bands here are moving away from dependence on Britain and America. Most musicians seem to feel that Holland has copied the Brits too long and now they want to sing in Dutch and develop a style of their own. *Stichting Popmuziek Nederland* was set up in 1974 and goes some way to solving at least some of the problems of new bands, mainly with the help of a f250,000 government grant. They provide a fully-equipped recording studio and the all-important contacts in the music biz, as well as freely distributing independent releases. As far as a place to play is concerned, *Paradiso* and the *Melkweg,* while excellent venues in themselves, have long been bastions of the rock establishment, and you're more likely to catch new Dutch music at *Mazzo* on Mondays, *Maloe Melo,* or a number of other places all listed below. Watch out for the so-called multi-media centres, such as *Meervaart* and *Fizz,* which offer a variety of entertainments all under one roof. Apart from posters in the hipper bars, the usual organs are good for up-to-date listings – *Uitkrant, Amsterdam This Week,* etc. If you're a real enthusiast, the leading Dutch music paper is *De Oor* (The Ear).

Paradiso, Weteringschans 6   f2.50 for one month's membership plus a varying admission price (f5–10 depending on who's playing): with the Melkweg, a survivor from the sixties explosion, but one which has made a more definite effort to move with the times. Housed in a converted church off Leidseplein, this is where big names tend to play, and people come here to see bands, buy dope, and generally pose around.

Melkweg ('Milky Way'), Lijnbaansgracht 334   The most notorious Amsterdam nite-spot and the one that is most hard to categorise. The first time you go it'll cost you f11 (f6 plus a further f5 for three months' membership, free if you have a student or CJP card), which leaves you expecting quite a lot. The place itself is a fun-palace that lives by its reputation, a bewildering maze of rooms that offer everything from Concert Hall to Restaurant to Tea Room to Film Theatre. There's live music most nights but a lot of people just hang out in the Market, where you can buy sweets, snacks and a large selection of different types of dope, all reasonably priced in pre-wrapped little bundles – the cheapest deal you could get when I was there was one for f10. The dope is shipped in by the Dutch authorities – a way of keeping down street-dealing and the black market – and the Melkweg is a government-funded outlet for the stuff. If you want to buy, you'll find this (with *Paradiso* – another government 'shop') by far the most reliable place to do it.

The Gym, Beursstraat 3 (prices vary according to who's on)   Behind the Beurs, and one of the top Amsterdam venues. A variety of musics throughout the week – Monday: Jazz, Tuesday: Salsa, Wednesday: Blues, Thursday: Reggae, Friday: New Wave, Saturday: Disco.

De Ijsbreker, Weesperzijd 23, f10   Concentrates on modern jazz and electronic and experimental music. Interesting.

Maloe Melo, Lijnbaansgracht 160, free   One of the best places in Amsterdam to see a band, though most of the ones that play here you'll probably never have heard of. Small, crowded and smoky, with the accent on R&B.

De Meervaart, Osdorpplein 67, prices range from about f5 to around f15   A multi-media centre, with music and theatre and a great deal else.

Oktopus, Keizersgracht 138   Squatters' bar with cheap drinks, videos, and intermittent bands. Opens at 2100 and makes for a good night out.

De Snelbinder, Tuinstraat 237   As well as nightly discos, live music on Thurs, Fri, Sat.

Cafe de Pieter, Sint Pieterspoortsteeg 29   Bar with bands on Wednesday. Open till 4 am.

Odeon, Singel 460   Puts on 'night concerts' on Thursdays, Fridays and Saturdays. These start at midnight and finish much later.

Bimhuis, Oudeschans 73, f7.50–12.50   The city's major jazz venue. Gigs on Wednesday, Thursday, Friday, Saturday.

De Kroeg, Lijnbaansgracht 63, free   Next door to Maloe Melo – bar with jazz and salsa most nights. Starts late.

The Run-Inn, Keizersgracht 402   Laid-back piano bar.

De Engelbewaarder, Kloveniersburgweg 1 59   Good bar with jazz on Saturday and Sunday evenings, from 2000.

Cab Kaye's Jazz Piano Bar, Beulingstraat 9   Jazz piano nightly, from 2000.

Joseph Lamm Jazz Club, Laagte Kadijk 35   Trad jazz, jam sessions. Sundays at 2100.

Classical

Concertgebouw, Van Baerlestraat 98 (021 71 83 45 Box Office open Monday-Saturday 1000–1500)   Obviously, *the* place to see a concert in

Amsterdam. Open every day except Monday, ticket prices vary from
nothing for weekly lunch-time concerts, to f37.50 for Bernard Haitinck
and the Concertgebouw orchestra, though certain selected summer
concerts can be cheaper. Also watch out for the *July jazz festival,* which
usually draws most of jazz's big names.

Odeon, Singel 460   Classical concerts on Tuesdays and Sundays.

Opera can be heard at the Stadsschouwburg – check press for details.

To suit other tastes

Soeterijn Theatre, Linnaeusstraat 2   Ethnic music on Tuesdays – from
SE Asia, Latin and South America.

De Schutter, Voetboogsteeg 13   Folk and country music every Thursday
evening.

Nieuwe Kerk, f5   Organ concerts on Sunday afternoons at 1500.
Thursday evenings too in July and August.

Oude Kerk, f5   Organ concerts during the summer – Tuesday evenings.

Westerkerk, f5   Summer organ concerts – Monday evenings at 2000.

The Vondelpark

Named after the 17th-century poet, the Vondelpark is Amsterdam's most
popular park: pushing its way between the smart Oud West and Zuid
districts, it's the venue for some great, **free outdoor concerts** in the
summer months. Sunday's the day when everyone and his dog turns up
to hear the bands play, taking in the music either crushed in the arena
or sprawled around the park's ponds. A laid-back pop festival atmosphere
prevails, supported by the sundries usually found at such events – food,
drink and a small market offering haircuts and dope plants as well as the
more normal stuff. Incredibly, the city council provides the facilities,
cleans up afterwards and also organises most of the week's events. There's
classical music on Wednesday at 1200, **children's theatre** at 1500 hrs,
folk/jazz on Thursdays at 1900, **theatre** on Fridays at 2100 and **bands**
on Saturdays and Sundays, starting at 1400 – check the posters around
town for specific listings.

DISCOS AND CLUBS

Most of the city's discos open around ten and stay open till at least four
in the morning. Admission varies, but unless there's something special on
expect to pay between f5 and f12.

Mazzo, Rozengracht 114   Sparse hi-tech interior – mirrors everywhere
and flashing video screens. Technically a club, but you can join for one
night only. Normally just a disco but live bands every Monday.

Okshoofd, Herengracht 114   Claiming to be 'the most swinging talk-
and-dance-o-theque in this (or possibly any other) world' the Okshoofd

is in reality down-to earth and fairly ordinary. Restaurant/video room open on Friday and Saturday.

Richter 36, Reguliersdwarsstraat 36   Outrageously smart and trendy. This is where Holland's bright young things come to dance.

Flora Palace, Amstelstraat 24   The place to go if you like your music funky. Videos and gay nights on Mondays.

Odeon, Singel 460   One of Amsterdam's most widely-frequented discos. Housed in a renovated theatre, good music, sporadic live bands.

De Koer, NZ Voorburgwal 155   Small, very fashionable and *very* cliquey. You'll have to fight to get accepted here.

De Snelbinder, Tuinstraat 237   Unpretentious, and definitely out of favour with Amsterdam's hip crowd. Live music at weekends, and rooms where you can watch TV, drink in peace, play pool or just relax.

Schakel 49, Leidsedwarsstraat 49   No entrance fee and fairly mainstream music. Tourist joint.

Fizz, NZ Voorburgwal 163   Multi-media entertainment including food, games, video and disco.

CINEMAS AND THEATRES

The usual **cinema** chains show the standard releases, with an audible sound track and Dutch subtitles when the film is in English. Admission is about f10 and a weekly list of movies is pinned up in many bars or can be found in the usual periodicals.

As well as the forty or so mainstream cinemas, Amsterdam has many **Film Theatres** showing arthouse movies and experimental or independent productions.

Amsterdams Filmhuis, Ceintuurbaan 338 is the major film theatre, showing political and art films on two screens and publishing its own magazine, *Lampier du Cinema*. If you can tolerate the noise from downstairs the **Melkweg**, Lijnbaansgracht 243 is popular, usually offering a season of works from one director or theme. Like the Melkweg the **Shaffy** complex at Keizersgracht 324 has a film theatre and often works with the Melkweg in presenting themes. More specialised are the **Filmmuseum Cinematheek**, Vondelpark 3, which presents early films and the classics, and the **Soeterijn** at Linnaeusstraat 2, which mainly shows third world films. **Desmet**, Plantage Middenlaan 4 is a refurbished Art Deco cinema, premiering films produced by Holland's three independent companies, and **Kriterion**, Roeterstraat 170, **Nickelodeon**, Kleine Gartmanplantsoen 14 and **Jean Vigo**, Lijnbaansgracht 235 are worth keeping an eye on for their 'quality' presentations.

Amsterdam has a profusion of **theatres** and theatre groups, and if you're prepared to look around there's always something happening in English. Productions are as diverse as the theatres numerous, and the best way of finding out what's on is by checking the listings of *Amsterdam This Week* or, more critically, *The Paper*. The main venues are the **Mickery** at Rozengracht 117; **The American Repertory Theatre (ART)** at Kerkstraat 4, and **Shaffy Theatre** Keizersgracht 324. **ESTA,** the English Speaking Theatre of Amsterdam, doesn't have a fixed venue, but its productions come well recommended.

The **Uit Buro** on Leidseplein (corner of the Stadschouwburg) will help with tickets (generally around f10, occasional student reductions) and also co-ordinates the *Amsterdam Summer Festival* in June and July.

THE GAY SCENE

Amsterdam's gay life is unbeatable: people come from all over to sample its selection of bars, restaurants, hotels, saunas – the list is endless – specifically catering for homosexuals. You'll find most of the action centred on the area around Rembrandtsplein and Muntplein, from the Amstel across as far as Kerkstraat; plus one or two places in NZ Voorburgwal and Warmeosstraat. As well as all this there are a number of information centres and organisations that hand out advice and useful tips for those both gay and new to the city.

COC, Rozenstraat 14   The nationwide gay organisation with branches all over the country – help, advice, coffee shop and notice-board for both men and women.

Shorerstichting Consultatie-Bureau Voor Homofilie, Wolvenstraat 17   Free and confidential advice and information. Legal, social and personal problems all dealt with.

Spartacus, publishers of the well-known gay guide to the world are based, appropriately enough, in Amsterdam. They're always ready to answer queries and provide first-hand practical info for first-time visitors to Holland. You can reach them on 95 09 50, Monday to Friday.

Man to Man, Spuistraat 21   Information centre, meeting place and cinema. They also put out the definitive Dutch *gay guide* – obtainable from bookshops and some bars and hotels.

The great thing about most of the **bars** is that you don't have to be gay to enjoy them – they're among the friendliest, most relaxed places to drink in town. Some are more intimidating and are strictly reserved for gay men and/or gay women. Here's a very brief selection of bars which are principally for gay men, though gay women are by no means excluded.

Amstel Taverne, Amstel 54   Probably the best established gay bar in town. Always packed, and at its most vivacious in summer when people crowd out onto the street

Company, Amstel 106   Leather bar, very popular later on in the evening.

Chez Manfred, Halvemannsteeg 10   A tiny bar but the Amsterdam gay scene at its gregarious best.

April, Reguliersdwarsstraat 37   Probably the best out of what is a streetful of gay bars. A little further down is **Viking,** a lot less comfortable and mainly for the disco crowd – open till 5am at weekends. **Downtown,** at number 31, is cosier and also serves food.

Wells Fargo, NZ Voorburgwal 101   Western style saloon and one of the more renowned gay bars. Large, loud and convivial. **Why Not,** at NZ Voorburgwal 28, bills itself as 'the place to meet a boy', but is not nearly so pleasant or lively.

Argos, Warmeosstraat 15   Apparently 'the oldest leather bar in Europe'. Hard-line and sometimes a bit heavy. **Casa Maria,** in the same street, is friendlier and more laid-back.

Many Amsterdam **hotels** are run by gay couples, and some make gay visitors particularly welcome. Kerkstraat and the environs of Leidseplein are the best places to look, but more specifically **Seven Bridges** at Reguliersgracht 31 is an amicable place with singles from f40, doubles f60. **Tabu,** Marnixstraat 386, is not exclusively gay, but sympathetic – singles from f35, doubles f50.

WOMEN'S GROUPS AND CENTRES

Women's groups in Amsterdam are among the best organised in Europe. Though they concentrate on problems facing women in Holland, they're always glad to hear from interested visitors from other countries. The **Vrouwenhuis** at Nieuwe Herengracht 95 is the co-ordinating women's centre and the best place to find detailed information on feminism in Amsterdam and throughout the country. They'll also put you in touch with some of the more specialised groups like the *Feminist-Socialist association* and *Grapevine* for single parents. The Vrouwenhuis is open daily 1400–1700, tel. 25 20 66.

Amsterdam has many restaurants and cafés specifically intended for women and which often exclude men. If you want to meet other women in relaxed surroundings then the **Vrouwenrestaurant Zus,** Goudsbloemstraat 52, for women travelling through or living in Amsterdam, is one of the best places, serving vegetarian food from 1730–2100 (closed Mondays). Of the Vrouwencafes, **Saarein,** Elandstraat 119, is the foremost, open from noon every day (2000 on Mondays) and exclusively for women. Try also the smaller and quieter **Vivre la Vie** at NZ Voorburgwal 171, **Harmonia,** Kerkstraat 346 and **Orka,** Koveniersburgwal 21.

Two other useful addresses: **COC** at Rozenstraat 14 is Amsterdam's gay info centre/bar/disco and reserves Saturdays for lesbian women, and **Xantippe,** Prinsengracht 290 is an excellent feminist bookstore.

THINGS

Airport Schipol, south-west of the city. Until the rail link to Amsterdam CS is completed, you have to be content with trains to Amsterdam Zuid or Amsterdam RAI. Alternatives are taxis – which can cost as much as f40 – or the KLM bus, which is both inexpensive and frequent and only takes thirty minutes to Centraal Station.

Babysitting Roeterstraat 170 (tel. 23 17 08).

Banks Most banks are open Monday-Friday 0900–1600. If you want cash at any other time the GWK office at the station is open until late evening, seven days a week. Failing that, the VVV will change money, though for a paltry rate.

Books Most bookshops stock at least a few Penguins, but the best selections of English books are to be found at *Allert de Lange,* Damrak 62, or *The English Bookshop,* Lauriergracht 71. The *AB Bookshop* in Spui is especially good for foreign newspapers and magazines and *De Slegte* are at Kalverstraat 48.

British Council Keizersgracht 343.

Canal Trips If you can stand the tourists and the canned commentary, the best way to see canal houses is, logically enough, from a canal. Trips cost f7.50 and last around 45 mins – they leave from Stationsplein and Damrak.

Car Hire *Avis* (Keizersgracht 485), *Budget* (Overtoom 121), *Europcar (Overtoom 51), Hertz* (Overtoom 333).

Car Repairs *ANWB,* Museumplein 5 (tel. 73 08 44), accident breakdown (26 82 51). All night petrol station, Marnixstraat 250.

Chemists Geldersekade 84, Damstraat 2, Rozengracht 67, Utrechtsestraat 86.

Consulates American (Museumplein 19), British (Koningslaan 44).

Dental Treatment Louwesweg 1 (tel. 15 69 36). Phone between 0830 and 1200.

Help and Legal Advice JAC, Amstel 30, give it free (Mon, Tues, Thurs, Fri 1000–2200; Sat, Sun, Wed 0900–2200).

Hospital Treatment Ambulance 555 5555. The most central hospital is the *Onze Lieve Vrouw Gasthuis,* Eerste Oosterparkstraat 179 (tel. 599 9111).

Launderette The most central one is at Warmeosstraat 30.

MAIC *Maatsch Advies en Uit Centre* – JW Brouwersplein 9, near the Concertgebouw. Info on courses and accommodation as well as general advice for those new to the city.

Markets *Albert Cuyp*, Albert Cuypstraat (general Monday-Saturday), Waterlooplein (flea market Monday-Saturday), *Singel*, off Muntplein (flower market Monday-Saturday), *Looier*, Elandsgracht (antiques Monday-Saturday), *Nieuwmarkt* (antiques May-September, Sundays),

Oudemannhuispoort, off OZ Achterburgwal (books Monday-Friday).

The Pill   Obviously it's best to stock up if you're coming for any length of time, but should you run out while you're here the *Aletta Jacobhuis,* Overtoom 323 (Monday-Friday 0900–1600/1900–2115) will be able to provide you with some.

Police   Emergencies 22 22 22. HQ – Elandsgracht 117 (tel. 559 9111).

Post Office   NZ Voorburgwal 182 (Monday-Friday 0830–1800, Thursday till 2030, Saturday 0900–1200). For telephones use the back entrance – open day and night.

Supermarkets   The most central place to stock up on food is a place on Leidsestraat – I can't remember the name or address. Other than that, there are night shops (open 1700–2400) at Amstelstraat 30 and Overtoom 478.

Swimming   Indoor pools at Heiligeweg 19 and Marnixplein 5; outdoor at Hobbemastraat 26.

Travel   *NBBS* are on Dam Square and *Transalpino* and *Magic Bus* are just around the corner in Rokin, at numbers 44 and 38.

VVV   Stationsplein and Rokin. Stationsplein office open daily 0900–2300.

What's On   the *Amsterdam Uit Buro,* in the Stadschouwburg building, is the main place to buy tickets, pick up information, etc. A number of magazines are good for listings: *Amsterdam This Week* is as up-to-date as the name suggests and is put out free by the VVV. *Uitkrant* is an Uitburo publication and appears monthly. Otherwise, *The Paper* (see p.14) does the best listings in town, though you have to pay for it. Finally, if you're staying at a student hotel or campsite you're likely to be handed a copy of *Use It* – a valuable guide to just about every aspect of the city.

Wholefood shop   *Manna,* Spui 1 and Quellijnstraat 153.

TRAVEL DETAILS

Trains

Roughly three trains an hour from Amsterdam Centraal to Haarlem (15 mins), Leiden (32 mins), The Hague (45 mins), Rotterdam (1 hour 5 mins), Dordrecht (1 hour 45 mins). One train an hour to Vlissingen (2 hours 40 mins). The connection to the Hook of Holland ferry (1 hour 20 mins) stops at Haarlem, Leiden and The Hague. Also trains to:

Hilversum (2 an hour; 20 mins),

Maastricht (1 an hour; 2 hours 30 mins),

Leeuwarden (1 an hour; 2 hours 25 mins),

Groningen (1 an hour; 2 hours 25 mins),

Arnhem (2 an hour; 55 mins),

Utrecht (3 an hour; 40 mins),

Hoorn (2 an hour; 40 mins),

Alkmaar (2 an hour; 30 mins).

International trains

Cologne (1 an hour; 3 hours 15 mins), Hanover (4 daily; 5 hours), Antwerp (1 an hour; 2 hours 15 mins), Brussels (2 an hour; 3 hours), Paris (8 a day; 6 hours), Luxembourg (11 daily; 6 hours via Brussels, 7 via Maastricht), London (2 daily; 10 hours).

Buses

Amsterdam CS–Volendam (NZH bus 110/112; 30 mins), Amsterdam CS–Edam (NZH bus 112; 30 mins), Amsterdam CS–Marken (NZH bus 111; 40 mins), Amsterdam Station Zuid–Haarlem (CN bus 142; 1 hour 15 mins), Amsterdam Weesperplein–Muiden (CN bus 136/138; 30 mins), Amsterdam Weesperplein–Naarden (CN bus 136/138; 1 hour), Amsterdam Weesperplein–Haarlem (CN bus 137; 1 hour 15 mins), Amsterdam CS–Leiden (CN bus 145; 2 hours), Amsterdam Muiderpoort–Utrecht (CN bus 120; 1 hour 35 mins), Amsterdam Amstel–Lelystad (VAD bus 154; 1 hour).

Chapter two
NORTH HOLLAND AND TEXEL

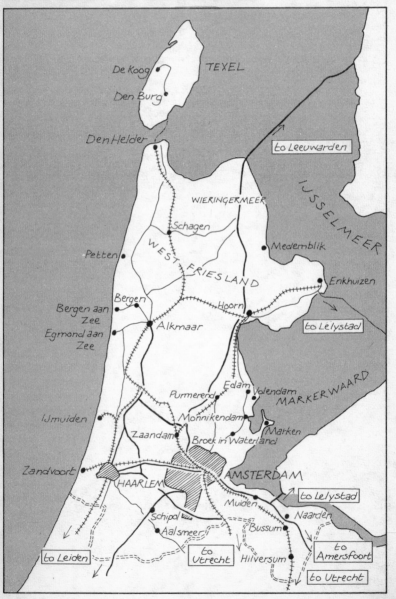

Until the 17th century most of **North Holland** was punctured by innumerable small lakes which poached vital land from the farms around them. A great many of these were reclaimed in the early 1600s by Jan Adriaanszoon, a pioneering engineer who came to be better known as 'Leeghwater' (Empty-water), and Beemster, Purmer, Wormer and Schermer, among several others, became important farming areas and weekend retreats for the wealthier Amsterdam merchants. All of this has shaped what you see today. Hazlitt said that 'Holland is perhaps the only country which you gain nothing by seeing. It is exactly the same as the Dutch landscapes of it,' and this is probably truer of North Holland than any other province. So much of it is green and water, topped by trees and the odd church, and all covered by a boundless sky.

The surface of North Holland was due to increase in 1980, with the completion of the **Markerwaard**, the final polder in the Zuider Zee scheme, but it met with such intense opposition from the towns most likely to be affected that the plan has now been shelved. Marken, Volendam, Edam and Hoorn all wanted to keep their waterside positions, and not end up incarcerated in yet more expanses of green flatness. The ring-dyke connecting Enkhuizen and Lelystad remains and is well-used, but the draining of the area within is unlikely ever to take place now.

Amsterdam sprawls south into suburbs and dormitory towns, and there's little of interest there. Apart from Amsterdam itself, **Haarlem** is the main target as far as monuments go. North of Amsterdam is a favourite of the day-excursionists, but while you can miss the twee costume-villages of Marken and Volendam, **Hoorn** and **Enkhuizen** further north have a decayed greatness that is pleasant if not exactly stunning. Everything in this chapter is within easy reach and day visits are always conceivable. Even **Texel**, in the far north, is only an hour and a half from Amsterdam, and if you're after a bit of peace and quiet, it's one of the most worthwhile journeys you can make.

AMSTERDAM TO HILVERSUM

East of Amsterdam, **Muiden, Naarden** and **Hilversum** are similar only in their lack of cheap accommodation. Unless you're heading to Utrecht or further east, each is really a day trip from Amsterdam. They're easy to get to and of the three, Naarden is the best bet for a day out.

MUIDEN is squashed around the Vecht, a river usually crammed with pleasure boats and dinghies sailing out to the Ijsselmeer. Most of the sightseeing is done by weekend sailors eyeing up each other's boats, but **Muiderslot** (Monday-Saturday 1000–1600, Sunday 1300–1600), a castle more storybook than stronghold, is the place to head for. In the 13th century it was the home of Count Floris V. A sort of aristocratic Robin Hood, he favoured the common people at the nobles' expense, the nobles replying by kidnapping poor Floris, imprisoning him in his own castle and stabbing him to death.

Destroyed and rebuilt in the 14th century, Muiderslot's interior is now a restoration of the period of a more recent occupant, the poet Pieter Hooft. He was chatelain here from 1609 to 1647, a sinecure that allowed him to entertain a group of literary and artistic friends who became known as the *Muiden Circle,* and included Grotius, Vondel, Huygens and other Amsterdam intellectuals. The (obligatory) guided tour costs f3.50 and is centred around the characters of the Muiden Circle – a recreation of the 17th century which is believable and likeable, two things period rooms generally aren't.

Look at a postcard of **NAARDEN** and it seems the town was formed by a giant pastry cutter: the double rings of ramparts and moats, unique in Europe, were engineered between 1675 and 1685 to defend Naarden and the eastern approach to Amsterdam. They were still used into the 1920s and one of the fortified spurs is now the wonderfully explorable **Fortress Museum** (Monday-Friday 1000–1630, Saturday and Sunday 1200–1700; f2.50), whose claustrophobic underground passages show how the garrison defended the town for 250 years.

Naarden's quiet centre is peaceful rather than dull. Most of the small, low houses date from after 1572 when the Spaniards sacked the town and massacred the inhabitants, an act designed to warn other towns and villages in the locality. Fortunately they spared the late Gothic **Grote Kerk** (afternoons only, closed Friday; f2.50) and its superb vault paintings. Based on drawings by Dürer, these twenty wooden panels were painted between 1510 and 1518 and show an Old Testament scene on the south side, paralleled by a New Testament story on the north. To study the paintings without breaking your neck, borrow a mirror on entrance. A haul up the Grote Kerk's **tower** (last tour 1530; f2) gives the best view of the fortress island and, less prettily, Hilversum's TV mast.

If you've never heard of Jan Amos Komenski or Comenius, a polymath and educational theorist of the 17th century, it's unlikely that the **Comenius Museum** (Tuesday-Sunday 1400–1600; free) at Turfpoortstraat 27 will fire your enthusiasm for the man. A religious exile from Moravia (now in Czechoslovakia), Comenius lived in Amsterdam and is buried in Naarden. To the Czechs he's a national figure, and they donated most of the exhibits in the museum as well as building his **Mausoleum** in the *Waalse Kapel* on Kloosterstraat – a building permanently on loan to the Czech people.

In the 19th century a rail link turned **HILVERSUM** into a dormitory suburb for wealthy Amsterdammers, and the well-heeled smugness they created continues: their villas have been flashily converted into studios for Dutch broadcasting companies, and behind the neatly trimmed hedges and net curtains live Hilversum's more-than-comfortably-off. In the middle of all this tidy bourgeois greenery is Dudok's **Raadhuis** of 1931, a deceptively simple progression of straw-coloured blocks rising to a clock tower, the eye drawn across the building by long slender bricks. The Raadhuis is open to the public during office hours (ask at reception for info) and if you've any interest in modern architecture, go in and explore. It's a series of lines and boxes, marble walls margined with black like an uncoloured Mondriaan painting, all coolly and immaculately proportioned. Dudok also designed the interior decorations, and though some have been altered, his style confidently continues, even down to the ashtrays and light fittings.

Dudok was Hilversum's muncipal architect and the **Information Centre** on Kerbrink publishes a walking tour of the many other buildings he designed in the town (their free town map is also the best available). The VVV near the station will help with pensions, but as there's no accommodation going for less than f27 a night, you'll probably want to move on.

NORTH OF AMSTERDAM

The polders immediately north and the towns that line the Ijsselmeer are a favourite for day-trippers from Amsterdam; umpteen bus companies run excursions from the capital. **MARKEN** is usually their first stop, a former island in the Zuider Zee that was largely a closed community – its biggest problem being the genetic deficiencies caused by close and constant inter-marrying – until it was joined to the mainland by road, the first victim of the Markerwaard scheme. Now more accessible, its character has been artificially preserved. The harbour is brightly painted in Marken colours, local costumes and clogs are still worn and gangs of tourists wander around, led by informative guides - something the locals no doubt appreciate, judging by the number of tourist-junk shops here. They take no notice though, and go on with their everyday chores, hardened to the multi-national groups gathered outside their windows. A fishing village before, Marken must have felt the pinch when the Zuider Zee was closed off. The solution, unfortunately, was this.

The road follows the dyke as far as **VOLENDAM**, a larger village which retains some semblance of its fishing industry in conjunction with the more lucrative business of tourism – into which it has thrown itself wholeheartedly. This is everyone's 'picture-book' view of Holland: fishermen in their baggy trousers sit idly in strategic positions along the harbour wall, while women scurry around, clad in familiar winged lace caps; the Volendam costume is the well-publicised one that all foreigners know and associate with the Dutch. The people here too must be making more money than they ever made from fishing. Piped music all around the harbour completes an effect which, on the whole, is best forgotten.

So close to Volendam as to be virtually the same place, you would expect **EDAM** to be just as bad, especially considering its reputation for the small red balls of cheese which the Dutch keep for export. Actually, it's quite a relief after the mob-rule of Volendam; an absurdly picturesque little town that is more a dormitory suburb of Amsterdam than a major cheese-producer. Apart from its intrinsic charm, the thing to see is the **Grote Kerk** – an enormous building almost wholly rebuilt after a fire in 1602, and with some remarkable stained glass dating from that time. If Edam has a centre then it is Damplein, where stands the 18th-century **Raadhuis**, which Sacheverell Sitwell described accurately as 'sensible, solid and in no hurry', though inside it's far from sensible, a superabundance of luxuriant stucco work. Across the bridge in a distinctive step-gabled building, there's a small **museum** (daily 1000–1200/1330–1630), and the **VVV** are in the leaning Speeltoren, in Kleine Kerkstraat.

The northern part of North Holland is known as West Friesland – the result of Charlemagne's 'Lex Frisonum' which, when he couldn't control the rebellious Frisians, divided the whole area into three. Since then, none of these regions have had much in common: the east is now known as Groningen and the west has retained its original name, while the central part – Friesland itself – is the only one that has really kept a regional identity.

HOORN, the ancient capital of West Friesland, 'rises from the sea like an enchanted city of the east, with its spires and its harbour tower beautifully unreal'. So wrote E. V. Lucas in 1905, and Hoorn is still very much a place that you should either arrive at or leave by sea, though you probably won't get the chance to do either. In the balmy 17th century it was one of the richest Dutch ports – what the poet Vondel referred to as the trumpet and capital of the Zuider Zee – handling the important Baltic trade and that of the Dutch colonies. From here the East India Company was run, Tasman went off to discover Tasmania and New Zealand and in 1616 William Schouten sailed out to navigate a passage around South America, calling its angry tip 'Cape Hoorn' after his native town. All of this is hard to detect in today's quiet provincial town. The harbour silted up in the 18th century, making Hoorn one of 'the dead cities of the Zuider Zee', and the creation of the Ijsselmeer was the last straw: the harbour is now no more than a yacht marina, and elegant streets and houses only a faint echo of an astonishingly illustrious past.

Hoorn is small, manageable and doesn't demand more than a day. And while it hasn't anything of special interest, apart from the Westfries Museum, it's a good place to drift around aimlessly; there's plenty to stumble upon by chance, particularly towards the station, where you'll find quiet canals and almshouses. The centre is **Rode Steen** (literally 'red stone' – where the scaffold was), and here stands J. P. Coen, founder of the Dutch East Indies empire and very much honoured as one of the bright lights of the 17th century. On the corner is the VVV who do a free map and walking tour but guard their lists of rooms carefully. If you decide to spend more time here, you can either try *De Magneet*, Kleine Oost 5, for f27.50, or the VVV will book you a private room for f22.50 plus f3.50 booking fee.

The **Westfries Museum** is next door (Monday-Friday 1100–1700, Saturday and Sunday 1400–1700; f1.50), its heavily ornamented façade dominating the unassuming square with the coats of arms of Orange-Nassau, West Friesland and the seven major towns of North Holland. Formerly the government building of those towns, it's a historical reminder of Hoorn's past glory plus a regional museum for the whole West Frisian area. Most rooms are furnished convincingly in 17th-century style and are devoted to aspects of local history, all vividly communicating the unbelievable affluence of the time.

In Kerkstraat, the **St Jans Gasthuis** – a delightful building with a so-called 'trap-gable', tapering to a single window and built at an angle to the main body – puts on temporary exhibitions for the museum. Opposite, the **Grote Kerk**, a 19th-century church that was put up after its predecessor was lost in a fire, is in a dreadful state of disrepair and when I was there had been taken over by a water-sports supplier. By now it may have been demolished. . . .

For **eating and bars** try Breestraat, behind the Grote Kerk; or the shopping streets of Kruisstraat and Kerkstraat. A **steam train** runs twice a day in the summer between here and Medemblik – f8 single, f13 return. Times from the VVV.

Another 'dead city', **ENKHUIZEN** declined at the end of the 17th century and now repeats much the same sort of attractions as Hoorn, though its museums are decidedly more impressive and a major pull. The **VVV** is at the station and they'll let you have a rough map and book you a **room** for f20 plus fee, or there are two **campsites** just north of the old town and easily walkable. The cumbersome **Dromedaris** tower – a 16th-century left-over from the town walls – marks the old harbour, and now houses rooms and a cheap restaurant.

The **Zuider Zee Museum** is why most people come here – since 1983 split into *Binnen* and *Buiten,* indoors and out. The **Buitenmuseum** was opened in 1983 as an attempt to capture salient examples of a lifestyle destroyed with the building of the Afsluitdijk, and place them in a realistic setting. Cottages, farmhouses, a tannery, a smithy and countless other original buildings have been brought from 39 different locations on the Ijsselmeer to form a representative sample of life on the Zuider Zee in the 19th century. It's a project that has been in the making for 40-odd years, and you may wonder how it pays for itself. The answer is that it doesn't – you do, to the tune of f7.50. Extortionate, but if you have the money, worth seeing (open April-October, daily 1000–1700; no museumcards). The only way to get there is by boat, which you can pick up at the jetty by the railway station.

If the price seems too much, the **Binnenmuseum**, Wierdijk 18 (Monday-Saturday 1000–1700, Sunday 1200–1700; f3.50; closed January) is good consolation. Forerunner of the open-air section, this has existed since 1950 and has a good collection of fishing vessels and equipment, and Zuider Zee arts and crafts, such as regional costumes and painted furniture from Hindeloopen – all lovingly displayed. Owing to the popularity of the other museum, I suspect they're going to run this one down over the next few years, so expect some big changes.

During the summer, you can take **boats** to Urk and Stavoren from behind the station. There are three boats a day to Urk and two to Stavoren – f8 single and f13 return. For times, check with the VVV.

MEDEMBLIK is just a few miles up the coast, but there's not much to entice you there. Though one of the most ancient towns in Holland and seat of the pagan Frisian kings until the 7th century, the only sign of it all is the **Kasteel Radboud**, named after the most famous of them and a much restored 13th-century fortress that sits graciously by the harbour. Otherwise, Medemblik survives as a yachting centre and very little else.

If you're heading towards the enclosing dyke then you'll cross the **Wieringermeer polder** – first of the Zuider Zee polders and a corner of land created in the 1920s when the island of Wieringen was connected to the mainland and the area behind it reclaimed. During their occupation, and only three weeks before their surrender, the Germans flooded it, boasting that they could return Holland to the sea if they wished. After the war it was drained again, leaving a barren treeless terrain that had to be totally replanted. Almost 40 years later, it's virtually back to normal and offers a familiar scene – Patrick Leigh Fermor's 'flat geometry of canals and polders', leading up to the Afsluitdijk and away into Friesland.

The sluices on this side are known as the *Stevinsluizen,* after Henry Stevin who, amazingly, had the idea of reclaiming the Zuider Zee around 1600, but was constrained by the small problem of not having the technology to do the job. The dyke was eventually built to a plan by Cornelis Lely and finished in 1932. Near the Den Oever end stands Mari Andriessen's statue of Lely, who died before he could see his vision completed. Further along, at the point where the barrier was finally closed, is an observation post on which an inscription reads: 'A nation that lives is building for its future.'

HAARLEM

Despite being only eight miles from Amsterdam, **Haarlem** has a character of its own. Here they speak a refined kind of Queen's Dutch, and the city has an air of quiet affluence, remarkably independent of the dubious excesses of the nearby capital. Don't believe the Amsterdammer claim that Haarlem is parochial and rather snobbish, it is both unfair and unfounded. The Frans Hals Museum, in the almshouse where the artist spent his last – and for some his most brilliant – years, is worth a day trip in itself, though you really need longer to do justice to Haarlem's churches, museums and *hofjes*. The **VVV** is at the station (Monday-Saturday 0900–1930, Sunday 1100–1400) and they have an excellent map and free lists of **rooms**, though you're more likely to find somewhere cheap to stay in neighbouring ZANDVOORT – try *Jeugdhotel Casa Blanca*, Oosterparkstraat 33 (open April-November; f25). There's a **Youth Hostel** in Haarlem at Jan Gijzenpad 3, and a couple of **campsites** among the dunes at Bloemendaal-aan-zee (bus 81). For cheap **food** try *Time Out*, Kreisstraat 43 (from f8) or *De Ark*, Nieuwe Heligland 3 (from f10) – both of which have a good selection of Dutch dishes. **NBBS** are at Kruis Weg 66 and there's a branch of **De Slegte** at Grote Houtstraat 100.

For a long time the residence of the counts of Holland, Haarlem was sacked by the Spanish under Frederick of Toledo in 1572. After a siege of seven months, the revenge exacted by the inconvenienced Frederick was terrible, being the massacre of almost the whole population, including inevitably the entire Protestant clergy. Recaptured in 1577 by William the Silent, Haarlem went on to enjoy its greatest prosperity in the 17th century, becoming a centre for the arts and home of a flourishing mannerist school of painters.

At the core of the city is **Grote Markt** – an open space flanked by perhaps a greater concentration of Gothic and Renaissance architecture than any other Dutch square. At one end stands a statue of Laurens Coster, who, Haarlemmers insist, is the true inventor of printing, though Gutenberg is generally acknowledged as more likely. He stands in the shadow of the **Church of St Bavo** finished in the early 16th century and familiar from Berckheyde's many views of it, from which it has changed little; only the black-coated burghers are missing. It dwarfs the cluttered maze of streets and houses around it and serves as a landmark from almost anywhere in the city. Having said that, you still can't fail to be deeply impressed by the sheer height of the interior which, combined with the mighty Christian Muller organ that literally covers the west wall, make St Bavo's beauty more breathtaking than serene. Stripped of almost any kind of ornamentation, the church gives the impression that it has lost an inner skin, leaving only the bare bones which impress with

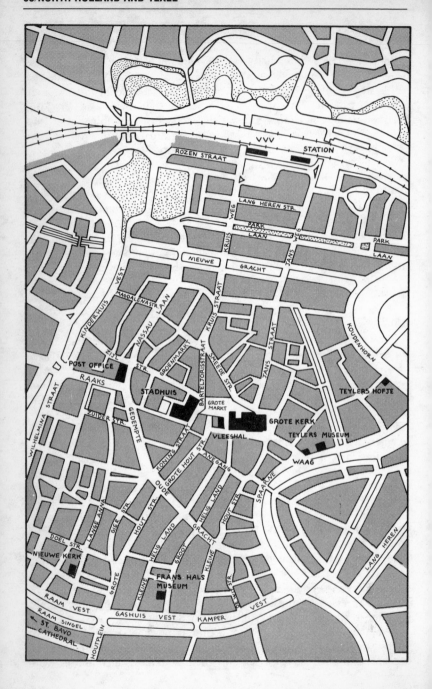

their structural power. The organ alone stands out from this, said to have been played by Handel and Mozart and one of the largest in the world, with 5,000 pipes and a riot of baroque embellishment. Beneath is Xaverij's lovely group of draped marble figures, representing Poetry and Music giving thanks to the town patroness for her liberality. In the choir a late 15th-century view of the church is traditionally though dubiously attributed to Geertgen tot Sint Jans, and there are memorials to the 19th-century Dutch poet Bilderdijk, and the painters Pieter Saenredam and Frans Hals, all of whom are buried here.

When I was there St Bavo's was being thoroughly restored and was only half open. Though definitely worth a visit now, you'll have to wait until 1986 before you can see the place in its full glory. Attached is the **Vismarkt**, and opposite that, Lieven de Key's **Vleeshal**, decorated profusely with step-gables, heads and obelisks and perhaps the epitome of the northern Renaissance in its cheerful opulence. Both buildings are now annexes of the Frans Hals Museum, with regular exhibitions of modern art.

The **Stadhuis** confronts St Bavo's from the other end of the square. The date 1630 on the front refers to the last rebuilding, but much of the place dates back to the 14th century and recalls various styles; with two different gables, a rampart front, a spire and a balcony on which it's not hard to imagine the burgomaster emerging to placate the angry mob. Nowadays you can only visit the Great Hall (Monday-Friday office hours).

The **Teylers Museum**, at Spaarne 16 (Tuesday-Saturday 1000–1700; f2.50), is Holland's oldest museum, founded in 1778 by wealthy local philanthropist Pieter Teyler van der Hulst. Its strength lies in the versatility of its collection, which should appeal to scientific and artistic tastes alike. Apart from a good selection of fossils, bones and crystals, there are rooms full of weird and wonderful instruments and apparatuses, including Van Marum's enormous electrostatic generator of 1784. All this H. G. Wellsian technology, the purpose of much of which remains obscure, reinforces the Victorian feel of the museum, while a portrait of the benevolent Teyler surveys all. As well as scientific exhibits, there are sketches and line drawings by Michelangelo, Raphael, Rembrandt and Claude among others. These are covered as they need to be protected from the light, but don't be afraid to pull back the curtains and have a look. There are also rooms devoted to 19th-century Dutch painters, with some good work by Breitner, Israels and Weissenbruch, and 18th-century painters, in particular Hendricks, who was keeper of the art collection of the museum.

On the opposite side of town is Van Campen's **Nieuwe Kerk**, which was built on to Lieven de Key's bulbed and typically Dutch tower in 1649. Not only do the two not fit together, but the interior – in the shape of a Greek cross within a square – is symmetrical with a soberness that is quite chilling after the soaring heights of St Bavo. Just beyond here and much less self-effacing, the Roman Catholic **Cathedral of St Bavo** demands to be seen (March-October 0930–1200/1400–1630). One of the largest ecclesiastical buildings in Holland, it was designed by Joseph Cuijpers and built between 1895 and 1906, and can best be described as 'post neo-Gothic'. Broad and spacey inside, the exterior is a host of cupolas and turrets, which crowd around the apse in a way reminiscent of Byzantine churches or mosques. The whole structure is surmounted by a distinctive copper cupola, the effect only slightly spoilt by two staid west towers added in the late 1920s.

Frans Hals and the *hofjes*

E. V. Lucas said that **Frans Hals** 'stands alone in his gusto, his abundance, his surpassing brio'. He was right: Hals's work is normally characterised by a tremendous vivacity and, though unfortunate enough to be roughly contemporary with Rembrandt and constantly outshone by him in popular opinion, Hals is arguably one of the greatest ever portraitists, showing a sympathy with his subjects and an ability to capture fleeting expressions that even Rembrandt lacked. On top of that, he was probably the most original of all 17th-century Dutch painters, his bold impressionistic brush-strokes and lighting bridging a stylistic gap of 300 years. Seemingly quick and careless flashes of colour form a coherent whole at a distance, a technique that was peculiar to him at the time and gave us a set of 17th-century figures that are curiously alive.

Hals was probably born in Antwerp, the son of Flemish refugees who settled in Haarlem in the late 1580s. Unfortunately, his extant work is relatively small – some 200 paintings and nothing like the etchings, sketches and studies left behind by Rembrandt. It seems unlikely, though, that Hals was any less prolific and, not a fashionable painter until the 19th century, a lot of his work must have been lost before it became collectable. The **Frans Hals Museum**, Groot Heligland 62 (Tuesday-Saturday 1000–1700, Sunday/Monday 1300–1700; f2.50), retains the most complete collection of his 'corporation pieces' or group portraits anywhere, and is meaningfully housed in the **Oudemannhuis**, where the aged Hals is supposed to have lived out his last years on a council hand-out, destitute, despite a successful painting career. Successively sued by the town's tradesmen and the women who had his illegitimate children, his constant money problems seem to have been the result of his lifestyle rather than any lack of success as a painter.

The museum begins with Van Scorel's *Baptism of Christ* and a good group of paintings by the **Haarlem Mannerists**, including works by Carel van Mander. His output was small and he was more the 'éminence grise' of the Mannerist school, shaping the styles of the other painters represented here. Cornelisz van Haarlem best embodies these guidelines: *The Marriage of Peleus and Thetis* is his most important work here, with more attention given to the arrangement of elegant nudes than to the subject.

Frans Hals was a pupil of Van Mander, though he seems to have learned little more than the barest rudiments of painting from him. Like all great painters the only style you can recognise in his work is his own. The paintings in the west wing established his reputation as a portraitist, and show various civic guards – usually a bloated and unruly lot – in mid-banquet. These military companies got together during the Spanish wars, but by the early 17th century were more like social clubs for the wealthier sections of the community. Hals himself was a member of the Haarlem Militia Company of St George for a time and he painted them in 1616. All of these works are most remarkable for their composition, which for the first time made the group portrait a unified whole instead of a static collection of individual portraits: Hals's figures are carefully arranged, but so cleverly as not to appear contrived. In the *Officers of the Militia Company of St George* (1639) the artist appears in the top left-hand corner – one of his few self-portraits.

Darker and more akin to Rembrandt, the *Governors of the St Elizabeth Gasthuis* (1641), leads on to the culmination of the museum which is, fittingly, the portraits of the *Regents* and *Regentesses of the Oude-mannhuis* itself. Beautifully lit, these are Hals's most ambiguous works and represent the height of his achievement, commissioned when he was in his eighties and some say he had lost his firm touch. That he hadn't is clear, and any previous acquaintance pales in comparison with actually seeing these paintings; I, for one, was over-awed by their sinister life, which puts you in mind of Van Gogh's remark that 'Frans Hals had no less than twenty-seven blacks'.

Haarlem has a greater number of **hofjes** than most Dutch towns; proof of its 17th-century prosperity and an example of the extraordinary Dutch liberal tradition. They were generally founded by wealthy citizens for elderly women who could normally look after themselves but needed help with money, food and fuel. The **Oudemannhuis** is different only in that it was for men. Otherwise it's fairly typical in style and you'll see its peaceful courtyard repeated with slight variations all over town – a functional and unpretentious form that has real charm. Most of the other *hofjes* are still inhabited, so you're confined to the courtyard, but the women who sit around seem used to the odd visitor and won't throw you out. Ask at the VVV for details on where to find them. The only one that really stands out is the **Teylers Hofje**, the most recent and definitely the grandest. Built in the 18th century by the city's most famous benefactor for rich women – only they could afford to stay here – its grandiose portico with Doric columns seems utterly out of place.

The monied Haarlem suburbs quickly give way to the thick woodland and rugged lunar landscape of the *Kennemerduinen national park* (access – apply VVV), which stretches down to the sea. BLOEMENDAAL-AAN-ZEE is the grandiose name for a group of shacks that house the usual ice-cream trade and a little further south is **ZANDVOORT** – one of the major Dutch resorts and an unfortunate agglomeration of modern and faceless blocks that rise up out of the dunes. As seaside resorts go it's pretty standard – crowded and oppressive in summer and depressingly dead in winter – and there's no real reason to come here except as a base for Haarlem. Zandvoort also means something else to the Dutch: championship motor racing, and the continual hum from the nearby circuit provides a backdrop for everyone's sunbathing. If you do come, and manage to fight your way through the crush to the water, watch out as it's a little murky and ominously close to the smoky chimneys of IJMUIDEN to the north.

NORTH FROM HAARLEM

On the northern outskirts of Haarlem is **SPAARNDAM**, well-known for its statue commemorating the little boy who saved the whole country from disaster by sticking his finger in a hole in the dyke. There's no truth in this tale at all, but it had a sufficient ring of reality for an American writer to weave a story around it – and create a legend. Few Dutch people know the story but despite this a monument to the heroic chap was unveiled in 1950; more, it seems, as a memorial to the opportunistic Dutch tourist industry than anything else.

Cheese is as Dutch as clogs and windmills, and in **ALKMAAR**, every Friday at ten between May and September, coachloads of expectant tourists are dumped on Waagplein to watch the **Cheese Market**, which ranks as possibly *the* Dutch tourist spectacle. As its dates suggest (and though the VVV will try to convince you otherwise) the whole ritual is obviously preserved for touristic reasons; an anachronism that is a guaranteed drawer of the crowds. If you want to see anything be sure to get there early, as by ten the mob is already several people deep. Golden discs of Gouda lie in rows and piles, awaiting the men who will barter for them and the unfortunates who have to carry them around. Everything happens on Friday in Alkmaar and the rest of the week it's exceptionally quiet. If you don't want to see the cheese market – and frankly, you wouldn't be missing much – this is a better time to come. Though there isn't a great deal to see, it's a pleasant enough place to spend a day or two. Along with a cheese museum, the **VVV** is in the **Waag** – a structure that was not built as a weigh-house, but as a chapel dedicated to the Holy Ghost. In the late 16th century it was converted to its present use, and the magnificent east gable was added, shortly after the town's famous victory against the Spanish in 1573, when they withstood a long siege by Frederick of Toledo. With some justification, they have never let anyone forget it, and everywhere there are reminders of the defeat that was the beginning of the end for the Spaniards. The **Stedlijk Museum** in Doelenstraat (Monday-Thursday 1000–1200, 1400–1700, Friday 1000–1700, Sunday 1400–1700), has pictures and plans of the siege, as well as a *Holy Family* by Honthorst and portraits by Caesar van Everdingen, a local and very much minor 17th-century figure who followed the Mannerist style of the Haarlem painters. At the other end of Langestraat in Verdronken Oord, the **cafés** *De Pilaren* and *Stapper* are the closest you'll ever come to action in Alkmaar. If you're staying, the **Sleep-In** is here too, at number 12 (open in July and August, f6.50). **Campers** should take bus 168/169 from the station to the edge of town.

Bus 168 goes on to **BERGEN**, a cheerful village where there has been a thriving community of artists since the expressionist Bergen school of the early 20th century. There are still many artists here and a disproportionate number of galleries for a place of this size; if you're interested, visit the **KCB** next door to the VVV – a small gallery that displays work by local artists, who also sell their work at the Friday evening **art market**. A collection of Bergen school paintings is on permanent display at the Smithuizen Museum, Van Renesselaan 42, Castricum (phone first for an appointment).

Still on a 168 bus, you finish up in **BERGEN-AAN-ZEE**, a bleak, mostly post-war coastal resort on the edge of a desolate stretch of dunes. About two miles to the south is **EGMOND-AAN-ZEE** which despite its historic associations is no less God-forsaken. The remains of the counts' castle are inland at **EGMOND-AAN-DEN-HOEF**, but these two seaside towns, which incidentally can get very crowded in summer, have little to recommend xcept their beach and dunes.

At the northernmost tip of the province is **DEN HELDER** – a town of around 60,000 which was little more than a fishing village until 1811, when Napoleon recognised its strategic importance and fortified it as a naval base. Since then it has remained the principal Dutch naval town: an uninteresting muddle of ugly modern architecture with a seedier older quarter towards the harbour, a sort of Dutch Chatham. The only possible reason for coming here is to sail to Texel, and you might as well take bus 3 from the railway station to the harbour and miss out the town altogether. **Boats for Texel** leave every half an hour in season and cost f7.50 return (cars – f33.50), the journey taking a mere fifteen minutes. Try to avoid hot summer weekends – I saw the queues.

TEXEL

About half of **Texel** has been reclaimed from the sea, changing its shape dramatically over the years. Until the draining of the North East polder in the 19th century, it looked like a misshapen hand with the large and swollen thumb of the dunes to the west. Now the unbroken line of beach and dunes merges through dense green woods into acres of rich farmland, traversed by dykes, now overgrown and marked by thick chains of trees. Texel is incredibly pretty and diverse, and though the packed ferry may fill you with feelings of dread, the island is large enough to absorb even the heaviest influx of holiday-makers.

The first thing to do when you arrive is to get yourself mobile, and the best way to get around is by **bike**; buses are both infrequent and expensive. Take the bus from the ferry-port, which is in the middle of nowhere, to **DEN BURG**, where you can hire bikes at *Zegel*, Parkstraat 16. Den Burg is the main town – just one central street leading up to a small shady square where you'll find the **VVV** (Monday-Friday 0900–1800, Saturday 0900–1700). They have a list of rooms at around f20, but hotels are expensive and accommodation can be a problem in peak season. There are, however, heaps of **campsites**, mostly dotted around DE KOOG, and two **Youth Hostels**, on either side of Den Burg on the roads

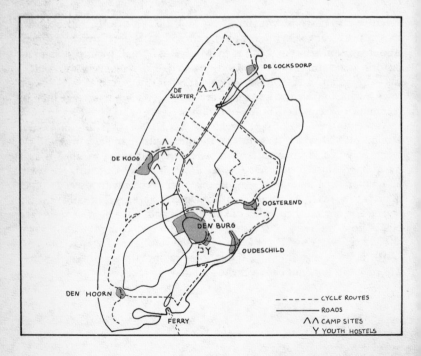

to Oudeschild and De Koog. VVV booklets include a cycle-route and bird-route – Texel is one of the most important breeding grounds in Europe and the birds are protected in sanctuaries all over the island. Though you can see them well enough from a distance, real enthusiasts who want to visit the places themselves have to get permission from the VVV.

DE KOOG is the main resort and accordingly horrific for most of the summer. Easy to avoid: if you want to explore the beaches and dunes you can head towards **DEN HOORN** – a tiny village surrounded by bulb fields in spring – where there are some really deserted spots, including a nudist beach in the south-west corner. Failing that, cycle north to **DE SLUFTER**, where many people prefer not to go because it *is* so remote – scrubby dunes meet vast stretches of sand and as far as you can see, there is rippling water and soaring birds.

Lastly, **OUDESCHILD**, south-east of Den Burg, is worth a quick look if only for its **Beachcombers Museum** (Tuesday-Saturday 1000–1700; f2.50), a fascinating collection of marine junk recovered from offshore wrecks – everything from aeroplane engines to messages in bottles.

TRAVEL DETAILS

Trains
Amsterdam–Haarlem (3 an hour; 15 mins), Amsterdam–Alkmaar (2 an hour; 30 mins), Amsterdam–Hoorn (2 an hour; 40 mins), Amsterdam–Enkhuizen (2 an hour; 1 hour), Amsterdam–Den Helder (2 an hour; 1 hour 7 mins), Haarlem–Zandvoort (2 an hour; 10 mins), Haarlem–Alkmaar (2 an hour; 25 mins) Alkmaar–Hoorn (2 an hour; 25 mins), Hilversum–Utrecht (3 an hour; 20 mins), Hilversum–Amersfoort (2 an hour; 15 mins).

Buses
Muiden–Naarden (CN Bus 136/138; 30 mins), Hoorn–Edam (NZH Bus 114; 25 mins), Hoorn–Medemblik (NZH Bus 140/141/144; 45 mins), Alkmaar–Harlingen–Leeuwarden (1 an hour; 1 hour 50 mins, 2 hours 30 mins).

Boats
Enkhuizen–Stavoren (May-Sept: 3 a day; 1 hour 20 mins), Enkhuizen–Urk (May, June and Sept: 2 a day, July and August: 3 a day; 1 hour 30 mins), Den Helder–Texel (2 an hour; 15 mins).

Chapter three
SOUTH HOLLAND AND UTRECHT

South Holland is the most densely populated province of the Netherlands, with a string of towns and cities that make up most of the **Randstad** or rim-town. Careful urban planning has stopped this from becoming an amorphous conurbation, however, and each has a pronounced identity – from the refined tranquillity of **The Hague** to the seedy low-life of **Rotterdam**'s docklands. All the towns have good museums and galleries; some, like The Hague's **Mauritshuis**, Leiden's **Museum of Antiquities** and Rotterdam's **Boymans-van Beuningen** outstanding. Since it too now forms part of the Randstad, we've also included **Utrecht** here, again a city rich in galleries.

Historically, South Holland is part of what was simply **Holland**, the richest and most influential province in the country. Throughout the Golden Age Holland was far and away dominant in the political, social and cultural life of the Republic, most of the other provinces being little more than backwaters. There are constant reminders of this pre-eminence in the buildings of this region: elaborate town halls proclaim civic importance and even the usually sombre Calvinist churches allow themselves little excesses – the later windows of Gouda's Janskerk a case in point. All the great painters either came from or worked here, too – Rembrandt, Vermeer, Jan Steen – a tradition that continued into the 19th century with the paintings of the Hague School.

Uniformly flat, the countryside is brightened only by rainbow flashes of bulb fields. Towns are linked by an efficient rail network, and, more cheaply, buses on similar routes. Hitching is also simple – none of South Holland's towns are more than 13 miles apart.

SOUTH TO LEIDEN THROUGH THE BULB FIELDS

HAARLEM stretches a long arm down to the dull residential town of HEEMSTEDE, on the edge of the Haarlemmermeer polder: once a large lake reclaimed in the mid-19th century after an especially violent storm inundated land from Leiden to Amsterdam. The main road cuts south across the heart of the Dutch bulb industry – centred on a thin strip of land between the dunes to the west and the polders to the east. **Tulips** are another purely 'Dutch' commodity, the stuff of songs and tourist mythology. It's a business that began when Carolus Clusius, a 16th-century botanist, brought a collection of flowering bulbs all the way from

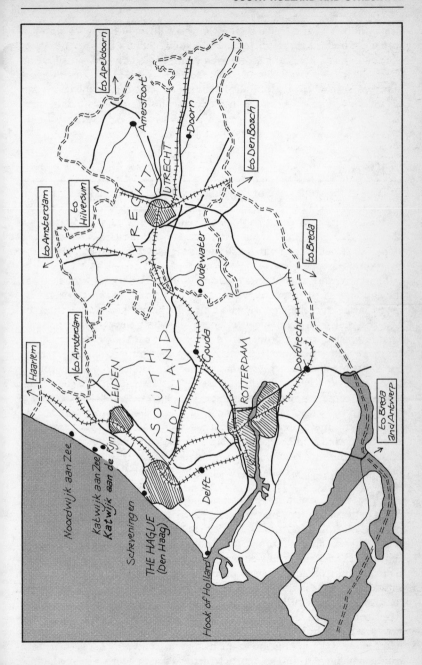

to Apeldoorn

to Den Bosch

to Amsterdam

to Hilversum

to Breda

Amersfoort

Doorn

UTRECHT

U T R E C H T

Oudewater

to Amsterdam

Haarlem

S O U T H

Gouda

ROTTERDAM

Dordrecht

to Breda and Antwerp

LEIDEN

H O L L A N D

Noordwijk aan Zee

Katwijk aan Zee
Katwijk aan de Rijn

Scheveningen

THE HAGUE
(Den Haag)

Delft

Hook of Holland

Asia Minor, and they have thrived on the sandy soil here ever since. In spring the bulb fields are in full and dazzling bloom – mile upon mile of neat blocks. It's here that Mondriaan could have derived his inspiration in this rigorous division of pure colour which, like a De Stijl painting, is more remarkable for its formality than for any intrinsic beauty. You can see the flowers at closer range in the **Keukenhof** gardens at **LISSE**, open daily in the spring. If you're especially interested the **AALSMEER** flower auction begins at 7.30 am every weekday.

LEIDEN

Situated at the confluence of the canalised branches of the Rhine, **Leiden** is a series of islands. A stately city, home of Holland's most prestigious university and a dozen or so good museums, it has the air of academia about it; as E. V. Lucas wrote, 'the sense of commercial enterprise dies away: whatever they are at Amsterdam, the Dutch at Leiden cease to be a nation of shopkeepers'.

The University was a present from William the Silent: a reward for the courageous townspeople who had just endured a year-long siege by the Spanish, emerging victorious when William cut the dykes around the city and sailed in with his fleet for a dramatic eleventh-hour rescue. That happened on 3 October 1574 and every year the people of Leiden commemorate it with appropriate revelry. They traditionally eat herring and white bread – since this is what the fleet are supposed to have brought with them – and *hutspot* or stew, which was apparently found simmering in the abandoned Spanish garrison. The university quickly became a major centre of Protestant scholarship, and you can still visit its first home today. It stands on Rapenburg – a dignified canal that, together with Steenschur and Breestraat, marks the edge of medieval Leiden. This is one of the pleasantest parts of town, a network of narrow streets that converge on a central square and the **Pieterskerk**, Leiden's principal church.

A large brick structure, this is now only used for exhibitions, concerts, and a Saturday antique market, giving it an empty warehouse-like atmosphere as most of the fixtures have been removed. What remains, however, is impressive. The beautifully simple Renaissance rood screen stands in the choir that is high and well proportioned, built over some thirty years by Rotger of Cologne, a mason probably more renowned for the Cologne cathedral and the churches of Kampen. Sundry famous names are buried here, in keeping with Leiden's host of eminent sons – among them John Robinson, 'father' of the Pilgrim Fathers, who lived in a house on the site of what is now the **Jan Pesijn Hofje**, next door to the church. He had been a curate in England at the turn at the century but was suspended from preaching in 1604. A belief in the Puritan ideals of freedom of worship led him to flee with his congregation to pursue a less tarnished form of worship in the more tolerant atmosphere of Holland. Settling in Leiden, Robinson acted as pastor to growing numbers but still found himself at odds with the establishment. In 1620, a hundred of his followers – The Pilgrim Fathers – sailed via Plymouth for the freedom and abundance of America. Robinson died before he could join them. If you want to find out more, take a look at the **Pilgrim Fathers Documentation Centre** at Boisotkade 2a, part of the city archives and a mine of information on Robinson's group during their stay in Leiden.

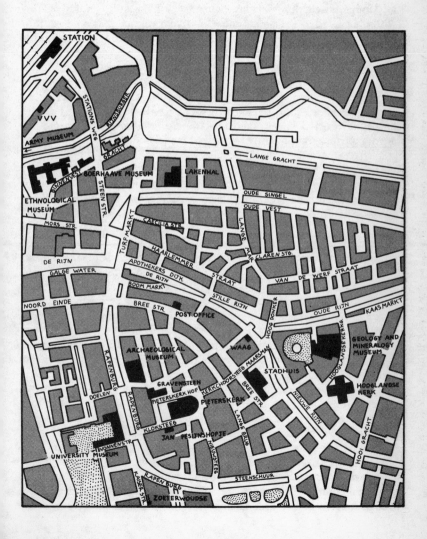

Breestraat signals the edge of Leiden's centre proper, flanked by the long front of the late 16th-century **Stadhuis**, which was almost wholly destroyed by fire in 1929. The façade is all that remains, tacked on to a 1930s structure but by itself a perfect example of early Dutch Renaissance architecture with the profusion of fussy ornament popular at the time. Behind, the two Rhines converge at the busiest point in town and a sequence of bridges lead through a flurry of activity to the pedestrian Haarlemmerstraat.

If you had stopped after crossing Nieuwe Rijn, you would have found the **Hooglandsekerk** (Monday-Thursday 1000–1600, Friday 0900–1200), dedicated to St Pancras and a light, high church that is delightfully plain without being spartan, and thankfully doesn't have the secularised atmosphere of the Pieterskerk. On a central pillar is Verhulst's epitaph to the heroic Burgomaster Van der Werff, who led the citizens of Leiden during the siege of 1564. When the situation got so desperate that most people were all for giving in, Van der Werff, no doubt remembering the massacre of Haarlem, offered his own body to them as food. The invitation was rejected but it succeeded in instilling new vigour into the flagging citizens, humbled by his selfless leadership.

Leiden's museums

Leiden's museums are varied and comprehensive enough to merit a section to themselves. It's possible to spend several days here trudging from one to the other and rarely seeing daylight; something that isn't recommended. The following listings should make it easier to be more selective.

The **Rijksmuseum Van Oudeheden**, Rapenburg 28 (Tuesday-Saturday 1000–1700, Sunday 1300–1700; f3.50) is Leiden's star attraction. The principal Dutch archaeological museum, much of its huge collection is in storage, though a new extension project is under way that will double its size in ten years. Exhibition rooms are grouped around a main hall, where stands the *Temple of Taffeh* – a present from the Egyptian government in gratitude for the Dutch part in the UNESCO excavations in Abyssinia in the 1960s which succeeded in uncovering submerged Nubian monuments. The conditions the Egyptians placed on their gift led to it being set up here, in a former open courtyard that was specially converted so that no-one has to pay to see it, temperature and humidity are carefully regulated, and the lights overhead simulate the passage of the sun. Originally dating back to the 1st century AD, the temple was modified in the 4th century for the worship of Isis, eventually being sanctified as a Christian church 400 years later.

Once through the entrance hall, the museum really begins with remains of the temple to Nehellania – local Roman goddess of seamen – which were uncovered in Zeeland. The Egyptian collection is staggering, beginning with wall reliefs from tombs and temples and continuing upstairs with a set of mummies and sarcophagi as complete as you're ever likely to see outside Egypt. The second floor is specifically Dutch – an archaeological history of the country, and inevitably not as interesting as what has come before.

Leiden's municipal museum is housed in the old **Lakenhal** on Oude Singel (Tuesday-Saturday 1000–1700, Sunday 1300–1700; f2) and contains a picture gallery devoted to natives of the town. The 16th century is represented by Cornelius Engelbrechtsz, a triptych by Lucas van Leyden and canvases by Jacob van Swanenburgh, the first teacher of the young Rembrandt. Another room concentrates on Rembrandt himself and the Leiden painters who were associated with him – among them Jan Lievens (with whom he shared a studio) and Gerrit Dou, who initiated the Leiden tradition of small, minutely finished pictures. Upstairs, the original Lakenhal is kept in much the same way as it would have been when Leiden's cloth trade was at its height, and forms the greater part of the museum.

Walking towards the station, you come to the **Museum Boerhaave**, (Tuesday-Saturday 1000–1700, Sunday 1400–1700; f3.50), named after a 17th-century Leiden surgeon and an absorbing, if brief, guide to scientific developments over the last three centuries, with particular reference to Dutch achievements.

Next door is the **Rijksmuseum Voor Volkenkunde** (as Boerhaave), the national ethnological museum, which, while it has a more than complete section on Indonesia and the Dutch colonies, gives most other parts of the world a less than thorough showing. Basically, this is a memorial to Holland's colonial past and worth a visit for just that. Apart from Indonesia, there are good sections on the South Pacific and Australasia, China and Japan.

The **Royal Army and Weapon Museum** (Monday-Friday 0930–1700, Sunday 1300–1700; f2.50) at Pesthuislaan 7, has a good display of weaponry, uniforms and military accoutrements; which may sound supremely dull but isn't, even if you're not an enthusiast. It attempts to show a military history of the Netherlands, from the wars with Spain up to the Dutch imperialist ventures of the 1950s – which are shown in surprisingly candid detail.

Finally the **Rijksmuseum van Geologie en Mineralogie** (Monday-Friday 1000–1700, Sunday 1400–1700; free) has a display of minerals, fossils, bones and skeletons; and the **Academisch Historisch Museum** (Tuesday, Wednesday, Thursday 1300–1700; free) devotes itself to the history of the university and student life through the ages.

Some practical details
The VVV are at Stationsplein 210 (Monday-Friday 0900–1900, Saturday
0900–1800, Sunday 1000–1400), and have a list of **hotels and pensions**,
cheapest of which is *Witte* (f20) at Witte Singel 80. They also have a list
of private **rooms**, which they only hand out if everything else is full. The
nearest **campsite** is Koningshof, a couple of miles out of town at Rijnsburg
– bus 40 and a ten-minute walk. The nearby resorts of KATWIJK and
NOORDWIJK have a larger and cheaper selection of places to stay –
both of their respective VVVs have lists. In Katwijk, the *Rosmerta* is
billed as being 'suitable for youths'; Jan Tooropstraat 4. The cheapest in
Noordwijk are *Maaike* and *Bernadette*, next door but one to each other
in Quarles van Ufford Straat.

Eating doesn't pose too many problems. Here's a list of likely places:
Mensa de Bak Student restaurant in Kaiserstraat, at the end of
Rapenburg.
Repelsteetje, Breestraat 19 Set menu, changed every day, f10.
Vegetarian.
Menuet, Marsmansteeg 23 Indonesian, from about f7.50. Closes
about 7.30 pm.
Eethuisje de Engelenbak, Lange Mare 38 Dutch food from about
f9.50.
Pizzeria dal Sulcitano, Haarlemmerstraat 270 Pizzas from f7.

COC Soos, Caeciliastraat 18 is described as a 'very active' gay centre
and bar, women only on Friday nights.

Due to the number of students around, bookshops tend to be more
than usually well stocked with **English books**. There's a *De Slegte* at
Breestraat 73 and second-hand stuff at *Siveris*, Princessekade 3. **NBBS
travel** are to be found at Breestraat 53.

Katwijk and Noordwijk
KATWIJK-AAN-ZEE is the stock Dutch seaside town: not as crowded
as Zandvoort nor with the pretensions of Scheveningen, but equally
uninteresting. That's not, however, to say it's unpopular, but if the
weather's hot enough and you're looking for a beach to stretch out on,
the dunes to the north and south provide access to some vast untouched
expanses. Just north, and regarded with some awe by Charles Tennant,
who called them 'nothing short of an act of madness', are the **Katwijk
Sluices**, finished in 1807 to prevent the consistent damming up of the
Oude Rijn. They regulate the flow of the river, without which the whole
of this area would be returned to the quagmire it was before. Scarcely
three miles further up the coast is NOORDWIJK-AAN-ZEE, a patchy
place of recently-built egg-box apartments belittling the terraces of the
tiny town centre behind. Apart from serving as a cheaper base for seeing
Leiden, there's nothing for you here.

THE HAGUE

In its urbane atmosphere **The Hague** is quite different from any other Dutch city. Since the 16th century it's been the political capital of the Netherlands, creating a rivalry with commercial Amsterdam that continues today. Unlike the newly-rich Amsterdam merchants, however, The Hague's politicians and statesmen were confident of their own importance and felt no need to brag their wealth in flamboyant building. Most of the city's canal houses are sedately classical, and there's little of the riotously individual architecture found in Amsterdam. In 1859 Matthew Arnold wrote, 'I never saw a city where the well-to-do classes seemed to have given the whole place so much of their own air of wealth, finished cleanliness, and comfort; but I never saw one, either, in which my heart would so have sunk at the thought of living.' Things haven't changed much: today's 'well-to-do classes', the diplomats in dark Mercedes and multi-national businessmen, ensure that most of the city's hotels and restaurants are firmly in the expense account category, and the nightlife is similarly packaged.

You don't need more than a day, though, to see the famed **Mauritshuis** collection of Dutch art. Though the Mauritshuis itself is currently closed for restoration the core of the collection can be seen at the **de Witt house**, and the modern art of the **Gemeente Museum** is also definitely worth a look.

If you're coming to The Hague by train you'll arrive at either the **Centraal station** or **Den Haag H.S. (Hollands Spoor)**. From the Centraal station it's a short walk to the VVV (Monday-Saturday 0900–2100, Sunday 0900–1800) office at Julianaplein 7 and thence to the centre. From Den Haag H.S. a 5, 8 or 9 tram takes you to the centre, a 12 to the VVV. Despite being the country's third largest city, almost everything worth seeing is in easy distance from the centre, but if you intend to use the city's buses and trams the VVV sells the standard Strippenkaart and a *Dagkaart*; best bet if you're only here for the day.

The centre

Right at the centre, and the oldest part of the city, is the medieval **Binnenhof** or inner court. Count William II built a castle here in the 13th century, and the settlement that grew around it became known as the Count's Hedge – *'s Gravenhaage,* still the city's official name. Now home of the Netherlands' two-chamber parliament, the Binnenhof is an irresistible tourist focus, though in fact there's little to see save the **Ridder-zaal** (Hall of the Knights) a slender-turreted structure used for state occasions. It's been a court room, market and stable, and so repeatedly replaced and renovated that little of the 13th-century original remains.

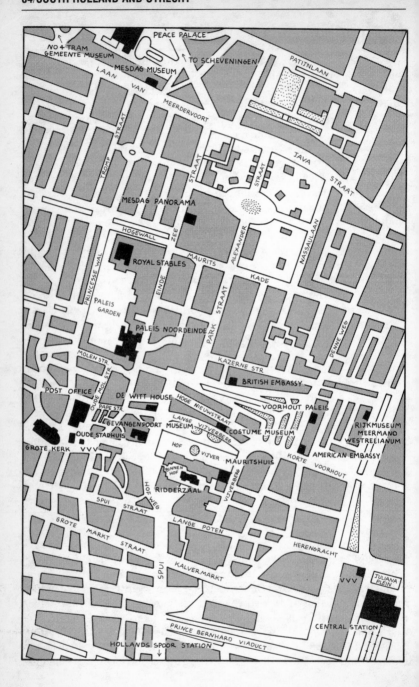

A guided tour of the Ridderzaal and one or other chamber of parliament costs f3.50 and starts at Binnenhof 8a.

Flanking and mirroring the Binnenhof is the **Hof Vijver** lake, on whose far side is **Lange Voorhout**, the most distinguished of The Hague's diplomatic quarters. A wooded corner enclosed by the stately Voorhout palace and the British and American embassies, it feels like a dignified remnant of the 1890s, disdaining the little antique market held between the trees on Thursdays.

Off to the other side of the Binnenhof is the **Paleis Noordeinde** (no admission), one of several royal buildings that lure tourists to The Hague. The city has been the home of the Dutch royal family since the mid-19th century, and despite the present queen's attempts to demystify the monarchy, there's no deterring the enthusiasts who fill the expensive 'Royal Tours' around the peripheries of the palace and the queen's other residence just outside town, the *Huis ten Bos*.

Of The Hague's churches, easily the best is the St Jacob's or **Grote Kerk**, a hall church with an exhilarating sense of breadth and warmly decorated vaulting. The one thing you can't miss, as it's placed where the high altar should be, is the memorial to the unmemorable admiral Obdam, hero of the little-remembered battle of Lowestoft, but keep an eye open for the Renaissance pulpit: like the one in Delft's Oude Kerk, with carved panels framing the apostles in false perspective.

North of the centre the **Peace Palace** (Monday-Friday – tours at varying times, check with the VVV; f2) is home to the Court of International Justice and, for all the wrong reasons, a monument to the futility of war. The palace was built in 1913, instigated by an earlier conference for the suppression of war and a $1½ million donation from Andrew Carnegie. The purpose of the conference had been to 'help find a lasting peace and, above all, a way of limiting the progressive development of existing arms', an aim which, two world wars and a massive arms build-up later, seems deeply ironic. It's with an inescapable sadness that you view the palace and its grandiose yet pitiful symbols of peace. Even by the time the various countries' donations of tapestries, urns, marble and stained glass were arriving, war was inevitable, and in one of the small courtrooms irony again intrudes on an individual level: a picture of Victory remains unfinished, its artist killed in the Great War. Though the guides point out the riches of the palace, all in all it's a cheerless afternoon out.

The Mauritshuis collection

Once the home of statesman Johan de Witt, the **de Witt house** at Kneuterdijk 6 temporarily contains a selection of the Royal Picture Collection of Flemish and Dutch painting of the 15th to 18th centuries. The **Mauritshuis**, the collection's usual home, is undergoing a restoration that will hopefully improve its rather cramped galleries. William V started the collection in the 18th century, and though only a few of the hundreds of paintings are on exhibit here the selection shows its character as well as some of its most famous masterpieces.

Best known of the **Rembrandts** is the *Anatomy Lesson of Dr Tulp,* the artist's first commission on moving to Amsterdam at the age of 26. By the peering pose of the 'students' who lean over the corpse, Rembrandt solved the problem of emphasis falling on the body rather than the subjects of his portrait, who were in fact members of the surgeons' guild. Hopefully Tulp's skills as an anatomist were better than his medical advice, which included recommending that his patients drink fifty cups of tea a day. The other famous painting here is the *View of Delft* by **Vermeer**, a tranquil, detached work, though the dispassionate photographic quality it has in reproduction is oddly lacking in the large, poorly preserved canvas.

Though there are only a couple of Jan Steens in the exhibition, **Adriaen Brouwer**'s low-life scenes show the less sophisticated side of genre painting. His sordid subjects, as in *Peasants' Brawl,* apparently came from personal experience – he spent much of his short life in either tavern or prison.

Of the earlier works, three stand out: **Holbein**'s *Portrait of Jane Seymour* was one of several pictures he painted for Henry VIII, who sent him abroad to paint possible wives. Holbein's vibrant realism was later to land him in hot water: an over-flattering portrait of Anne of Cleves swayed Henry into an unhappy marriage with his 'Flanders mare' that was to last only six months. The **Flemish Primitive painters** are represented by a moving *Christ brought down from the Cross* by van der Weyden and a sombre *Portrait of a Man* by his pupil, Memling.

Though most of the work will remain on display, some of the lesser paintings may change before the reopening of the Mauritshuis, scheduled for 1985. The de Witt house is open all week and it'll cost you f3.50 to get in if you don't have a museumcard.

The Hague's other museums and galleries

Arguably the best and certainly the most diverse of The Hague's other museums is the **Gemeente Museum** at Stadhouderslaan 41 (Tuesday-Saturday 1000–1700, Sunday 1300–1700; f2; bus 4 or tram 10). Designed by Berlage, its confused and awkward layout doesn't help you find your way around the large and varied collection. Outstanding though are the *musical instruments*, with particularly beautiful harpsichords and early pianos. There's detailed English info, taped music of the relevant periods and even (upstairs) a harpsichord you can play if temptation's too great.

The museum's collection of *modern art* also suffers by being frustratingly arranged, but persevere for it gives a good account of the development of Dutch painting through the Romantic, Hague and Expressionist schools to the De Stijl movement. **Mondriaan**, most famous member of the De Stijl group, dominates the gallery: the museum has the world's largest collection of his paintings, though much of it consists of (deservedly) unfamiliar early works painted before he evolved the abstraction of form into geometry and pure colour for which he's best known. In addition to all this the Gemeente has a reputation for first-rate temporary exhibitions, so allow plenty of time to explore.

If you've only time or inclination for one of The Hague's many other museums, then the **Gevangenpoort** or Prisoners' Gate Museum (Monday-Friday 1000–1700, Saturday/Sunday 1300–1700; last tour 4 pm; f2.50) is the most central. Originally part of the Binnenhof's fortifications, it was used as a prison until the 19th century, and now contains an array of instruments of torture and punishment centred around its Chamber of Horrors. As well as the guillotine blades, racks and gibbets, the old cells can be seen, including the comfortable *ridderkamer*. Here Cornelis de Witt, Burgomaster of Dordrecht, was imprisoned before he and his brother Johan, leader of the States of Holland, were dragged out and murdered by a mob in 1672. The brothers were shot, beheaded and cut into pieces which were then auctioned to the crowd; Johan's tongue is preserved for a macabre posterity in the Gemeente Museum. The museum is understandably popular so join the queue about fifteen minutes before each half-hourly tour.

Mesdag's unremarkable seascapes are occasionally tinged with an unlikeable bourgeois sentimentality, but his **Panorama** (Monday-Saturday 1000–1700, Sunday 1200–1700; f2.50; no museumcards), a huge painting of Scheveningen, is undeniably an achievement. Completed in four months with help from his wife and the young Breitner, the painting is so naturalistic it takes a few moments for the skills of lighting and perspective to become apparent. Near the Panorama is the house Mesdag bought as a home and a gallery. At the time it overlooked one of his favourite subjects, the dunes, and it is now preserved as the **Mesdag Museum** (Monday-Saturday 1000–1700, Sunday 1300–1700; f3.50), containing his collection of paintings – including many from the Hague School who, like Mesdag, took the seascapes of the nearby coast as their subject. There's also work by Corot, Rousseau, Delacroix and Millet though none of the paintings represent the artists' best achievement. My favourites are the florid and distinctive paintings by Mancini whose oddly disquieting subjects are reminiscent of Klimt.

The **Bredius Museum** at Prinsengracht 6 (Tuesday-Saturday 1400–1700; f1) offers a cross-section of 17th-century Dutch painting, with works by Rembrandt, Jan Steen and van Ostade; plus a pornographic little picture by Adriaen Brouwer.

The **Prince William V Gallery** (Monday-Friday 1100–1400; free) has paintings by Rembrandt and Paulus Potter (among others) exhibited as they would have been in the 18th century, squeezed together in a cramped patchwork. Though faithful to the period this makes viewing difficult to eyes trained by spacious modern galleries.

The **Meermanno-Westreenianum Museum** (Monday-Saturday 1300–1700; free) has a small collection of remarkably well-preserved illuminated manuscripts and bibles; the **Costume Museum** (Tuesday-Saturday 1000–1700, Sunday 1300–1700; f2) disappointingly concentrates on the 18th century, but is well arranged in rooms of the period; finally the **Madurodam Model City**, heavily plugged by the tourist authorities, is both trite and expensive (f5) – visit, if you must, between 9.30 am and 10.30 pm (tram 9).

Eating and sleeping

Both are expensive: for **food** you'll really do best to slum it in one of the fast food places, or try the popular *De Apendaans* at Herenstraat 11. **Accommodation** in Den Haag proper is difficult to find: the small *Minema* pension, Dedelstraat 25, f28 is often full, as is the *Hotel Neuf,* Rijksweg 119, f30. SCHEVENINGEN'S pensions are slightly cheaper and there's a better chance of getting a room. Try *El Cid, Huis Rosa* or *Berkhout,* all in Baadhuisweg and around f25. The **Youth Hostel** at Monsterweg 4 is some 8 km out (51 or 53 bus from the Centraal Station) and Duinhorst, the nearest **campsite**, 3 km (91 bus from the VVV office). By far the easiest solution if you're visiting between mid-June and the end of August is to use the nearby student flats in **Delft** as a base; only a quarter of an hour away by train (see p. 92).

A day by the sea: Scheveningen

Scheveningen, an upmarket coastal resort, is packed at the first hint of sunshine. Fading from fashionability after the 19th century, it's been revamped around the Pier entertainment complex and the Kufhaus casino, where you'll need passport and tie if you're thinking of blowing your last few guilders. All the people I mentioned Scheveningen to were sceptical of its value for money – I didn't like it either; it looked like a slick and sterilised Margate. If that's to your taste, take a 1, 7, 8 or 9 tram, or 22 bus.

Hague listings

Bikes   can be hired from either station for f5.50 a day + f200 deposit.
Car hire   Hertz Rentacar, Van Stolkweg 2, tel. 55 99 00
Embassies   Australia: Koninginnegracht 23, tel. 63 09 83
Britain: Lange Voorhout 10, tel. 64 58 00
Canada: Sophialaan 7, tel. 61 41 11

Eire: Dr Kuyperstraat 9, tel. 63 09 93
USA: Lange Voorhout 102, tel. 62 49 11

Feminism The *Vrouwenhuis* at Anna Paulownastraat 15 is a meeting place and information centre; open from 7 pm.
Wil Kattenburg at Het Zieken 189 and *Butterfly* at Laan Van Meedervort 53 are both women's bars.

Gay scene Many gay bars of which *Boko* and *Venice,* both on Nieuwe Schoolstraat are the best known. *Trefcentrum* at Stationsweg 112 has a gay disco with a women's night on Sundays.

Hospital 22 21 11 (Ambulance).
45 53 00 (General medical care).

Markets General: Grote Markt, Herman Costerstraat (Monday/ Friday/Saturday).

Food: Markthof, Gedempte Gracht (Monday/Tuesday/Saturday).

Antique and curio: Lange Voorhout (Thursday).

Morning after pill 63 09 63.

Student travel NBBS, Schoolstraat 26.

VVV Main office, Julianaplein 7. Information centre, Groenmarkt.

What's On A fortnightly magazine on events and entertainments in The Hague and environs. Free and useful. Available from the VVV and elsewhere.

DELFT

Only a few minutes from The Hague by train, **Delft** has considerable charm: gabled red-roofed houses stand beside the tree-lined canals and the muted colours of pavements, brickwork and iron bridges give the town a faded, placid tranquillity – a tranquillity that from spring onwards is systematically destroyed by tourists. They arrive in their air-conditioned coachloads and descend to clog the narrow streets, buy an over-priced piece of gift pottery and snap the spire of the Nieuwe Kerk. And beneath them all, the gift shops and tea rooms, old Delft itself gets increasingly difficult to find.

Why is Delft so popular? Apart from its prettiness, the obvious answer is **Delftware**, the clumsy and monotonous blue and white ceramics to which Delft gave its name in the 17th century. Original designs were stylised copies of Chinese ceramics imported by the Dutch East Indies Company but the patterns quickly evolved into domestic traditions of landscapes, animals and comic figures. By the early years of the 18th century, the town's craftsmen had become confident enough to create vases, jars and even ornamental musical instruments – a good collection of which is in the Rijksmuseum in Amsterdam. Delftware, eventually in polychrome as well as traditional blue and white, fell out of fashion in the late 18th century and production stopped following the French occupation. A revival occurred some years later, and today in the gift shops Delftware has once more found a profitable niche. Most of the modern pieces are cheap mass-produced copies but there is still 'real' Delftware too, made in the traditional fashion and sold at great price, though if you like the stuff seconds are on sale at reduced prices in the factories. *De Pocelyn Fles* at Rotterdamseweg 196 run tours throughout the day should you want to see the process and/or buy. Also, the **Huis Lambert van Meerten Museum** at Oude Delft 119 (Monday-Saturday 1000–1700, Sunday 1300–1700; f1), has a large collection of Delft (and other) decorated tiles.

A second reason for Delft's popularity must be the **Vermeer** connection. The artist was born in the town in 1632 and died here too – leaving a wife, eleven children and a huge debt to the local baker. He had given the man two pictures as security, and his widow bankrupted herself trying to retrieve them. His famous *View of Delft,* now in The Hague, is only sporadically identifiable in the town today: the tourists are shunted around on canal trips to seek something of it, but you'll do a lot better on foot – it's not a difficult place to find your way about. The **Markt** is the best place to start – a central point of reference with the Renaissance Stadhuis at one end and the Nieuwe Kerk at the other. Lined with cafés, the VVV office, rip-off restaurants and Dutch teenagers offloading disco music on ghetto-blasters, it really gets going with the Thursday general market and, if you're reading this on a Wednesday evening, reckon on moving off elsewhere.

The **Nieuwe Kerk** (Monday-Saturday 0900–1700; f2; tower f2 extra) is new only in comparison with the Oude Kerk, as there's been a church on this site since 1381. Most of the original, however, was destroyed in the great fire that swept over Delft in 1536 and the remainder in a powder magazine explosion a century later; an explosion, incidentally, which also claimed the life of the artist Carel Fabritius, Rembrandt's greatest pupil and (debatably) himself the teacher of Vermeer. The most striking part of the restoration is in fact the most recent – the 100m spire, replaced in 1872, from whose summit you can gain a wide view of the red-roofed town. Unless you're a Dutch monarchist the church's interior is uninspiring: it contains the burial vaults of the Dutch royal family, the latest addition being Queen Wilhelmina in 1962. Only the mausoleum of William the Silent is of any interest, designed in the early 17th century by Hendrik de Keyser, architect also of the Stadhuis opposite.

South of the Stadhuis, signs direct you to the **Koornmarkt**, one of the town's most characteristic 17th-century streets. At number 67 is the **Museum Tetar van Elven** (Tuesday-Saturday 1100–1700; f1), slightly drab in appearance but an authentic period restoration of an 18th-century patrician house. It was the studio and home of Paul Tetar van Elven, a provincial and somewhat forgettable artist/collector. **Wynhaven**, another interesting old street, leads to the Hippolytusburt and the Gothic **Oude Kerk** (Monday-Saturday 1200–1600), arguably the town's finest building. Simple and unbuttressed, with an unhealthily leaning tower, it's the result of a succession of building from c.1250 to the 16th century. The vaulting, strong and unornamented, proves interiors don't have to be elaborate to avoid being sombre. Pride of the church is the pulpit of 1548, intricately carved with figures emphasised in false perspective. Most striking though is its modern stained glass depicting and symbolising the history of the

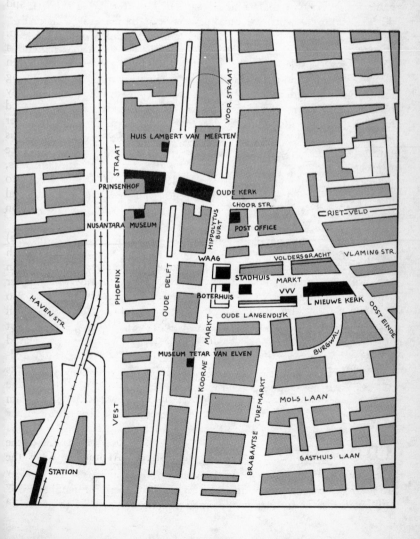

Netherlands, the 1945 Liberation in the north transept, for example. If you're curious about the tombs – including that of Admiral Maarten van Tromp, famed for hoisting a broom at his masthead to 'sweep the seas clear of the English' and sailing up the Medway – take a look at the 'Striking Points' pamphlet available on entrance.

Opposite the Oude Kerk, flanked by gardens, is the former convent of St Agatha, or **Prinsenhof** as it came to be known (Monday-Saturday 1000–1700, Sunday 1300–1700; f2). This too is well worth a visit, housing Delft's municipal art collection, a fine group of works including paintings by Aertsen and Honthorst. It has been restored in the style of the 1580s, an era when the building served as the base of William the Silent in his Dutch Protestant revolt against the Spanish. From here William planned actions against the Imperial Catholic troops of Philip II, achieving considerable success with his *Watergeuzen*, or sea-beggars, a kind of commando-guerilla unit initially operating from England. Here too he met his death at the hands of a French assassin who had inveigled himself into William's presence. The shots that passed through him, made by three pellets welded into one, left their mark on the Prinsenhof walls and can still be seen. For f1.90 you get in here and also gain admission to the nearby ethnographical **Nusantra** and **Huis Lambert van Meerten Museums**.

A real bargain if you want to stay in Delft between May and September are the **Student Flats** at floor 9, Krakeelhof, Jacob van Bierenlaan (tel. 015 13 59 53), south of the station. Singles are f11, doubles f18, and if you stay for more than four nights prices go down. At these prices it's worth using Delft for exploring the rest of South Holland. **Pensions** are small and likely to be full in season. Only two have single rooms: *Van Leeuwen*, Achterom 143 (f23) and *Rust*, Oranjeplantage 38 (f25). Of the remainder, *De Kok* at Houttuinen 15 is the largest with doubles from f50.

You'll have to look hard to find **restaurants** and **bars** not exclusively tourist-geared. Cheapest food is served at the *Mensa*, Nieuwelaan 76, closed Saturday and Sunday. *Alcuin*, Oude Delft 57 (1730–1915, closed Saturday) and *Eetafel Tyche*, Oude Delft 123 (Monday-Friday 1715–1915) both have meals for around f7. The newly-opened *Café Monroe* near the Oude Kerk is the current hang-out of Delft youth.

Once you've had enough of Delft's packaged prettiness, Rotterdam is the next logical stop.

ROTTERDAM

Rotterdam is the largest port in the world. As you approach the water-front huge cranes rise up on the horizon, the machinery for handling 300 million tonnes of fuel, grain and materials needed or sold by western

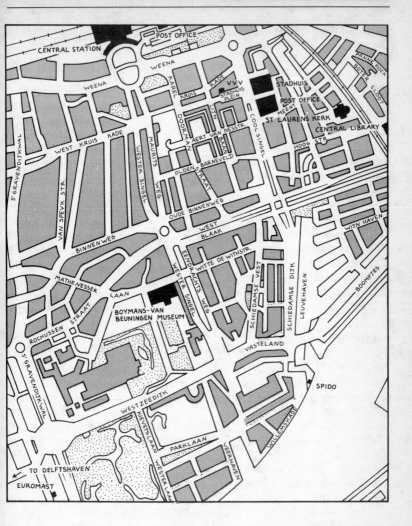

Europe each year. Totally destroyed by wartime bombing, the city's docks and centre were quickly and imaginatively rebuilt, its Lijnebaan the first of Europe's pedestrian shopping precincts. This prospect of docks and shops probably sounds unalluring, but Rotterdam is a surprisingly likeable place: in the **Boymans-van Beuningen Museum** it has one of the best – and most overlooked – galleries in the country, and between the central modernity and dockland sleaze is **Delftshaven**, an old area that survived the bombs. There's not much else, but redevelopment hasn't obliterated Rotterdam's earthy character: the prostitution and dope peddling are for real, not for tourists, and if you want to avoid the high spots of the low life, stick to the centre.

Getting around and somewhere to stay
Rotterdam has a large and confusing centre but the **Central Station** is the hub of a useful tram and metro system that makes getting around a lot easier. Near the station at Mauritsweg 29 the **Sleep-In** at f6 per night is the cheapest place to stay. Central **pensions** include *Sehlmeier*, Oldenbarneveldtstraat, 3 or 8 tram (f25) and, good for doubles, *Bavris*, 's-Gravendijkwal 70 (from f55). The **Youth Hostel** is at Rochussenstraat 107 (tram 4 from Central Station), the nearest **campsite** at Canaalweg 84 (33 bus from Central Station).

The Boymans-van Beuningen Museum
(Tuesday-Saturday 1000–1700, Sunday 1100–1700; f4)
The **Boymans-van Beuningen Museum** is Rotterdam's one great attraction. Amid the enormous collection of paintings, from Flemish Masters to Pop Art, it's impossible not to find something to your liking, and the selection that follows is necessarily brief and biased by my own tastes. You can get to the museum on a 5 tram, or from Eendrachtsplein metro.

The first entrance on Mathenesserlaan leads to the modern paintings, best known of which are the **Surrealists**. De rigueur for student bedrooms in the 1970s, it's difficult to appreciate **Salvador Dali**'s *Impressions of Africa* as anything more than the painting of the poster; the frightened artist behind the easel has become part of our storehouse of images – and is no longer surreal. Other works by **Magritte**, **Ernst** and **de Chirico** give a good sample of a movement now waning in appeal. Surrealism was never adopted by Dutch artists though the 'Magic Realism' of **Carel Willink** has its similarities in the precise, hallucinatory technique he uses in *Self Portrait with a Pen* to distance and disconcert the viewer. **Charley Toorop**'s *Three Generations* is also realism with an aim to disconcert – the huge bust of her father, Jan, looms in the background, dominating the painting.

The **Van der Vorm collection**, a mixture of 17th- and 19th-century works, has two contrasting **Rembrandts**: an analytic *Portrait of Alotte Adriaensdr*, her ageing illuminated but softened by her white ruff, and the gloomy indistinct *Blind Tobias and his Wife* painted twenty years later. A series of small galleries contains most artists of the Impressionist, Barbizon and Hague Schools: **Weissenbruch**'s *Strandgezicht* stands out, a beautiful gradation of radiant tones.

The old building has the museum's earlier paintings and an excellent Flemish and Nederlandish religious art section. **Hieronymus Bosch**, famed for his nightmarish triptyches, is represented here by more mainstream works: usually considered a macabre fantasist, Bosch was actually working to the limit of his native tradition's confines, where Biblical themes were depicted as iconographical representations, heavily loaded with symbolism. The imagery of Bosch's *St Christopher* – the dragon, the broken pitcher – lurks in the background, as it does in the form of a tempting brothel in *The Wanderer*. Bosch's technique never absorbed the influence of Renaissance Italy – his figures in *The Marriage Feast at Cana* are static and unbelievable, uncomfortably arranged around a distorted table. Other works here include paintings by **van Scorel, Memling, Bruegel**'s *Tower of Babel* and the sublime *Glorification of the Virgin* by **Geertgen tot Sint Jans**.

Continuing through the old buildings you reach the small collection of **Dutch Genre** paintings. With middle-class tastes rather than church patronage dictating subjects, 17th-century painters began to depict unidealised real life situations. Initially humorous like **Jan Steen**'s *Extracting the Stone* or *The Doctor's Visit,* they quickly developed a sophisticated moral content: **Gerrit Dou**'s *The Quack,* ostensibly just a captured moment, is full of small cameos of deception – a boy catching a bird, the trapped hare – that comment on the quack's sham cures.

Further paintings by **Rembrandt** in the 17th-century section include *Titus at his Desk,* a deeply personal study of his son, quite unlike his formal portraits. Most of the work of Rembrandt's pupil **Fabritius** was destroyed in the Delft explosion that killed the artist in 1654. His *Self-Portrait* is a rare surviving work, and uses the reverse of Rembrandt's usual technique – the subject here in shadow, the background lit.

The city

Other than the seemingly endless Lijnenaan precinct, Rotterdam's centre offers little. A massive restoration of the St Lawrence Kerk has left it cold and soulless: more exciting is the redevelopment of the **Blaak** area nearby, and the hi-tech New Central Library, descending in a cascade of escalators to the grubby general market. On a rather lonely corner of a park, the **Euromast** was originally just a drab grey observation platform thrown up in 1960. The Spacetower was added later, its revolving lift rising on the outside of the 185-metre tower. The view is spectacular, but at f9.50 no less than you'd expect. One way of exploring the **waterways** you see from the Euromast is on the *Spido cruises* that leave from Willemsplein (5 tram or Leuvehaven metro). They vary in duration and interest but are most impressive at night, when the illuminated ships and refineries gleam like Spielberg spaceships.

If nothing in the city centre can exactly be called picturesque, **DELFTSHAVEN** goes some of the way to make up for it. You can get there by tram 6 or on foot from Coolsingel metro, and the uncrowded, unhurried streets and a cluster of small museums make a startling break. Once the harbour that served Delft, it was from Delftshaven that the

Pilgrim Fathers set sail in 1620, changing to the more reliable Mayflower in Plymouth before beginning their voyage to America; their final prayers before departing were said in the church in Voorhaven. Many of the buildings along the canal are restored or converted 17th-century warehouses: the **Dubbelde Palmboom Museum** at Voorhaven 12, once a jenever distillery, is now a historical museum with a well-mounted if unexceptional collection of objects made in the city. Two other museums worth a quick visit are the pewter workshop in the **Zakkendragerhuisje** at Voorstraat 13 and the **Atlas van Stolk print collection** at Aelbrechtkolk 12. Entry to all the museums is free but they close on Mondays.

Out of Rotterdam: the Delta Expo

A Spido cruise for f38 or, more realistically, a bus trip will take you 22 miles to **HARINGVLIETDAM**, a 1½ mile barrier completed in 1970 and the showpiece of the Delta Project. In 1953 an unusually high spring tide and strong winds broke the dykes of south-west Holland, flooding the polders and drowning 1835 people. With their usual flair for doing things thoroughly the Dutch began a fifteen-year plan to close off the estuaries and protect the low-lying land. Closed, the massive sluices of Haringvliet also stop salt water creeping up the estuary and force the Lek, Waal and Maas rivers to push silt out of Rotterdam's sea canal. This huge and clever piece of engineering is celebrated in the impressive **Delta Expo** (April-October daily 1000–1700; f2.50), an exhibition showing the development of the Delta Project and the Netherlands's long history of attempts to control the sea. There's plenty of English info and you even get to visit the interior of one of the dam's sluice gates that can allow 20 million litres of water a second into the sea.

Eating and drinking

One sure non-rip-off **restaurant** is *De Eend* at Mauritshuisweg 28, about the cheapest sit-down meal in town at around f7. Otherwise use the centre's many *stokbrood* and snack bars unless you can afford a mainstream restaurant, of which the VVV has a long list. At f15 the *Statenhof*, Bentinckplein 1–4, is about the cheapest of several vegetarian restaurants, though the out-of-centre *Voedingshuis Kralingen,* Lambertusstraat 100 (tram 1 or 7 towards Kralingen) has a better reputation. West of the centre, *Drie Ballons,* Tiendstraat 4, and *Melief Bender,* le Middellandsstraat 34a, are good brown cafés, with *Jan de Jong,* Drievriendenstraat 26, popular with gay women. Also near here are Rotterdam's two best **gay bars**, *After Dark,* Coolsestraat 33 and, nearby, *Loge 52.*

Arena, Westkruiskade 26, is Rotterdam's attempt at Paradiso and *Double Diamond,* corner of Westkruiskade and Westersingel, dubiously proclaims itself as an English pub. *Dizzy,* 's-Gravendijkwal 127, is a good and popular **jazz café** and *Otto* across the road its disco partner. Good for **live music** and described as a 'real hang-out' is *Parkzicht*, Kievitslaan 25, near the Euromast park.

Rotterdam listings
Consulates British, Parklaan 18, tel. 36 15 55.
USA, Vlaasmarkt 1, tel. 11 75 60.
Feminism Bookstore and information – *Emma,* Westersingel 27b.
Football Feyenoord stadium – NS Stadion train station or 49 bus, both from Central Station.
Markets General – off Grote Markt, Tuesdays and Saturdays.
Antique and curio – Grote Kerkplein, Tuesdays and Saturdays.
Student travel NBBS, Meent 126.
Police Haagseveer 23, tel. 14 14 14.
VVV Stadhuisplein 19. Also kiosk at Central Station.

DORDRECHT (DORDT)

A friendly and likeable town, Dordrecht, or **Dordt** as it's usually called, has a confusion of shabby buildings and gentle dilapidation that stop it being just another tidy show-piece. Though there's little enough to see, it's a congenial place, first and foremost a working harbour for the cruisers heading inland on the river Maas. If you want to familiarise yourself with the centre, the **VVV** at Stationsweg 1 (Monday-Saturday 0830–1930, Sunday 1000–1600) publish the oddly-named 'Strolling around the Old in Dordrecht' but you'll do just as well to wander. The **Grote Kerk** (Tuesday-Saturday 1000–1200/1400–1600; f1) provides a good landmark; its leaning tower, topped with incongruous 17th-century clocks, is visible all over town. Inside there's an elaborately carved choir, but scale the tower itself for a great view of Dordt and its surrounding waters. Near the church at Nieuwe Haven 29 is the **Mr Simon van Gijn Museum** (open all week; f0.50), a superior house museum with some amusing 19th-century toys.

The **Dordrecht Museum** at Museumstraat 42 (all week; free) has the town's main collection of paintings, including work by locally born Nicolaes Maes, Jacob Cuyp, Ferdinand Bol and the later and lesser Ary Scheffer whose works here include *Mignon Pining for her Native Land,* a much reproduced painting that understandably struck a chord in the sentimental hearts of the 19th century. Breitner's *Lauriersgracht 1890* is among a small collection of Amsterdam and Hague School paintings.

Behind the Groothoofds Poort, a decorated city gate, the rivers Merwede, Noord and Oude Maas stretch out as a grey expanse of water so crammed with ships passing from the Rhineland and Rotterdam that it must be the busiest river junction in Europe. It's best at night when you can sit at one of the cafés and watch the dark barges glide past like powerful sinister sea creatures.

For a quiet town Dordt has some good **bars**: try *Avontuur* at Voorstraat 193 – pints, stone floors, good atmosphere. Also in the centre are *Kaper* and *Bombardon* – live music and haircuts – and *Puree,* a dope-smokers' bar. Best places for cheap **food** are in Voorstraat, including the vegetarian *De Gellukkige Mus* (Monday-Friday 1800–2000) and the more expensive but highly recommended Italian *Costa d'Oro* at 444. Other than the VVV list of pensions there's little private **accommodation**. The **Youth Hostel** at Noordendijk 382 is fairly central, but if you're **camping** and don't mind being stuck on an island where drink is frowned upon, *De Kliene Rug* at Loswalweg 1 is a great place run by genuinely friendly people. Get the VVV to phone first then take an 8 bus to Stadspolder, walk 15 minutes to the jetty, yell and wave furiously and a boat will come and pick you up.

Around Dordrecht – the Biesbos and Kinderdijk
On 18 November 1421 the sea defences gave way and the 'St Elizabeth flood' formed what is now the Hollands Diep sea channel and the **Biesbos** or 'reed forest'. The sea destroyed 70 towns and villages and it's estimated that over 100,000 people were drowned. The 40 square miles of islands, marshes and lakes are now a nature reserve and can be visited from Dordrecht which at f12 for a four-hour trip is overlong and overpriced. The VVV also run trips to **Kinderdijk** ('child's dyke') supposedly the place where a child floated to safety in the flood. If you want to see **windmills**, this is the place: there are nineteen here, built around 1740 to drain water from the Alblasserwaard polders. From April to September (not Sundays) one mill can be visited, and on Saturdays they're all put into operation.

NORTH OF ROTTERDAM: GOUDA AND OUDEWATER

The canals, *markt* and churches of **GOUDA** seem so totally Dutch that its similarity with a hundred and one other towns might initially be off-putting. But Gouda has two things going for it: the St Janskerk and its famous cheese. It's on Thursdays between June and September (conveniently coinciding with the tourist season) that the cheeses are sold in the traditional market around the 17th-century **Waag**. As you'd expect, coaches roll in to savour the moment and unless you're wildly interested in it all, Thursdays are best avoided.

Surprisingly, Gouda's **Markt** is the largest in Holland, the prominent Gothic Stadhuis no doubt reducing impressions of size. Just off here is the **St Janskerk** (Monday-Friday 0900–1700; f2), a large church with some superb stained glass. As well as being intrinsically beautiful, the windows show the way religious art changed after the Reformation. The Biblical themes executed by Dirk and Wouter Crabeth when South Holland was still Catholic have an amazing clarity of detail and richness of colour. Their last work, *Judith Slaying Holofernes,* is perhaps the finest, the story unfolding in intricate perspective. The post-Reformation windows are more secular, generally celebrating civic pride. *The Relief of Leiden* shows William the Silent retaking the town from the Spanish, though Delft takes prominence – no doubt because the town paid for the window.

Gouda is best around its medieval church; **Jerusalemstraat** has a variety of old houses and the **St Catherine's Hospice** is a likeable conglomeration of 16th-century rooms and halls. It's also the municipal **Museum** (Monday-Saturday 1000–1700, Sunday 1200–1700; f2), whose paintings by Pieter Pourbus the Elder and a 15th-century silver chalice are highlights of a mixed collection. Gouda's other museum is the **De Moriaan** at Westhaven 29 (Monday-Saturday 1000–1230/1330–1700, Sunday 1200–1700; f1.50), a collection showing just about every variation on the theme of pipes possible – the town was once the country's largest producer of clay pipes.

Utrecht is only a bus ride away, and if you've time **OUDEWATER** en route is worth stopping off for as well. A compact and delightful town, it holds a unique place in the history of Dutch witchcraft, and its **Heksenweg** or *witches' weigh house* is a strange reminder of early anti-feminism.

It's estimated that over a million people were burned or otherwise murdered in the widespread witch hunts of the 16th century, and not only from superstition and fear: anonymous accusation to the authorities was an easy way of removing an enemy – or even a wife at a time when there was no divorce. The methods of 'trial' by fire and water are well known, that by weighing less so: the theory was that a witch would have to be light in order to fly on a broomstick, so many towns used the Waag to weigh women accused. If their weight didn't accord with a figure derived from their height, prosecutions proceeded.

Oudewater's *Waag* gained its fame from the actions of Charles V who saw a woman accused of witchcraft in a nearby village. The weighmaster, who'd been bribed, stated that the woman weighed only a few pounds. Charles ordered the woman to be weighed in Oudewater where the officials proved unbribable, pronouncing that the woman weighed eight stone and acquitting her. The probity of Oudewater's weighmaster impressed Charles and he granted the town the privilege of issuing certificates, valid throughout his empire, stating that 'The accused's weight is in accordance with the natural proportions of the body.' Once in possession of the certificate one could never be brought to trial for witchcraft again. Not surprisingly, thousands of people came from all over Europe for this life-saving piece of paper, and to Oudewater's credit, no one was ever found to weigh less than the 'natural proportions' indicated.

You can still see the original rope and wood balance used in the *Waag* and be issued with a certificate in olde-worlde English that states nothing, but does so very prettily. The Heksenwaag and its small museum closes on Mondays and costs f1.25.

UTRECHT AND AMERSFOORT

'I groaned with the idea of living all winter in so shocking a place,' wrote Boswell in 1763, and **UTRECHT** still promises little as you approach: surrounded by familiar shopping complexes and industrial development, the town only begins to reveal itself in the old area around the Dom Kerk, roughly enclosed by the Oude and Nieuwegracht. These distinctive sunken canals date from the 14th century and their brick cellars, used as warehouses when Utrecht was a river port, have been converted to pricey cafés and restaurants. Though the liveliest place to be, they don't disguise Utrecht's provinciality: just half an hour from Amsterdam, all the brashness and vitality of the capital have gone and it's for museums and churches rather than nightlife that the town is enjoyable.

Focal point of the centre is the **Dom Tower**, at 112m the highest

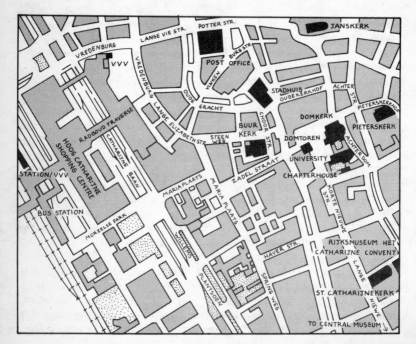

church tower in the country. It's one of the most beautiful too, soaring unbuttressed lines rising to a delicate octagonal lantern added in 1380. A guided tour (daily 1030–1600; f1.50; no museumcards) takes you unnervingly near the very top, from where the gap between tower and Gothic **Dom Kerk** is most obvious. Only the eastern part of the great cathedral remains, the nave having collapsed (with what must have been an apocalyptic crash) during a storm in 1674. A major restoration means the Dom will be closed until 1986 but you can still walk through the **Kloostergang**, the 14th-century cloisters that link the cathedral to the chapter house, now part of the university.

Utrecht's other churches are really only worth a visit if you're passing: oldest is the **St Pieterskerk** (Friday/Saturday 0900–1200/1400–1600), a shabbily maintained building that's a mixture of Romanesque and Gothic styles with 12th-century paintings and reliefs. Until her death in 1514 the **Buurkerk** was the home of one Sister Bertken, who was so ashamed at being the illegitimate daughter of a cathedral priest that she hid away in a small cell here – for 57 years.

Housing the national collection of ecclesiastical art, the **Catherine Convent Museum** (Tuesday-Friday 1000–1700, Saturday/Sunday 1100–1700; f2) has a mass of paintings, manuscripts and church ornaments from the 9th century on, brilliantly exhibited in a complex built around the old convent. This excellent collection of paintings includes work by **Geertgen tot Sint Jans, Rembrandt, Hals** and, best of all, a luminously beautiful *Virgin and Child* by **van Cleve**. Part of the convent is the late Gothic St Catherine's church, its radiant white interior enhanced by lovely floral decoration.

Utrecht's other important museum, the **Centraal**, is near the end of Nieuwegracht at Agnietenstraat 1 (Tuesday-Saturday 1000–1700, Sunday 1400–1700; free; bus 2). Its claim of '25,000 curiosities' seems a bit exaggerated, but it has a good collection of paintings by Utrecht artists of the 16th and 17th centuries. **Van Scorel** lived in Utrecht before and after he visited Rome and brought the influence of Italian humanism north. His paintings, like the vividly individual portraits of the *Jerusalem Brotherhood*, combine the style of the high Renaissance with native Dutch observation. The central figure in white is Van Scorel himself: he made a trip to Jerusalem around 1520, accounting for his unusually accurate drawing of the city in *Christ's Entry into Jerusalem*. A group of painters influenced by another Italian, Caravaggio, became known as the Utrecht School. They adapted his chiaroscuro technique to genre subjects like Honthorst's *The Procuress,* developing an erotic content that would itself influence later genre painters like Jan Steen and Dou. Even more skilled and realistic is Terbrugghen's *The Calling of St Matthew*: a beautiful balance of gestures dramatising Christ's calling of the tax collector.

Gerrit Rietveld, the De Stijl designer, was most famous for the *zig-zag* and *Rietveld* chairs in the applied art section. Part of the De Stijl philosophy was that their approach could be used in any area of design, though Rietveld's angular furniture is probably better to look at than sit on. Out of town, his **Schroder House** at Prins Hendriklaan 50 (no admission) continues the organic union of lines and rectangles characteristic of the movement.

By now the **Musical Box to Barrel Organ** collection should have found an unusual home in the Buurkerk. If, like me, you can't stand blaring fairground organs, particularly in a church, you'll prefer the other part of the collection – ingenious musical toys and mechanical instruments. East of the centre at Johan van Oldenbarneveldtlaan 6 is the **National Railway Museum** (Tuesday-Saturday 1000–1700, Sunday 1300–1700; f2.50), with trains, coaches and trams waiting on Utrecht's disused railway station – little English info but enthusiastic attendants.

A few practical details

The **train** and **bus** stations both lead to the Hoog Catharijne shopping centre and a **VVV** kiosk that'll help with pensions (around f25) in the town; their booklets 'Utrecht', 'The Dom' and 'Other Churches' are also worth picking up. The **Youth Hostel** at Rhijnauwenselaan 14, Bunnic, Bus 40 is a little far out, but the well-equipped **campsite** at Arienslaan 5 can be reached by a 57 bus from the Central Station. **Restaurants** are mainly along the Oudegracht, the mostly vegetarian *De Werfkring* at 123 having the best reputation. A cheap **wholefood** alternative is *De Gronewaterman* at Springweg 6. The junction of Oudegracht and Wed has the town's best collection of **bars**, popular with students. *Cafe Graf Floris,* opposite the central Vismarkt, is a good place to hear the Dom Tower's carillon concerts, and the nearby *De Witte Ballons* at Vismarkt 12 has a lively atmosphere. The *Heksenkelder* is a **feminist bookstore** and bar with a restaurant at the rear – Oudegracht 261. The main **VVV** office is at Vredenburg 90 (Monday-Saturday 0900–1800, Sunday 1000–1800), where you'll also find the **general market** on Wednesdays and Saturdays.

Arriving at the station (VVV in station square) it's quite a walk to the centre of **AMERSFOORT,** so catch a no. 1 or 2 bus if you want to save your energy for the town itself. The best thing about Amersfoort is its medieval streets – the Muurhuizen or 'wall houses' built into the original defensive wall around the town – and the Havik, the town's old centre. Though most recent building is commendably congruous with earlier styles there's an inevitable shopping precinct that leads to the **St Joriskerk,** an unusual, predominantly Gothic building with nave and aisles of equal height; only the south porch and adjoining Buttermarket stop the monolithic exterior resembling an aircraft hangar. Like most churches of the period the St Joriskerk was an enlargement of an earlier building, but here the original Romanesque tower was left inside the later construction of the 15th century.

All that remains of Amersfoort's other church is the **Onze Lieve Vrouw Tower**; it was built by pilgrims visiting the Amersfoort Madonna, a small wooden figure thrown into a river by a young girl in the 15th century. In the manner of such things a dream commanded her to retrieve the figure, which subsequently showed miraculous powers, though unfortunately not miraculous enough to prevent the church's destruction in a gunpowder explosion of 1787. You can climb the tower in June and July from Thursday till Sunday for f3.50. North of the town are the ridiculously picturesque **Kopplepoort** a 15th-century gate that defended the town's waterways, and the **Flehite Museum**'s distinctly uninteresting collection of local antiquities.

TRAVEL DETAILS

Trains
Amsterdam–Leiden (3 an hour; 32 mins), Leiden–The Hague CS (3 an hour; 11 mins), The Hague HS–Delft (4 an hour; 10 mins), The Hague CS–Gouda (3 an hour; 20 mins), The Hague HS–Rotterdam (3 an hour; 20 mins), Rotterdam–Hook of Holland (2 an hour; 30 mins) Rotterdam–Gouda (3 an hour; 20 mins), Rotterdam–Dordrecht (3 an hour; 16 mins), Rotterdam–Utrecht (2 an hour; 45 mins), Dordrecht–Rosendaal (3 an hour; 22 mins), Amsterdam CS–Utrecht (3 an hour; 30 mins), Utrecht–Arnhem (3 an hour; 50 mins), Utrecht–Amersfoort (3 an hour; 15 mins), Utrecht–Den Bosch (3 an hour; 40 mins).

Buses
Utrecht–Oudewater (VAGU bus 180; 40 mins), Gouda–Oudewater (VAGU bus 180; 25 mins).

Chapter four
THE NORTH AND THE FRISIAN ISLANDS

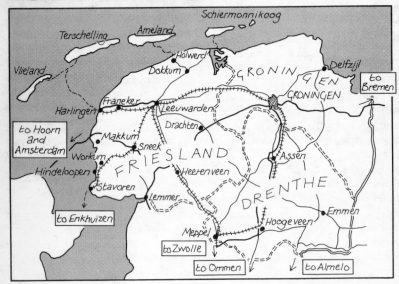

Opened in 1932, the **Afsluitdijk** bridged the gaping hole that was the Zuider Zee and made the north of the Netherlands much more accessible; suddenly Leeuwarden was signposted from Amsterdam and the little-visited provinces of **Friesland, Groningen** and **Drenthe** were on the map. Groningen, apart from its vibrant capital, has little to tempt you, and Friesland is the most rewarding of the three.

Over the years, **the Frisians** have remained resolutely independent and have managed to avoid complete absorption into the Netherlands, retaining their own language, literature and a concrete cultural identity that's a refreshing change from what is at times a pervasive uniformity in the rest of the country. The countryside is dead flat and very green, dotted with black and white cattle and long thatched farm houses, which are always crowned with the same white gable finial, known as an *uleburden*: a double-swan motif which is a symbol to keep away evil spirits. Before AD 1000, these low-lying areas were a prey to constant inundation by the sea and so houses and sometimes entire settlements would be built on artificial mounds or *terpen* (*wierden* in Groningen), which brought them high above the water level. It was a miserable sort of existence, as Pliny observed around AD 50 – 'Here a wretched race is found, inhabiting either the more elevated spots or artificial mounds where they pitch their cabins. When the waves cover the surrounding area they are like so many mariners on board a ship, and when again the tide recedes their condition is that of so many shipwrecked men.' Not surprisingly, the Frisians soon got pretty fed up with this kind of life and eventually got around to building dykes to keep the water out permanently. You can see what's left of the mounds in Friesland today, though in large settlements it's difficult since they have become obscured as the towns have outgrown them.

Friesland today remains Holland's outsider, pushing for limited forms of devolution that are quite presumptuous for such a small area. Its language probably bears more resemblance to English than Dutch and while it is recognised by the government as official, few people in the rest of the country understand it and it plays little part in commerce, industry or the media – even in Friesland itself. It is confined to being taught in schools here (though even this is a recent innovation) and is used by some people in everyday life.

If you venture this far north, try to get to the **Frisian Islands** – a fragmented extension of the sand bank that runs the length of North Holland. One of the few areas of the country you have to put any effort into reaching, the islands preserve a rare peace and an untamed, rather frightening kind of beauty. Four of the five belong to the province of Friesland and constitute an important nature area, with thriving communities of birds and a rich flora and fauna that have so far largely escaped the influence of man. The Dutch and German tourists who arrive here each summer are easily absorbed into the miles of beach and wild expanses of dune. Plans to build dykes connecting the islands to the mainland and reclaim the shallows all around were met with such resistance from naturalists and islanders that they have now been abandoned, and there's a strong feeling amongst the people here that they should remain as distinct from the Dutch mainland as possible. If money's tight **Ameland** and **Schiermonnikoog** are your best bet as they're nearer – and cheaper to reach.

Drenthe is the most sparsely populated and least visited of Dutch provinces, and it's not hard to see why. Inhabited since Neolithic times, it has come under the same variety of emperors, bishops and despots as most other parts of Holland, but though it took the winning side of the Protestants in the revolt against Spain, it wasn't awarded provincial independence until 1796. Despite that, it retained a fair amount of autonomy – probably because it was simply ignored – and today is a distinctive area, mostly heath and woodland with stretches of peat bog, that attracts only the most hardy travellers. The two towns of any size are unhappy places with only a couple of things that could conceivably bring you this far off the beaten track. **Assen** was only made capital because of its central position, and is irritating enough to have an excellent museum, **Emmen** is the best place to see Drenthe's most original feature – its *hunebedds* or megalithic tombs, the earliest sign of any civilisation in the Netherlands, probably dating from around 2500 BC.

INTO FRIESLAND

Just north of the Afsluitdijk, **HARLINGEN** is a small port and the first of the chain of towns that stretches across north Friesland into Groningen. More importantly it's the place to catch a ferry to the islands of VLIE-LAND and TERSCHELLING. Two or three ferries leave for each island daily, take about an hour and a half and cost f27 return; in addition there are three fast services to Terschelling daily. Though services exist between the islands, they're neither regular nor frequent. While you're waiting, take a wander round the centre's 16th- and 17th-century houses, part of a new conservation plan intended to retain the traditional aspects of Friesland with an eye to tourism. Look out for a small statue on the quayside: yet another of the boy who supposedly stuck his finger in a hole in a dyke to stop a flood.

After Texel (for which see p. 74), **TERSCHELLING** is both the most developed and most fashionable of the islands. With a scattering of hotels and campsites, it has a well-organised tourist infrastructure, and while this doesn't spoil the quiet of the island and its nature reserve to the east, **VLIELAND** is less popular and even more peaceful. Cars aren't allowed here and the best way to travel through the island's heaths and woodlands is by bike – the VVV have lists.

The shallows around have always been dangerous for large ships. Their most famous victim was the *Lutine,* which sank carrying gold and silver as wages for British troops stationed here during the Napoleonic wars. All that remains is at the bottom of the sea, and only the ship's bell was recovered – now in Lloyd's of London where it's still rung whenever a big ship goes down.

Some details

Terschelling has four **campsites**, of which *Cnossen* at Hooftweg 8, West-Terschelling is the largest and best equipped; in the same village you'll find the **Youth Hostel Hanskedune**. The main village is Midsland, with the VVV office at Hooftweg 1. Vlieland's **campsite** is at Kampweg 1, Oost-Vlieland. The VVV run birdwatching trips and holidays: if you're interested, the best time to come is the nesting season in May and June.

Back on the road to LEEUWARDEN. Until Napoleon closed its university in 1810 **FRANEKER** was a minor cultural centre and stopping-off place for rising academics on their way to Leiden. It's a quiet, moated town, the **Stadhuis** a mixture of Gothic and Renaissance styles, with its twin gables, octagonal tower and rich interior making it one of Friesland's most attractive buildings. What little else there is to see is mostly on **Voorstraat**: the VVV at number 49 is also the **Coopmanshuis Museum**, once the home of an 18th-century university curator and now a collection of bits and pieces relating to the university and its obscure alumni. The recently restored **Martenahuis** and **Waag** are nearby, and it's really just for these and Franeker's other buildings that it's worth stopping off.

LEEUWARDEN

The amalgamation of three *terpen* on a port on what was once the Middelzee, **Leeuwarden** was the residence of the powerful Frisian Stadholders, who vied with those of Holland for control in the United Provinces. These days it's the neat and faintly twee capital of Friesland, with an air of provincial prosperity and smug sense of independence. The suburbs are pretty bleak and everything of interest is confined to the compact town centre, which is almost entirely surrounded and dissected by water and can be walked across in twenty minutes.

Waagplein is the hub around which the rest of the town revolves – a long narrowing open space, cut by a canal and flanked by cafés and large department stores. North from here, in Grote Kerkstraat, is the house where **Mata Hari** spent her early years. A native of Leeuwarden, her name has become virtually synonymous with the whorish female spy. A famous and successful dancer, she was arrested in 1917 by the French on charges of espionage and shot, though what she actually did remains a matter of some debate. In retrospect it seems likely that she acted as a double agent, gathering information for the Allies while giving snippets to the Germans. As perhaps their most notorious indigene, the people of Leeuwarden seem to prefer this story, treating her more like a heroine than anything else; hence the recent candid statue of her in Over de Kelders. The **Frisian Literary Museum and Documentation Centre** now has its home here. Founded in 1959, this acts as a testament to the past, and a centre for contemporary Frisian literature. It mounts a variety of temporary exhibitions as well as permanent ones on Mata Hari and P. J. Troelstra, a Frisian socialist politician and poet who set up the Dutch Social Democratic party in 1890 and was at the head of the labour movement until 1924. The centre is well worth a visit if you're at all interested in the cultural history of the area, and is open Monday-Saturday 1000–1200/1400–1700.

The **Grote or Jacobin Kerk** (Tuesday-Saturday 1000–1100/1400–1700) has recently undergone a very large restoration and is probably looking better than it has done for some time, though it's still an unremarkable Gothic church. A victim of subsidence, the whole place tilts slightly towards the newer south aisle, where some less-than-complete 16th-century frescoes have been uncovered. The Roman Catholic church of **St Boniface** nearby, whose ornamented spire imposes itself on what is otherwise a rather flat Leeuwarden skyline, is a Cuypers neo-Gothic church of 1894. The spire was almost totally destroyed in a storm of 1976 and there were many people who wanted to pull the place down altogether – even to replace it with a supermarket. Fortunately the steeple was replaced at great expense and with such enormous ingenuity that everyone seems to be agreed now about leaving the church as it is. There are few Cuypers churches left in Holland but thankfully the current vogue seems to be for keeping them – for the time being at least. Retracing your steps down Grote Kerkstraat you come eventually to **Het Princessehof** – a house of 1650 and former residence of the Stadholder William Friso. The house is now a museum with a stunning collection of **ceramics**, including the largest collection of tiles in the world. As the museum is so big, it's useless to attempt any kind of explanation except to say, definitely don't miss it. One piece of advice – if you're really into ceramics you could

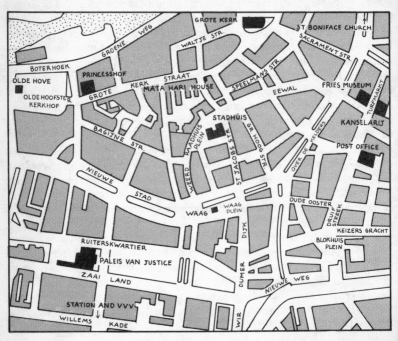

spend days in here; if not, be selective, as the sheer quantity of stuff on display is overwhelming (Monday-Saturday 1000–1700, Sunday 1400–1700; f2).

Around the corner is the **Oldehoofsterkerkhof** – a large square at the end of which stands the precariously leaning **Oldehove**, something of a symbol for the city and part of a cathedral started in 1529 but never finished because of subsidence. The early foundations form the basis of today's car park and the tower presides over all, a lugubrious mass of disproportion that defies all laws of gravity and geometry. To the right stands a statue of Troelstra, who looks impassively on, no doubt admonishing the city on their choice of architects. If you're brave enough you can climb the tower for a guilder (Tuesday-Saturday 1000–1630).

The **Fries Museum** (Tuesday-Saturday 1000–1700, Sunday 1300–1700; f3) is without doubt Leeuwarden's real attraction and one of the best and most important regional museums in the country. What Sitwell calls 'the continuing character of independence' of the Frisians is nothing new but interest in the language and history of the region only sprang up in the 19th century, when a society was formed that is the basis of the present museum. Highlights include rooms given over to the island of Ameland and, notably, the painted furniture of Hindeloopen – rich, gaudy and, for me at least, horribly oppressive. Most peculiar of all are examples of the bizarre headgear of 18th-century Frisian women – large cartwheel-shaped hats known as *Deutsche Muts,* and *oorijzers,* gold or silver helmets that were an elaborate development of the hat clip or brooch. As well as an indication of social standing, a young girl's first *oorijzer* symbolised her becoming a woman.

Opposite the Fries Museum stands one of the most striking buildings in Leeuwarden, the **Kanselarij**, a superb gabled Renaissance structure of 1571. You may notice that the gable and corresponding double stairway are slightly to the right, instead of being in the centre. This is because the building was supposed to be longer but the budget wouldn't stretch to it and the work had to stop where it was, making the Kanselarij a sort of 16th-century victim of public spending cuts. For the last four years it has housed the **Frisian Resistance Museum** (f1.50), annexe to the Fries Museum and a chronological exhibition tracing the early days of the Nazi invasion, through collaboration and resistance to the Allied liberation, with a variety of photographs and bits and pieces from the war years. The explanatory pamphlet you can ask for is an invaluable guide.

The **VVV** are at the station (Monday-Friday 0830–1900, Saturday 0900–1700) and have a list of private **rooms** that covers the whole of Friesland. Leeuwarden itself is not one of the cheaper places to sleep: there's only *Hotel 't Anker* in Eewal for f30, or *Pension H. Schippers,* Vervoerscentrum, Tesselschadestraat 57, for f25 – out of the centre to the south-west and a little difficult to find (turn left by the garage, into the car park and ask in the canteen). **Camping Kleine Wielen** is a no. 20 bus ride, about four miles out.

Eating: *Pizzeria Sardegna,* Grote Hoogstraat 28 has a selection of pizzas from f5, or the *Bombardon Eetcafe* in Sacramentstraat does a range of cheap dishes. *Het Bommelsteyn,* Korfmakerstraat 19, is also quite reasonable.

SOUTH OF LEEUWARDEN

Twenty minutes by train from Leeuwarden lies **SNEEK** (pronounced 'snake') – popular for its situation in the heart of the Frisian broads and in summer a lively town crowded with yachting enthusiasts. Expect it to be exceptionally busy during **Sneek Week**, the annual regatta which begins on the first Saturday of August, when the flat green expanses around here are thick with the white of slowly moving sails. Unfortunately, there's little of interest here for those who aren't into water sports but for those who are, **Sneekermeer** is the nearest centre – about six miles out. You can hire most equipment from *Camping De Potten.* Back in town, the **Martinikerk** is an unhappy Renaissance modification of 1681; the latest in a long line of churches that have stood on this site since 1150, the foundations of which you can see around it. The **Scheepvart Museum and Oudheidkamer**, at Kleine Zand 14 (Monday-Saturday 1000–1200/1300–1700; f2), has a well-displayed collection of models, paintings and all kinds of nautical items, plus a room devoted to the Visser family, who made a fortune in the 18th century, transporting eels to hungry Londoners.

Should you want to stay in Sneek, the nearest **campsite** is *De Dompi,* on the road to Sneekermeer, and the **VVV** (Monday-Friday 0930–1700, Saturday 0930–1200) in Kruize Broederstraat has free lists of **rooms** (f20–25).

Directly west is **MAKKUM**, a tiny place where they have made pottery they claim to be superior Delftware since the 17th century. The Tichelaar family have been among the main entrepreneurs all that time, and you can be shown around their ceramic works for f2.50 (Turfmarkt 7). Makkum varies from the bright and colourful, more akin to Delft, to delicate white fluted objects.

Heading south, **HINDELOOPEN** juts into the Isselmeer, displaying a neatness and quiet extreme even by Dutch standards. No more than a large village and something of an enigma, they used to speak their own dialect of Frisian here, and it was the birthplace of specific arts that never went further than its closely-drawn boundaries – a sumptuous costume, uniform architecture and, most famous of all, its painted furniture. A florid mixture of Scandinavian and Oriental styles, it gives the impression that they had the desire to paint just about everything in the house.

Countless shops sell copies in the main street, but you can see original examples in the small village **museum**. The best place though, is the Fries Museum in Leeuwarden, where whole rooms decorated like this are really overpowering.

A little further south is **STAVOREN**, probably the deadest of the dead cities of the Zuider Zee. Once a prosperous port, it's now a supremely uninteresting small town that you're only likely to visit to catch the **ferry to Enkhuizen**, which leaves roughly three times daily during the summer.

NORTH OF LEEUWARDEN

Bus 66 from LEEUWARDEN takes you to **HOLWERD**, a desolate spot from where you get the ferry to **AMELAND** – f9.75 return, and between April and September five boats a day. Between June and August, on Saturdays, there are lots more, but summer weekends can be pretty horrendous and are best avoided. The population – a mere 3,000 – goes up to a staggering 30,000 in the summer months though the nature of the island and its visitors is such that it's not hard to escape the onslaught. Most people tend to congregate and with the aid of a bike you can easily find more deserted spots. If you're feeling particularly adventurous, head for the eastern tip of the island, where you'll find miles of empty sands and dunes. **NES**, the principal village, snuggles amongst the green behind the enclosing dyke, a small cluster of cafés, hotels and touristy shops. It's a lively place in summer, not unpleasant – people breathing life into the place rather than spoiling it. The **VVV** (Monday-Saturday 0900–1200/1400–1700/2000–2100) are in the main street and they'll try to sell you their list of rooms – don't bother, try *Pension T. Oud,* Strandweg 12 (f22), or in the nearby village of BUREN, *Pension Kooiker,* Strandweg 14 (f20), or *P. H. Mosterman,* Hazeweg 12 (f19). You can hire **bikes** at M. Janszenweg 2 or *P. de Boer,* Strandweg 4, both in Nes, for around f5 a day.

A short bus ride north east of Leeuwarden is **DOKKUM** – a pretty moated little town where St Boniface met his death in 754, murdered while trying to convert the pagan Frisian hordes to Christianity. The people of Dokkum don't ever seem to have forgiven themselves for this callous act, and there are references to it all over town, in the form of churches, chapels and parks. An inoffensive and unashamedly dull place, Dokkum has nothing to keep you for more than a few hours.

The same bus takes you to **LAUWERSOOG**, where boats sail to the island of **SCHIERMONNIKOOG** – the smallest and most deserted of the islands and until the Reformation property of the monastery of Klarkamp, on the mainland. The island's name means literally 'island of the grey monks'. Nothing remains of them unfortunately, and Schiermonnikoog is just a concoction of long stretches of beach and dune – wild, uncultivated and very much a place to escape to. The boat costs f9.75 return and takes about fifty minutes to pick its way through the mud-flats. It's even possible to walk there – a pastime known as *wadlopen* and definitely not to be tried without a guide – ask at the VVV. You can't take a car as the only ones allowed on the island are those that belong to the inhabitants. Between April and October there are four boats a day and they drop you about two miles outside the only village, from where it's either a windy walk or there's a bus. Here you'll find the VVV, a couple of expensive **hotels**, a **Youth Hostel** and precious little else.

GRONINGEN

The province of **GRONINGEN** is a patchwork of industrial complexes and nondescript villages, but the city itself, benefiting from the presence of its large and prestigious university, has a cosmopolitan and vigorous feel quite unexpected in this part of the country. Apart from the Martini-kerk and a couple of good museums, there's little in the way of 'sights': Groningen was heavily bombed in the last war and is now an eclectic jumble of architectures with nothing of special interest. You visit Groningen more for its 'feel' and often there's a lot going on, particularly during term-time. It's a lively cultural centre for the whole of the northern Netherlands; an alternative to Amsterdam in what is one of the furthest corners of the country.

Centre of the city is the **Grote Markt,** an extensive open space that was at the heart of the war damage. It was reconstructed with little imagination and is today an ill-matched mix of fifties and sixties buildings, one of which houses the VVV (Monday-Friday 1000–1800, Saturday 1000–1600). The tiered and slightly leaning tower of the **Martinikerk** glowers anachronistically at the north-east corner of the modern square (Tuesday-Saturday 1200–1700; f1). Though the oldest parts of the church go back to 1180, most of it dates from the mid-15th century, the nave being a Gothicised rebuilding undertaken to match the choir. The vault paintings in the nave are beautifully restored and in the lofty choir there are two series of frescoes on the walled-up niches of the clerestory. On the right a series of eight depict the story of Christmas, beginning with an *Annunciation* and ending with a portrayal of the young Christ in the temple. On the left six frescoes complete the cycle with the story of Easter. The mainly 17th-century **Martinitoren** (Tuesday-Saturday 1200–1630) is, like most of its counterparts all over the country, the property of the city council, and it costs f1.50 to go up. It offers a view that is breathtaking in every sense of the word – fainthearts be warned.

Behind the church is the **Kerkhof**, the main haven of peace and quiet in the centre of town. On the corner there should be a **squat** – in a building which the local authorities want to demolish. When I was there

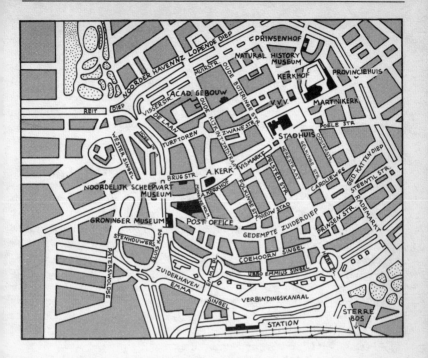

they had been resisting for about two years and seemed to think they could carry on longer, as long as they had the support of the local people. Pop in for a drink and a chat – it's a good place to make contacts.

Dutch maritime museums are two-a-penny, but one of the best equipped and most comprehensive is the **Noordelijk Scheepvart Museum** (Tuesday-Saturday 1000–1700, Sunday 1400–1700; f2.50), which traces the history of northern shipping with a variety of models and original artefacts. The **Niemeyer Tabalogisch Museum** is attached – much smaller and devoted to smoking, from 1600 to the present day. The Niemeyer name may ring a bell and here you can see the origins of those familiar blue tobacco packets.

Much more interesting, however, is the **Groninger Museum** at Praediniussingel 59 (Tuesday-Saturday 1000–1700, Sunday 1300–1700; f1). Apart from the oriental ceramics in the basement everything is displayed as representative of a period rather than a medium, and a mélange of arts and applied arts describe Groningen's history, from early *terp* culture to 20th-century painting. The small but impressive collection includes works by Lucas van Leyden, Ter Borch and some of the few extant paintings of Carel Fabritus. Local artist Jan Wiegers and his expressionist De Ploeg School conclude this part of the museum. Upstairs, expect to see enterprising and imaginative temporary exhibitions, on which the museum prides itself.

Living – a few points

If you're staying, then apart from **Camping Stadspark** – a ten minute ride on bus 12 from Grote Markt – the **Sleep-In** is the cheapest option, opposite the post office at Munnekeholm 2–4 (f6.50). There are a number of **hotels** for f25 a night. *Drogeristerij D.C. de Jonge,* Lange Der A 4 is the best, but if that's full there's *Hotel Tivoli,* Gedempte Zuiderdiep 67, *Pension Beekman,* Oosterweg 118, or *Hotel Wey,* Jozef Israelstraat 58.

The canteen **food** at the student *Mensa,* Oosterstraat 44 (Monday-Friday 1200–1330/1700–1900), is reliable, filling and very reasonable at f4.30, but if you want something a little more healthful, there's *De Eenhorn,* Ubbo Emmrisstraat 6a – vegetarian menus from f10. *Zelfbe-dienings,* Spilsluizen 9, do cheap meals for f8 (1700–1900). **Poelestraat** and the area around is a lively and popular part of town, with bars, discos and numerous snack-bars if you don't feel like a sit-down meal. Conversely, if you can afford a splurge try *De Pakhuis,* in a small alley off Peperstraat, where the food is good but not especially cheap.

Bands, normally including a few well-known names, play every Sunday in August in the **Sterre Bos,** a park to the south of the town centre. Info on this and other events can be gleaned from the *Groninger Zomer Manifestatie* or *Uit in Groningen,* both available from the VVV. A gay guide to the city is available from the **American Discount Book Centre** in Oosterstraat, price f2.50; where incidentally they also have a good selection of English books. **COC** are at Kraneweg 56 and **Dikke Trui,** Oude Ebbingestraat 82 is a women's bar, restaurant, theatre and art gallery that comes with a very high recommendation. Finally, if you're heading further east, **NBBS** are at Oude Kijk in 't Jatstraat 52.

SOUTH INTO DRENTHE

About ten miles south of Groningen is **ASSEN,** the dreary capital of Drenthe which would not deserve much more than a sentence here if it were not for the splendid **Drents Museum** (Tuesday-Friday 0930–1700, Saturday 1300–1700; f1). The archaeological section is its real strength – traditionally also the preserve of the archaeological department at Groningen and benefiting from the co-operation. The collection includes material on *hunebedds,* axes, urns and ceramics of Roman and Germanic origin, moor corpses and the **Pesse canoe** – the oldest water vessel ever found which, dated approximately at 6800 BC, looks its age.

The road south to **EMMEN** follows the Hondsrug Ridge of high ground, along which are several *hunebedds* or giant graves. Emmen itself has a couple of good examples: near the centre is a unique gallery-grave, said to be the tomb of a queen and made up of two burial chambers within an outer ring of standing stones. Another, about half a mile west of the station in the woods, is perhaps more impressive: a passage-grave – more intricate with a pronounced entrance – set in a clearing in the trees and ringed by standing stones. Otherwise Emmen is of no interest, an uninviting series of sporadic settlements interspersed with forest and farmland, and mostly visited for its zoo.

TRAVEL DETAILS

Trains

Stavoren–Sneek/Leeuwarden (1 an hour; 30 mins, 50 mins), Harlingen–Leeuwarden (2 an hour; 30 mins), Leeuwarden–Stavoren (2 an hour; 50 mins), Leeuwarden–Groningen (2 an hour, 50 mins), Leeuwarden–Zwolle (2 an hour; 1 hour), Leeuwarden–Amsterdam (1 an hour; 2 hours 30 mins), Groningen–Zwolle (2 an hour; 1 hour 10 mins), Groningen–Amsterdam (1 an hour; 2 hours 25 mins), Groningen–Bremen (2 a day, morning and evening; 2 hours 30 mins).

Buses and boats

Leeuwarden–Holwerd–Ameland (FRAM Bus 66; 5 boats a day; 2 hours), Leeuwarden–Lauwersoog–Schiermonnikoog (FRAM Bus 51; 4 boats a day; 2 hours 15 mins), Groningen–Lauwersoog–Schiermonnikoog (GADO Bus 63; 4 boats a day; 1 hour 55 mins). Harlingen–Vlieland (3 boats a day; 1 hour 30 mins), Harlingen–Terschelling (3 boats a day; 1 hour 30 mins). Stavoren–Enkhuizen (May-Sept: 3 boats a day; 1 hour 20 mins).

Chapter five
GELDERLAND AND OVERIJSSEL

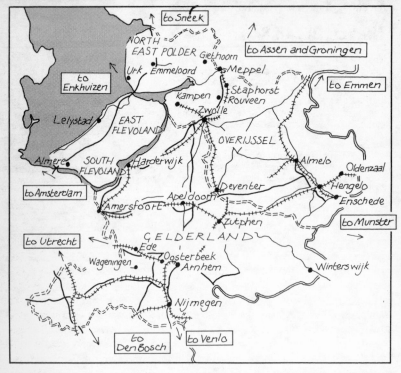

to Sneek

NORTH
EAST POLDER Giethoorn

to Assen and Groningen

Urk Emmeloord Meppel

to
Enkhuizen

to Emmen

Kampen Staphorst
Rouveen

Lelystad EAST Zwolle
FLEVOLAND

OVERIJSSEL

Almere SOUTH Harderwijk
FLEVOLAND

Almelo Oldenzaal

to Amsterdam

Deventer Hengelo
Apeldoorn Enschede

Amersfoort

Zutphen to Munster

to Utrecht

GELDERLAND

Ede

Oosterbeek Winterswijk
Wageningen Arnhem

Nijmegen

to
Den Bosch to Venlo

Gelderland and **Overijssel** make up the largest chunk of the eastern part of the Netherlands, but there's very little you can say about either. Of the Overijssel towns, **Zwolle** and **Kampen** display a faded and dreamy composure and, apart from the textile triangle of the eastern corner, are the province's largest centres. Further south, in Gelderland, Apeldoorn, Arnhem and Nijmegen are the main points of reference. **Apeldoorn** has for a long time been very much the preserve of Holland's pensioners, but **Arnhem**, while still suffering the effects of war damage and not much in itself, can prove a useful springboard for the scattered attractions nearby. Of these, the **Veluwe forest** is Gelderland's principal magnet, popular especially with the Dutch who head out here from the Randstad in droves to sample what is one of the more untouched parts of the country. Just north of Arnhem, the **Kroller-Müller Museum** lurks amongst the trees – the one thing you shouldn't miss in two provinces.

MEPPEL AND THE NORTH-EAST POLDER

MEPPEL is an exceptionally quiet, small market town on the south-west edge of Drenthe. If you do wind up here, there's nothing to keep you longer than it takes to change buses for the lakes to the west.

Bus 79 takes you to **GIETHOORN**, a village entirely composed of waterways and first settled by a group of wandering flagellants who dug peat for a living, giving the place its name when they uncovered a quantity of goats' horns. Their digging was so careless that it led to the formation of the lakes and channels that make Giethoorn what it is today – a series of islands, connected by footbridges, strung out along a central canal for about two miles. The bus drops you on the main road and you can walk into the village from here or take (f5) or hire (f15 an hour) a boat. It's a pretty dreadful place, long ago discovered by Dutch weekenders and German tourists, who swarm into the village in their thousands to jam the busy footpaths and the already congested waterways in search of a quaint, thatched northern Venice – such is the fascination of a water-town. Only in the evening do things look up, when the campers seem confined to camp and the day-trippers have all gone home, leaving behind them a peace you would have thought impossible during the day.

Several miles further west is the **North-East polder**, the second piece of land to be reclaimed in the Zuider Zee scheme. In 1936, the 35-mile-long dyke was finished and the land drained, giving 119,000 acres of new agricultural pasture. Only with the later polders have the government actively encouraged large-scale settlement and **EMMELOORD** is the one town of any size, first settled in 1948 in the dead centre. Apart from that there are a few tiny villages, and **URK** and **SCHOKLAND**, two former islands which were incorporated into the polder. As it was sinking into the sea, Schokland had been evacuated long before, leaving a ghostly place around which the land fell dry in 1941. You can still pick out the long, thin wooded shape with, at its north end, remains of the harbour and some deserted buildings. The **Ijsselmeer Polders Museum**, on the southern tip of the former island, has some interesting displays of archaeological and geological material found after the polder was drained (Monday-Friday 0900–1700, Saturday/Sunday 1000–1800).

URK was lucky – it retained its harbour and is today a thriving fishing port. It's a pretty, remarkably self-contained village, with a quayside that is a pleasant mixture of the functional and the picturesque. The people here preserve an austere Calvinist religion and still wear their local costume – authentic up to a point, but no doubt encouraged by the steady flow of tourists. There's a small local **museum** (Monday-Friday

0900–1300/1400–1800) and the **VVV** is well signposted. Between May and September you can take a boat to Enkhuizen: in peak season there are three a day, but check first with the VVV for times.

SOUTH TO ZWOLLE AND KAMPEN

STAPHORST has a bit of a reputation for being a haven of religious fanatics of the most extreme 'fire and brimstone' variety, though this seems to be more myth than fact. To be fair, the village does jealously guard traditions and a religious orthodoxy not found in the rest of the country: tourists are not encouraged, there's no VVV and, unlike such places as Marken and Volendam, the wearing of the multi-coloured traditional dress is totally genuine. However, during the week you'll find Staphorst very quiet and, apart from the houses painted in the local vicious-green and sky-blue, much like any other Dutch village. It's only alive here on Sunday morning, when everyone goes to church. Not being allowed to drive their cars they walk, and you'll see a lot of people wearing sombre Sunday dress all heading in the same direction, no doubt giving rise to the stories of people walking to church in long solemn processions. The facts, unfortunately, are more prosaic.

Staphorst runs eventually into ROUVEEN, both villages forming a continuous settlement that lines the road in the shadow of the motorway down to **ZWOLLE**: the small and compact capital of Overijssel. Its moated and still partly walled town centre revolves around **Grote Markt**, where you'll find the **VVV** (Monday-Friday 0900–1800, Saturday 0900–1230/1345–1700), which has information on **rooms**. Apart from **Camping Agnietenburg** (a 28/29 bus to the outskirts of town and then a two-mile walk), the **Sleep-In** is definitely the cheapest option at f7.50, though they have constant problems in finding permanent accommodation; by now they should be at Rode Torenplein. Failing that, there's *Pension Beniers*, Oosterlaan 6 (f30) or *Pension Dupont*, Bilderdykstraat 49 (f28).

In the centre of Grote Markt stands the **Grote Kerk**, dedicated to St Michael, dragon-slayer and patron saint of the town. If the exterior seems a little plain it's because it has been dogged by ill-luck in the past. Its tower was one of the highest in the country and, rather too efficient an expression of man's desire to get nearer to God, struck by lightning three times in 1548, 1606 and 1669. After the third time it was never rebuilt and eventually the bells were sold. Inside, the church has a familiar austerity, fashioned by the nature of Dutch worship, with the choir a bare and dusty forgotten corner and the seats arranged on a central pulpit plan. The pulpit itself is a beautiful piece of Renaissance carving, symbolising Jesus's words 'I am the true vine and my father the husbandman'. (July-mid-August Monday-Saturday 1000–1200/1400–

1700; other times of the year Wednesday 0930–1700).

Attached to the church is the **Hoofdwacht** of 1614, an elaborate ornately gabled building which once served as a guardhouse. In front of it executions once took place, and the words 'Vigilatae et Oratae' (Watch and Pray) were probably a chilling piece of advice to the crowds gathered to witness the bloody spectacle. The building now, appropriately enough, houses the police station.

The **Provincial Overijssel Museum** (Tuesday-Saturday 1000–1700, Sunday 1400–1700; f1) is close by at Melkmarkt 41 and is divided between two houses: the **Drostenhuis**, a rather run-down 16th-century mansion with an uncomfortable rococo pediment, and the **Gouden Kroon**, through the garden and used for temporary exhibitions. Compared to some of its provincial counterparts it seems unimaginative and disappointing – just the usual plod of period rooms put together in an unconvincing fashion – and the only memorable exhibits are some nice early 20th-century ceramics.

As far as **eating** is concerned, vegetarians can try *Rozemarintje,* Thorbecksgracht 63, where they do a menu for f7 or, for carnivores there's *Restaurant Pan,* Rembrandtlaan 4, who do one for f5. *Restaurant de Sassenpoort* is both more central and more expensive – from f10.

Just ten minutes by train from Zwolle, **KAMPEN** merits a close look if not a lengthy stay. A bold succession of towers and spires, it rises graciously out of the dull flat floodplain of the Ijssel. The towns on this river (Deventer and Zutphen are the others) enjoyed a period of real prosperity when, as members of the Hanseatic League, they had a virtual monopoly on the important Baltic trade. By the 16th century though, Amsterdam was mopping up everywhere, pinching the trade of medieval ports already in difficulties and profiting at their expense. The Ijssel towns were no exception and when Amsterdam was approaching the height of its glory they had gone into a long, slow decline.

Kampen retains some fragments of its past wealth along Oudestraat, the main street which runs the length of the ribbon-like town centre. Roughly half way down are the **Oude** and **Nieuwe Raadhuis**. Best bit of the old one is the *Schepenzaal* or Magistrates' Hall, with a stone *chimneypiece* of 1545 – a grandiloquent, self-assured work, carved by Colijn de Nole in praise of Charles V, though with its typically Renaissance depictions of Justice, Prudence and Strength, really as much in praise of the town as anything. Next to it is the *Magistrate's bench* – the work of a more obscure local carpenter who apparently didn't get on with de Nole at all. Angry at not getting the more important job of the chimney-piece, his revenge can still be seen on the left-hand pillar, in the satyr who is facing the chimney and laughing evilly. For a more detailed description, pick up the glossy booklet on your way in – entry through the Nieuwe Raadhuis.

At the far end of Oudestraat stands the **Bovenkerk,** a lovely Gothic church with a light, spacious sandstone interior. Generally regarded as one of the most important of Dutch medieval churches, its choir with thirteen radiating chapels was the work of Rotger of Cologne, a member of the Parler family of masons, and whose greatest triumph was Cologne Cathedral. In the south transept an urn contains the heart of Admiral de Winter, a native of Kampen who fought to rid his country of what he considered to be the yoke of the House of Orange, taking part in the French invasion of 1795 that instigated the Batavian Republic. The rest of him lies in the Pantheon in Paris. Nearby, the **Koornmarktspoort** is one of three surviving town gates and the scene of temporary exhibitions of modern art. Another, the **Broederspoort,** houses the local **museum** (Tuesday-Saturday 1000–1700; f1).

Finally, the **Kampen cow**: it hangs from a tower in Oudestraat for much of the year and is an offbeat symbol for the town. Kampenites are unfortunate enough to be the butt of the Dutch equivalent of 'Irish jokes', and the cow is the result of a story that plays on their reputation. When grass began to grow at the top of the tower local farmers asked if they could graze their cattle up there, and the result was – the cow. The **VVV** is almost next door (Monday-Friday 0900–1700, Saturday 1000–1400, Tuesday half-day) and should you want a bed for the night the cheapest is at *Hotel de Steur* (f28).

A NOTE ON FLEVOLAND

In Flevoland the Dutch landscape reaches new heights of boredom; so much so that the government actually pays people to come and live here. **LELYSTAD** is where most of them end up – a characterless grid of building, imposed on the polder's flat desert of green. Named after the engineer who conceived the scheme to reclaim the Zuider Zee, not even financial enticements would make most people come here, but if you've a passing interest in land reclamation there is at least one reason. **Informatiecentrum Nieuwland** (Monday-Friday 1000–1700, Sunday 1300–1700) gives the background on the Zuider Zee plan, with photos, models, films and slides, most of which are in English and give some clue to what's likely to happen here in the future. Bus 143 runs regularly from Kampen to Lelystad (50 minutes).

TWENTHE

Heading into eastern Overijssel, you realise how far you have left the typical Dutch polder landscape behind. The countryside is still fairly flat, but thickly wooded and slightly undulating. The principal towns of this region, known as Twenthe, are **Almelo**, **Hengelo** and **Enschede**, primarily industrial centres. Their prosperity lay in textiles but now, usurped by cheap east European and far eastern imports, trade is down and they are declining. Enschede has around 15 per cent unemployment and the towns in nearby Germany (which used to depend on this region for jobs) are in an even worse position. In a sense, these are the 'red-brick' heartlands of Holland: like the north of England, a monument to the glory of the industrial revolution and a depressing reminder of changing times.

None of that inspires a visit, and a stay of any length is not recommended. However, an excellent museum and some interesting 1930s architecture make **ENSCHEDE** worth a detour if you have the time. Laid waste by fire in 1832, the town has an ugly modern centre, mostly refashioned as a large shopping precinct. The **VVV** is at Markt 31 (Monday-Friday 0830–1900, Saturday 0900–1700), and they'll let you in to the **Grote Kerk**, though it's a much rebuilt Romanesque structure that's a lot more interesting outside than in. More exciting is the **St Jacobuskerk** across the road, built on the site of a previous church that was totally lost in the fire. Consecrated in 1933, it's normally kept closed, but if you call at the presbytery next door someone will open up the place for you. It's worth the trouble, as the church is very beautiful, built in a domed and cloistered neo-Byzantine style, with some good modern sculpture and stained glass. The **Stadhuis**, a little way down Langestraat, was finished in the same year, and is very much an architectural landmark in its brick and copper 1930s grandeur. No expense was spared in construction, and the interior is richly decorated with mosaics and, again, stained glass. Both buildings are powerful symbols of civic pride in a city restored after almost total destruction.

The **Rijksmuseum Twenthe** (Tuesday-Saturday 0900–1300/1400–1700, Sunday 1400–1700; f3) is north of the centre at Lasonersingel 29 – across the railway by the station, first right, first left and follow the road to the end. As well as the usual space given over to applied arts, in the form of tiles, clocks, furniture and archaeological finds, this museum's main attraction is its collection of Dutch painting from the 17th to the 20th century, one of the best, and certainly one of the most complete in the whole country.

For the **Textielmuseum** (Tuesday-Saturday 1000–1200/1400–1700, Sunday 1400–1700; f1.50) follow De Klomp east and turn right into Espoortstraat. It's a small museum, housed in a former mill-owner's residence and attempting to illustrate the development of the early cottage industry into the post-industrial revolution big business that textiles became. It can be seen in half an hour and seems uninspired, but its failings are more the result of lack of funds and space rather than any dearth of imagination. There has been talk of a move to bigger premises but for the moment the museum stays where it is.

INTO GELDERLAND: DEVENTER, ZUTPHEN AND APELDOORN

When Gerrit Groot founded the Brotherhood of Common Life there in the late 14th century, **DEVENTER** was known as a centre of learning. The Brotherhood was a semi-monastic collective that espoused tolerance and humanism, and it was for progressive attitudes like these that the town was widely regarded – Erasmus studied here and Thomas à Kempis was one of Groot's first pupils. Little of the academic atmosphere survives, however, and Deventer is today a colourless provincial town, not worth much more than a quick look if you're changing trains.

There's not a great deal to see: the tower of the **Grote Kerk** rises cumbrously over the houses nearby, capped with a cupola that was added in the 17th century by De Keyser. Worth glimpsing are the vault designs and murals, some of which are especially brightly restored. The **VVV** is a few steps away on Zandpoort, and in front of it the **Waag**, a late Gothic edifice which retains an ancient dignity despite something of a rickety appearance nowadays. It houses the town **museum**, which has paintings by Ter Borch – ex-burgomaster of Deventer – a collection of antique bicycles and numerous other articles of local, if not exactly universal, interest.

Less than a century ago, Baedeker's handbook could describe **APEL-DOORN** as 'a prosperous village', which gives some indication of just how fast the town has grown to its present size of 140,000. Its great claim to fame is the Paleis Het Loo and this has turned the place into one of the Netherlands' main tourist centres and an extensive garden city that sprawls languidly into the countryside around. Its appeal, however, is hard to find: Apeldoorn likes to regard itself as *the* Dutch royal city, with a strong sense of snobbish elitism and a slow stately pace that is largely the result of its ageing visitors. The one annual show of life is the **Jazz in the Woods** festival in early June.

The **Paleis Het Loo** (Tuesday-Sunday 1000–1700; f3.50) stands on the northern edge of town, linked to the station by buses 102/104. Built in 1685 by William III, it was the favourite residence of Queen Wilhelmina, who lived there until her death in 1962. No longer used by the Dutch royals – they have an ultra-modern apartment somewhere in the grounds – it has been restored as a national museum and should be open to the public by now.

The palace apart, Apeldoorn has little to hold you. Its centre is a small soulless shopping precinct, dissected by the main Hoofdstraat. At the top end of this, opposite the Grote Kerk, is the **Van Reekum Museum** (Tuesday-Saturday 1000–1700, Sunday 1300–1700; f1), the only other conceivable attraction, with exhibitions of contemporary art and design.

The **VVV** are at the station and have maps and free lists of **rooms** (from about f20). Otherwise, if you need to stay, there's a **Youth Hostel** at Asselsestraat 330 (buses 2/4 from the station) or **Camping de Veldekster** – south-west of the centre, bus 110. Inevitably, cheap **eating** is difficult and you have to fall back on either pizzas from *Ristorante Tipico* in Kapel-straat, or vegetarian at *Lust je nog Peultjes,* at the bottom end of Hoofdstraat, where they do a menu for f7.50.

While too small to warrant any major stay or detour, ZUTPHEN is ideal for a day's visit if you're based for any length of time in one of the nearby larger towns, like Arnhem. A sleepy little place with a dispropor-tionate concentration of historic buildings, Zutphen's almost 'museum-piece' centre hides an illustrious and sometimes torrid past as a rich medieval port. Sir Philip Sidney, the English poet, soldier and courtier, and perhaps the personification of the accomplished Renaissance man, was wounded here while fighting with Leicester's forces against the Spanish in 1586. When suffering from a wound that was to prove fatal, he offered his drink of water to a dying soldier, uttering the now common-place words 'thy need is greater than mine'; there's a memorial to him in Coehoornsingel.

At the centre of town the 15th-century Wijnhuis houses the **VVV**, and half-way down Zaadmarkt the **Museum Henriette Polak** (Tuesday-Friday 1000–1700, Saturday 1000–1230, Sunday 1400–1700; f0.75) has an excellent small collection of 20th-century Dutch painting and sculpture, including works by Mari Andriessen and paintings by Jan Wiegers, as well as lots of lesser known artists from the 1950s and '60s. The same ticket gets you into the **Stedelijk Museum** which is housed in a 13th-century Dominican monastery near the station and has a fairly predictable selection of shards, armour and silverware. In the old refectory on the first floor there's an altar-piece of c.1400, originally from the **Grote Kerk** of St Walburga, an indifferent Gothic church on the other side of town, whose most impressive features are an extravagant brass baptismal font and its medieval **library**, the oldest in Western Europe. Built in 1565, it was used by monks, nobles and the local Latin school until the 19th century, and contains around 700 books and manuscripts, from early incunabula to later 16th-century works, many still chained to the lecterns on which they're kept. The collection also includes two handwritten volumes – one a beautiful 16th-century illuminated missal, and the other an original manuscript attributed to Thomas à Kempis. Because of these riches, visits have set times – check with the VVV.

ARNHEM

'Fortunes are made in Amsterdam and Rotterdam, but it is in Arnhem that they are spent and enjoyed' wrote Henri Havard, a 19th-century view of the city when it was the chosen watering-hole of the idle rich.

History had other plans for **Arnhem** it seems, and it's now better known as the place where thousands of British and Polish troops died in the Allied airborne operation of September 1944 (codenamed 'Market Garden'), an operation that gutted the greater part of the city. What you see today is a post-war reconstruction that's of less interest for itself than the museums on its forested outskirts, particularly the **Kroller-Müller Museum** which, with its array of Van Goghs and modern art, is alone worth a very considerable journey.

These days Arnhem is something of a pilgrimage for English visitors who flock here every summer to pay their respects to the soldiers who died, or to view the spots immortalised by the battle. Inevitably, the rebuilding has left it a patchy place, and the best part of the town is unquestionably the north-west area of the centre. The heart of this is **Korenmarkt**, a small square which obviously escaped much of the destruction and has one or two good façades: the streets around here are pleasantly seedy, full of restaurants and bars. The **Korenbeurs** now houses the Filmhuis, where Arnhem and Nijmegen stage a joint **film festival** during July and August.

Arnhem degenerates as you walk south-east towards the area most badly damaged by the fighting. Eventually you reach **John Frostbrug** – named after the commander of the battalion that defended it for four days. It's just an ordinary bridge, but it remains the symbol and the centre of people's remembrance of the battle, Dutch and British alike. Around its north end you can see the results of the devastation – wide green boulevards intersect the broad open spaces of haphazardly placed blocks and car parks. The church of **St Eusabius** stands at the east end of the bland, characterless **Markt** and the 15th-century **Stadhuis** crouches behind. Both buildings seem oddly naked in the unsympathetic expanses around them, and instead of being surrounded by clusters of medieval houses (pre-war photos do show it to be something like this), they proclaim themselves pristine monuments saved from the debris of war. The church is a 15th/16th-century structure surmounted by a valiantly attempted but rather obvious replacement tower. Services are no longer held here and the light, airy Gothic interior is stripped bare of all furnishings and wholly given over to exhibitions staged during most of the summer.

East of the city in the nearby village of Oosterbeek, the **Airborne Museum** (Monday-Saturday 1100–1700, Sunday 1200–1700; f2.75; no museumcards; bus 1 – direction Oosterbeek) is normally packed with British visitors and since 1978 has been housed in the former *Hotel Hartenstein,* where the British forces were besieged by the Germans for a week before retreating across the river, their numbers depleted by several thousand. With the use of an English commentary, photographs, original material and dioramas, this place informs on every aspect of

Operation Market Garden and its consequences in Arnhem. Roughly opposite, at the far end of Stationsweg, is the war cemetery for the thousands who died in the battle.

A few practical points
NBBS student travel are at Kleine Oord 6, and there are frequent daily **train** connections to both Amsterdam and Cologne. The **VVV** is at Stationsplein 45 (Monday-Saturday 0900–2000, Sunday 1100–1600) and they have maps, detailed information on the battle, and up-to-date cultural info in *Uit in Arnhem* (f1). **Accommodation** can be a problem unless you come in July or August when the **Sleep-In** is open – beds for f6 at Thomas à Kempislaan 15, bus 3 (direction Cranvelt). The **Youth Hostel** is a little further on at Depenbrochlaan 27 (same bus). Otherwise, apart from **Camping Warnsborn** (north-west of the centre, bus 11), the cheapest place is *Pension Warnsborn*, Schelmersweg 1, at f28. Buses 11 or 2 (direction Hoogkamp).

A note on **buses**: Arnhem has a rather odd system of trolley buses which describe a figure-of-eight pattern over town. This means there'll often be two buses at the station with the same number and different destinations, so it's important to get the direction as well as the number right.

Cheap **eating** isn't too much of a hassle and the streets around Korenmarkt are best for restaurants. Also, there's *Da Leone,* Nieuweplein (pizzas from f7.50); *Old Inn,* Stationsplein (Dutch food from f10); *De Zonnebloem,* Velperbuiten 15 (vegetarian menu at f10). *De Fink,* Bovenbeekstraat, is a spacious friendly bar of the brown variety – good for contacts.

AROUND ARNHEM: THE KROLLER-MÜLLER MUSEUM AND VELUWE PARK

Arnhem's real crowd-puller is the **RIJKSMUSEUM KROLLER-MÜLLER** (Tuesday-Saturday 1000–1700, Sunday 1100–1700), made up of the private art collection of the banking and shipping millionaires of the same name, and a complete survey of modern European art from Impressionism to Cubism and beyond. A low-slung building among the trees at the centre of the **Hoge Veluwe National Park**, it was built in 1938 by the Belgian architect van de Velde; entry is included in the price of admission to the park (see below). The bulk of the collection is in one long wing, starting with the most recent Dutch painters and working backwards. There's a good set of paintings, in particular some revealing self-portraits, by **Charley Toorop**, probably one of the most skilled and sensitive of 20th-century Dutch artists. Her unclassifiable father **Jan** also gets a good showing throughout the museum, from his pointillist studies to later

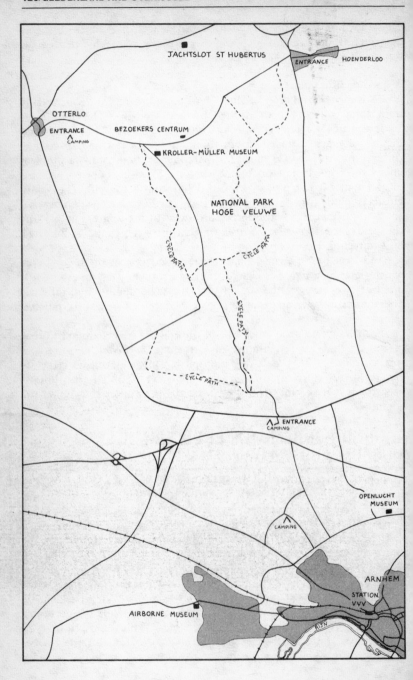

works more reminiscent of Beardsley and Art Nouveau. **Mondriaan** is well represented too, giving a good idea of the development of De Stijl, and there's a liberal sprinkling of the major Cubists. The whole building gravitates towards the **Van Goghs**, one of the most complete collections of his work in the world; housed in a large room around a central courtyard and placed in context with accompanying pictures by his contemporaries.

Outside, behind the main building, a **Sculpture Park** is spaciously laid out with works by **Rodin, Giacometti, Epstein** and **Barbara Hepworth**, all appearing at manageable intervals. Notable is **Jean Debuffet's** *Jardin d'email*, one of his larger and more elaborate jokes.

The **HOGE VELUWE NATIONAL PARK** makes up the south-east corner of the Veluwe. The nearest entrance is Rijnsburg, about six miles north of Arnhem, and there are others further north at Otterloo and Hoenderloo. Part sandy heath, part thick woodland, and once the private estate of the Kroller-Müllers, it's now the favourite playground of Dutch families during the summer months. The entry price includes the museum, though you have to pay extra if you have a bike or a car. If you don't, there are a number of ways you can get there: the best is to take the special summer bus (number 12, direction Hoge Veluwe, ten past every hour) which costs f7.40 for a day return and f5.50 for your entry ticket, all payable to the driver. Once in the park you can pick up one of the white bicycles that are left out for everyone's use. If the bus isn't running (check with VVV), you can either hire a bike or take a bus to Otterloo and walk to the park from there.

Best place to get off is the **Bezoekers Centrum** (visitors' centre) as this has information on the park and is the place to pick up a bike. Once you're mobile you can cycle around as you wish: apart from the museum the other thing to see is the **Jachtslot St Hubertus**, a hunting lodge built for the Kroller-Müllers by Berlage in 1920 (May-November Monday-Friday 1000–1200/1400–1700). Dedicated to the patron saint of hunters, the floor plan – in the shape of branching antlers – is representative of the stag bearing a crucifix that appeared to St Hubert while hunting, and each room of the sumptuous interior symbolises an episode in his life.

The **Netherlands Open Air Museum** was founded in 1912 to try to 'present a picture of the daily life of ordinary people in this country as it was in the past and has developed in the course of time' (Tuesday-Saturday 0900–1700, Sunday 1000–1700; f4.40; bus 3 – direction Cranvelt). Original buildings have been taken from all over the country and assembled here in a large chunk of the Veluwe forest, and represent an imaginative attempt to recreate the rural Dutch way of life over the past two centuries. Everything's been carefully reconstructed throughout, and the guide book explains all with academic attention to detail – at f5 worth every cent. It recommends three routes – red (1 hour), green (2 hours) and blue (4 hours); I suggest the green route with certain selected forays into other parts of the museum. The blue route is definitely only for fanatics of Dutch farmhouses.

NIJMEGEN

Spreading irregularly south from the Waal, **Nijmegen** is the oldest town in the Netherlands, first settled by the Romans, for whom it was an obvious strategic point since it marked the northernmost frontier of their empire. After their decline, the Franks invaded and Nijmegen later became one of Charlemagne's seats of government – from where he kept an eye on the still rebellious tribes of the north.

But for the French troops who almost wholly destroyed it in 1796, Charlemagne's **Valkhof palace** would have made Nijmegen a considerable tourist centre today. An enormous complex of chapels and secular buildings (originally completed in the 8th century and rebuilt in 1155 by Frederick Barbarossa, Holy Roman Emperor at the time) all that remains is a fragment of the Romanesque choir of the 12th-century palace chapel and a sixteen-sided chapel, built in c.1045 in imitation of the palatinate church at Charlemagne's capital, Aachen. The small chapel is complete, and would be lovely if not for the fact that it's normally full of people, piped choral music and paraphernalia on the Valkhof palace.

Nijmegen's importance as a strategic point continued to determine its rather chequered history as recently as 1944 when the bridges over the Waal here were a key objective of *Operation Market Garden* (see p. 124). They were taken by the Americans but the disaster at Arnhem and subsequent failure of the Allied troops to link up led to the city being in the front line for the rest of the war, and under constant shelling. All of this is vividly manifest in what you see here today. The old city was partially destroyed and has been replaced by a town largely designed to a new plan.

The **Grote Markt**, despite the pretty thorough devastation this area underwent, is surprisingly well preserved and in stark contrast to the modern shopping streets across the road. The gabled **Kerkboog** leads through to the peaceful precincts of the **Grote Kerk of St Stephen**, a much-renovated Gothic church which has some fine Renaissance woodwork. The tower, with its vaguely oriental spire, offers a commanding view over the surrounding countryside for a mere f0.30. The church will cost you another f0.60 (May-June Monday-Friday 1000–1230/1330–1700, Saturday 1000–1300; June-August Monday-Friday 1000–1700, Saturday 1000–1300, Sunday 1400–1700).

Behind the church, the huddle of medieval houses that sloped down to the Waal were totally destroyed in the war and have been replaced by a residential precinct on much the same pattern. A collection of neo-vernacular terraces, it's sad that such attempts at reconstruction are still a world away from the buildings around the church which, in spite of everything, have remained relatively unchanged. On the other side is the **Commanderie St Jan**, an authentically restored 17th-century building and now home to the municipal museum (Monday-Saturday 1000–1700, Sunday 1300–1700; free). Here you'll find a variety of exhibits with a local flavour, including innumerable paintings of Nijmegen and its environs, none particularly distinguished except Van Goyen's *Valkhof Nijmegen*, which used to hang in the town hall. Painted in 1641, it's a large picture depicting a shimmering Valkhof above the Waal: in sombre tones, pastel variations on green and brown, most of the picture is sky and water, lazily dancing before your eyes.

The **Rijksmuseum Kam**, east of the town centre at Kamstraat 45 (Monday-Saturday 1000–1700, Sunday 1300–1700; f3), is a small museum, devoted mainly to the Roman history of Nijmegen and founded by the eminent archaeologist G. M. Kam who died in 1922, donating his collection and the building to the country. Since then other artefacts have been added and the museum builds up a comprehensive picture of the first Roman settlement of Ulpia Noviomagus.

Finally, the **VVV** is, illogically, on the opposite side of town to the railway station, at St Jorisstraat 72 (Monday-Friday 0900–1800, Saturday 1000–1600, Sunday 1000–1400). They won't be able to find you a cheap room as there aren't any: apart from **Camping de Kwakkenburg** (bus 5) there's no Sleep-In, no Youth Hostel, and the only pension is *Catherina* (St Annastraat 64) at f35. Strangely enough, it's probably cheaper to stay in nearby Germany, where you can get a room for between 15 and 20DM.

As Nijmegen is a university city there are, however, plenty of cheap places to **eat**. Try the student *Mensa*, Prof. van Wielierstraat 8, south of the centre (buses 1/5/6/8). *Grietje Rietmeyer*, Ganzenheuvel 3 has a good variety of vegetarian food at around f10 and *Pizzeria Pinnoccio*, Molenstraat 99 does pizzas from f6.25.

TRAVEL DETAILS

Trains
Meppel–Zwolle (3 an hour; 15 mins), Zwolle–Kampen (2 an hour; 10 mins), Zwolle–Emmen (1 an hour; 1 hour 10 mins), Zwolle–Enschede (1 an hour; 1 hour 15 mins), Zwolle–Deventer/Zutphen (2 an hour; 25 mins, 35 mins), Zwolle–Amersfoort (3 an hour; 35 mins), Apeldoorn–Deventer (2 an hour; 12 mins), Apeldoorn–Zutphen (2 an hour; 15 mins), Zutphen–Arnhem (3 an hour; 20 mins), Arnhem–Amsterdam (3 an hour; 1 hour), Arnhem–Nijmegen (3 an hour; 15 mins), Arnhem–Cologne (15 a day; 2 hours).

Buses
Meppel–Staphorst (DVM Bus 28; 10 mins), Meppel–Giethoorn (NWH Bus 79; 30 mins; restricted service), Kampen–Urk (VAD Bus 141; 50 mins), Kampen–Lelystad (VAD Bus 143; 50 mins), Lelystad–Amsterdam (VAD Bus 154; 1 hour).

Boats
Urk–Enkhuizen (May, June and September: 2 a day; July and August: 3 a day; 1 hour 30 mins).

Chapter six

THE SOUTH

The South — a somewhat arbitrary grouping — covers the three widely disparate provinces of Zeeland, North Brabant and Limburg: **Zeeland** is a scattering of villages and towns whose wealth, survival, and sometimes destruction has long depended on the vagaries of the sea. Secured only when the dykes and sea walls of the Delta project once and for all stopped the chance of flooding, at their best they seem in suspended animation from a richer past. As you head across the arc of towns of **North Brabant** the landscape slowly fills out, rolling into a rougher countryside of farm-land and forests, unlike the precise rectangles of neighbouring provinces. Though the change is subtle, there's a difference in the people here too — less formal, more relaxed and for the most part Catholic, a fact manifest in the magnificent churches of **Breda** and **'s Hertogenbosch**. But it's in solidly Catholic Limburg that a difference in character is really felt.

European rather than Dutch, **Limburg** has only been part of Holland since 1830, but way before then the presence of Charlemagne's court at Aachen deeply influenced the region's identity. As Holy Roman Emperor, Charlemagne had a profound effect on early medieval Europe, revitalising Roman traditions and looking to the south for inspiration in art and architecture. Some of these great buildings remain, like Maastricht's St Servaas, and most have a wealth of devotional art that comes as a welcome change after the north. The landscape too has steepened sharply, and you're within sight of Holland's first and only hills.

ZEELAND

Zeeland's claw-like prongs jut out into the North Sea, a collection of sandbanks protected from flooding by the Delta dykes-barriers which also give the area its main lines of communication. Before they were completed in the 1970s, silting up and fear of the sea prevented any large towns developing, and Zeeland remains a condensed area of low dunes and nature reserves popular with holidaymakers and yachting types esca-ping the cooped-up conurbations nearby. Getting around isn't a problem, bus services making up for the lack of north-south rail connections, though undoubtedly the best way to see these islands is to cycle, a painless and anodyne experience. You can hire bikes in most towns (ask at VVVs) and many of the private operators will take your passport in lieu of a deposit.

The best thing to do on arrival at the bleak ferry terminal of **VLIS-SINGEN** is leave; a bus takes you to the train station, where there are hourly departures to Amsterdam (2 hours 40 mins) and intermediate stations. There's also a ferry service, outside the station, to Breskens, where you can go on by bus to Bruges. For anyone truly stuck for the night there's a **campsite** at Burg. van Woelderenlaan I (out of the ferry terminal, over the bridge to the end of Sloeweg and left), or **Pension Tromp** in P. Krugerstraat (f25) in Vlissingen itself. If you're waiting for a ferry go out to Middelburg on a cheap **Dagretour** ticket, it's better than sitting in Vlissingen all day.

Back in 1897 Baedeker reported that 'the rustic population of the neighbourhood is best seen on market day', and the women of **MIDDEL-BURG** still dress up for the Thursday market, the one big day in a town where very little happens. Though much destroyed by wartime bombing, Middelburg's concentric streets still centre on the markt and the town's best building, its huge **Stadhuis**. A lumpish structure, its Gothic façade is overloaded with sculpture and topped with an odd tower that seems to have crept up from behind; f1.50 will get you in to the tidily-restored

interior, though the adjacent **Vismarkt**, used for exhibitions of modern art, is free.

Like the Stadhuis, the **Abbey Churches** east of the centre have been massively restored after near total destruction in the war. How well this was done I wasn't able to find out, as the three churches, linked together and sharing the Lange Jan tower, were very solidly closed. There's an uninteresting museum, the **Zeeuws**, in the abbey grounds too, but restoration and desanctification seem to have taken their toll on the abbey's soul, and it's little more than pleasant today.

It's difficult to conceive of anything in Middelburg to stop over for, but if you find yourself needing a room the VVV at Lammerensteeg 5 has lists, starting at f22.

A 52 bus ride, and you're in **VEERE**, which sits on the coast, a tiny harbour of pretty houses that are a testament to a wealthy past. Following the marriage of the lord of the town to a daughter of James I of Scotland, Veere gained its riches from the monopoly it held on Scottish wool imports, only to die away into a backwater when the harbour silted up in the late 17th century. Statues of Veere's lords decorate its town hall, a building that's also the local **museum**. A lovely town, but again one to glimpse rather than spend any time in.

If you want to tour Zeeland, **GOES** to the east is a good place to start. Another quiet town, its few buildings of interest cluster around the Gothic Grote Kerk, and it's from the centre that buses run to most other parts of South Beveland. Travel up to **ZIERIKZEE** and you cross the elegant **Zeelandbrug**, at 5022 metres one of the longest bridges in Europe. A harbour town of medieval buildings, Zerikzee's landmark is it's aptly-named **Monstertoren**, the first 69 metres of a projected 207-metre tower abandoned when cash ran out in the 16th century. The western part of the island, **Schouwen**, is one of the better developed parts of the province, with a string of campsites through the dunes of the west coast, reaching a small nature reserve at Westerschouwen. The **VVVs** at Renesse and Haamstede will point you to the best accommodation.

HEADING EAST THROUGH NORTH BRABANT

The Netherlands' largest province, **North Brabant** sided with Maurice of Nassau against the Spaniards, splitting Brabant in two – the south today is part of Belgium. Catholic tradition is still strong in the region and in North Brabant's most interesting towns, Breda and 's Hertogenbosch, the great Gothic churches remain active centres of worship. Woodland and heath form most of the natural scenery, and the gently undulating arable land is distinctive in a country whose landscape is cursed with sameness. Main road and rail connections pass from west to east and north to Utrecht, though if you're driving or biking make sure you have a good map as the province's roads are notoriously unsignposted.

BERGEN-OP-ZOOM is the first of four towns that stretch east. Lying exposed on the Ooster Scheldt it's not surprising that it came under almost constant attack from the Spanish following the town's siding with the United Provinces in 1576. It was under siege well into the 17th century, and later damage during French and German occupations has flattened most of the old quarters. What's left is best around the Grote Markt, a café-lined square with the 15th-century **Stadhuis** and Keldermans's **Grote Kerk** looking on. Keldermans was also responsible for the **Markiezenhof**, now being restored as a museum. The remainder of the town is, like Roosendaal to the east, industrial or modernised. It's only when you reach Breda that you uncover a town with any individuality.

BREDA

Though there's little evidence of it now, **Breda** developed as a strategic fortress town, and has been badly knocked about since its capture by the Spanish in 1581. Much of the centre is taken over by a pedestrian shopping precinct, but it's in the area around the beautiful Grote Kerk that the town's character asserts itself. The best of the cafés are hard by in the Havermarkt, and on Tuesdays and Fridays stalls push close to the church for the lively **general market**. The Gothic **Grote Kerk** itself is the highlight of the town, its intimate interior generating a rare feeling of awe and exaltation. The short nave and high spacious crossing are mainly undecorated but in the north transept a 16th-century wall painting gives an impression of a colourful pre-Reformation interior discovered by recent renovations. Take a look also at the tombs, as one, that of Engelbrecht II, is magnificent. Engelbrecht was a Stadholder and Captain-General of the Low Countries who died in 1504 of consumption – vividly apparent in the drawn features depicted on his intensely realistic *mausoleum*. Four half-kneeling figures (Caesar, Regulus, Hannibal and Philip of Macedon) support a canopy that carries his armour, so skilfully sculpted that their shoulders sag slightly under the weight. It isn't known who executed the mausoleum, but it has grandeur and power without resorting to flamboyance; it's very moving. During the French occupation the choir was used as a stable but fortunately the 16th-century *misericordes*, showing rustic and comic scenes, survived. One or two of the carvings are recent replacements – but their subject should give them away.

Breda's two museums are near the church: the **Stedelijk en Bisschoppelijk Museum** at Grote Markt 19 is small and forgettable, but the **Ethnological Museum** on Kasteelplein (closed Mondays; f3.50) has a large collection that, for once, hasn't only been gathered from former Dutch colonies. Exhibits include particularly good Japanese rooms.

At the top of Kasteelplein sits the **Kasteel**: too formal to be forbidding, and much rebuilt since the *Compromise of Breda* was signed here in 1566 – an early protest against the Spanish domination of the Low Countries. Twenty-five years later the Spanish captured Breda, but it was regained in 1590 following a nifty trick by Maurice of Nassau's troops: the Spanish garrison was regularly supplied by barge with peat, so eighty men hid beneath the peat of a barge towed into the castle, overcame the Spaniards and retook the town. Today a military academy, there's normally no admission to the castle.

To the east at the end of Catharinastraat is the **Begijnhof**, built in 1531 and until recently the only *hofje* in Holland still occupied by Begijns. The one surviving sister no longer lives here, but a small museum of Begijn life remains in one of the houses. Some of the others are now used as commercial art galleries, rather spoiling the atmosphere of quiet retreat.

Breda's a good place to stay if you're touring the area: there's a **Sleep-In** at Hoek Claudius Prinsenlaan-Heerban (June-August, f7). Near the station, the **VVV** (Monday-Friday 0830–1800, Saturday 0830–1700, Sunday 0900–1530) offer the usual pension service at the usual prices, but if you opt for their **rooms** in private houses, ask for one that's central or you may end up in a nearby village. The closest **campsite**, *Liesbos,* is five miles out on the 111 bus. Best place to **drink** is the Havermarkt.

Two routes take you to 'S HERTOGENBOSCH or DEN BOSCH as it's almost always called. Unless you want to go to TILBURG, a dull textile town, or on to EINDHOVEN, the northern of the two is better.

DEN BOSCH

If Breda's Grote Kerk is Gothic at its most intimate and exhilarating, Den Bosch's **St Jan's Kathedraal** is Gothic at its most gloomy, the garish stained glass, c. 19th-century or modern, only adding to a sense of dreariness that hangs over the nave. Generally regarded as the finest Gothic church in the country, the cathedral, like Holland's other great churches, is currently undergoing restoration, closing off most of the choir for the next few years. You enter beneath the oldest and least well-preserved part, the western tower; blunt, brick-clad and oddly prominent amidst the wild decoration of the rest of the exterior. Inside, the most interesting features are around the nave. Alard Duhamel was one of St Jan's later master masons: he designed the brass *font* near the western entrance, and it's thought that the stone *canopy*, a weird twisted piece of Gothicism at the eastern end of the nave, was the masterpiece that earned him the title. It's as you're standing here that you first notice the extravagant Renaissance *organ case* that fills most of the west wall. Assembled in 1602, it was described by a Victorian authority as 'certainly the finest in Holland and probably the finest in Europe. . . . It would be difficult to conceive a more stately or magnificent design.' In the half-light of the cathedral the case seems as antique and petrified as the stone of the nave. It's still impressive though, and in comparison the *pulpit* of the same period can't help but fall a little flat, despite elaborate carving and sculpted tiers.

Much of the cathedral's early decoration was destroyed in the icono-clasm of 1629, including a number of works by **Hieronymus Bosch**, who lived in the town all his life. Only two Bosch panels remain (in the north transept) and even their authenticity is doubtful. What is more certain is that Bosch belonged to the town's *Brotherhood of our Lady,* a society devoted to the veneration of the Virgin, and as a working artist he'd have been expected to help adorn the cathedral. Sadly, there are no other paintings by Bosch in his home town. To see his work you really have to go to Ghent – or Spain's Prado.

Take away Den Bosch's cathedral and a pretty but not very interesting town remains. Best of its small museums is the **North Brabant Museum** (Bethaniestraat 4, closed Mondays; free) with a good-looking collection of art and antiquities, but really once you've seen St Jan's there's little to stop you moving on.

From DEN BOSCH it's easy to reach UTRECHT by road or rail, the countryside losing its rolling prettiness as you go north. As William Beckford commented in the 18th century, 'From Utrecht to Bois-le-Duc (Den Bosch) is nothing but sand and heath; no inspiration, no whispering foliage, not even a grasshopper.' The other main road and rail routes head down to the industrialisation of EINDHOVEN.

EINDHOVEN

In 1890 the population of **Eindhoven** was 4,500, in 1982 193,000: what happened in between was **Philips**, the electrical firm, and the name of Eindhoven's benign dictator is everywhere – on bus stops, parks and the high-rise office blocks north of the city. Philips also gave the town its single tourist pull, the **Evoluon** (open all week; f9; no museumcards; bus from central station), a science museum housed in what looks like a flying saucer from a 1950s B movie. Inside, the lift has you wide-eyed as you rise to a button pusher's paradise, which thankfully isn't just one big advert for the company. There are hundreds of exhibits to fiddle with but what was boring in physics at school is boring here and by the end of a tour you're numbed rather than blinded by science.

Eindhoven's rapid growth this century means there's little interesting old architecture. If you're a fan of neo-Gothic churches the **St Catharina** church was built by the doyen of the Gothic revivalists, P. J. H. Cuypers, late in the 19th century. The **Van Abbe Museum** (closed Mondays; f1) is a purpose-built gallery with an above average collection of modern art, mainly 20th-century paintings by Picasso, Klein, Chagall, Kandinsky and Bacon among others.

Two places to stay: the **Jeugd Hotel** at Paradise Laan 30 (f11 without breakfast) and the **Pension Den Boog**, Heilige Geestraat 46 at f19. There's an excellent **campsite** in wooded countryside at Landsard 15, but it's a long way out and a thirty-minute walk even from the nearest no. 7 bus stop.

There's nothing to lure you east of Eindhoven save the **National War and Resistance Museum** at OVERLOON, reached by a time-consuming train journey via modern VENLO and the cosy residentalism of VENRAY, where a bus service links train station to town. From here the only practical ways of reaching Overloon are by hitching or hiring a bike from Jacob's bike shop at the end of Radhuisstraat (f6 + f50 deposit or passport). Twenty minutes through fields of wheat and you're there. Overloon is an affluent little town, rebuilt following destruction in the last war when it was the site of a fierce battle in which 2,400 men died. The final stages took place in the woods to the east where hand-to-hand fighting was needed to secure the area, and it's on this site that the War and Resistance Museum (open all week; f5 + f1.25 for essential guidebook) now stands.

Its purpose is didactic: 'not merely a monument for remembrance, it is above all intended as an admonition and warning, a denouncement of war and violence.' This the museum powerfully achieves, with the macabre machinery of war forming a poignant prelude to the collection of documents and posters. A horrific series of photographs show the dead of the concentration camps, and a brightly, almost gaily coloured Buchenwald prisoner's uniform makes the holocaust real in a way that even the photos cannot. To tour the whole museum takes a couple of hours and the guidebook concludes with a breakdown of military and civilian losses and a moving epilogue: a sobering experience.

SOUTH INTO LIMBURG

Though the north part of Limburg between Venray and Venlo is more undistinguished moorland, bleak and boring, to the south the landscape gradually gains a profile that eventually becomes Holland's few hills. MAASTRICHT, the province's capital, is the place to head for, but en route a couple of towns might detain you. ROERMOND only became part of the Netherlands in 1813: until then it had been controlled either by the Spanish or the Austrian Habsburgs, who allowed freedom of Catholic worship. This religious tradition still gives the town its character.

The **Munsterkerk** (Friday-Saturday 0900–1200/1400–1800) is the largest and oldest of Roermond's several churches, a Romanesque slab greatly, perhaps overly, restored in the 19th century. Beneath its neo-Gothic decoration much of the original 12th-century form remains, but the best survivor of the period is the coloured marble tomb of the cheerfully dead Count Gerhard of Gelder and his wife. The whole church was built as a mausoleum for Gerhard, part of the abbey he'd founded in 1220, but after twenty-six years of restoration by local celebrity P. J. H. Cuypers it's as much his building as anybody's. There's a statue to the eminent architect near the church and the house at Andersonweg 6 where he lived and worked for much of his life is now the **Gemeentelijk Museum** (Tuesday-Saturday 1000–1700, Sunday 1400–1700; f1). As you'd expect, the main focus falls on Cuypers, but there's also a large gallery with changing exhibitions.

South-west of Roermond, **THORN** is hard to get to and I didn't bother; but if you like Baroque decoration the **Abdijkerk** has a profusion of it, including a particularly excessive high altar.

MAASTRICHT

A haphazard jumble of roofs spread across the left bank of the Maas – what Henri Havard called 'a charming disorder' – **Maastricht** has the air of a city in the heart of Europe, vibrant, alive and refreshingly un-Dutch. Situated in the bottom corner of a thin finger of land that reaches down between Belgium and Germany, the atmosphere of this small medieval centre, still partially walled, is unmistakably cosmopolitan, and three languages and currencies happily co-exist. It's a great town just to *be* in, wandering around soaking up the feel of the place, though that's not to say there's nothing to see. One of the oldest towns in the country, Maastricht's first citizens were Roman, and it was an important stop on the trade route from Cologne to the coast. They left relatively few traces, but the later legacy of Charlemagne is manifest in two churches that are among the best surviving examples of the Romanesque style in the Low Countries.

The **Markt** is at its busiest on Wednesday and Friday mornings, when people nip over the nearby borders for Maastricht's cheap general market. At the centre stands Pieter Post's **Stadhuis** of 1664; a square, grey lime-stone building that is particularly representative of the monumental Dutch civic architecture of the mid-17th century. It also illustrates a general and quite reliable rule – that 17th-century Dutch buildings were supposed to be seen from the front. The back is plain and grubby, while the other side, though by no means awe-inspiring, has the restrained kind of gran-deur typical of Post. Inside, the main hall is imposing, giving way to a rear octagonal dome supported by heavy arches. You can walk around fairly freely: open during office hours.

In the middle ages, the **Vrijthof** was the scene of the so-called 'Fair of the Holy Relics' – a seven-yearly showing of the bones of St Servaas which, while it brought pilgrims and plenty of money into the town, resulted in such civil disorder that it was eventually stopped. The square is bounded on one side by a line of cafés and opposite, absurdly close to each other, the churches of St Janskerk and St Servaas.

Dedicated to the first bishop of Maastricht, **St Servaas** (Monday-Saturday 1030–1800, Sunday 1230–1800) is possibly Holland's oldest

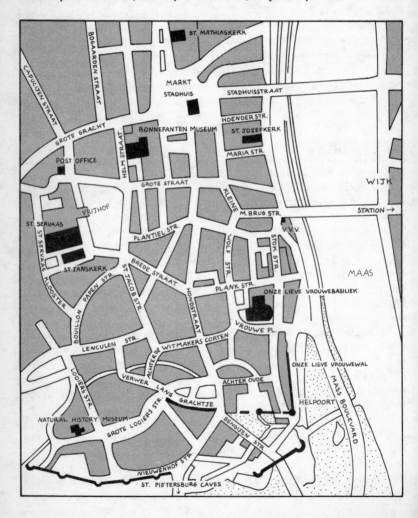

church, dating from AD 950 and the elaborate outcome of an earlier shrine. Most of it now consists of medieval and later rebuildings of the original. Inside, all is rich and imposing – round arches divide a nave lined with side chapels – and everything focuses on the apsidal choir, decorated with paintings from the 16th century. Only the crypt remains of the 10th-century structure and it's the most revered part of the church, containing the tomb of the saint himself.

When I was there the first phase of the present restoration was in progress – renovating the 15th-century Gothic cloisters – the main body of the church won't be finished until 1988, so be prepared for difficulties in getting in. The entry charge of f3.50 may come as a bit of a shock – it's because of the **Treasury**, which has iconography and reliquaries, including a copper bust reliquary of St Servaas, adorned with reliefs telling the saint's story.

Next door, and much overshadowed, is the **St Janskerk**, a compact Gothic church of the mid-14th century. It used to be the bapistry of St Servaas, which accounts for the proximity of the two, but except for a short interval, has been a Protestant church since 1632. St Jans is at least free to get in, but is unremarkable in just about every other way. Probably the best thing about it is the elegant tower – in restoration when I saw it and hidden in a cocoon of scaffolding.

The **Onze Lieve Vrouwekerk** (Monday-Saturday 1100–1700, Sunday 1300–1700) stands in a small square south-east of Vrijthof, peculiar in its fortified west front, with barely more than one or two slits for windows. First built around AD 1000, it's a mixture of styles, creating a distinctive beauty and a wonderful sense of solidly rooted height, the Gothic vaulting of the nave springing upwards from the capitals of a solid Romanesque base. The galleried choir is a masterpiece of proportion, raised and under a high half-dome, with a series of capitals exquisitely decorated with scenes from the Old Testament. Though the church itself costs nothing, the **Treasury** will set you back f2 for a predictable array of reliquaries and devotional articles.

Walking south from the Vrouwekerk you come across the remaining sections of the town walls – most were razed in the 1870s to allow the city to expand. The small streets around here enjoy an unbroken peace, grouped around the rapidly running river – a surprising novelty after the sluggish canals of the Dutch water towns, and once providing the energy for several 17th-century water mills.

Just off Vrijthof is the **Bonnefanten Museum** (Monday-Friday 1000–1200/1300–1700, Saturday/Sunday 1400–1700; f2.50), an interesting general collection of painting and applied arts. Flemish Masters are predominant – Bruegel, Van Dijk and Rubens – but there's also a large set of canvases by 20th-century Limburg artists. The applied arts section has some excellent Art-Deco ceramics, alongside more recent pieces from the Sphinx and MOSA firms, the tall chimneys of which you can see just west of town.

South of the city are the **St Pietersburg caves**, which guidebooks always seem to regard with some kind of awe, but aren't in fact all that marvellous, or even natural caves at all. The quarrying of marl – a kind of sandstone that hardens on exposure to the air – has been going on since Roman times, producing a network of cold, dank underground passages and chambers that you can be led around for f3.30 (no museumcards). During the war they were intended as air-raid shelters and were fitted out accordingly, though only in fact used in the last few days before Maastricht's liberation. On the walls are recent charcoal drawings, which usually illustrate a local story and act as visual aids for the guides. Apart from those and ten varieties of bat, there's little to see. Out of the systems, the Zonneberg is probably the best, here being the most evidence of wartime occupation and what everyone claims is Napoleon's signature on a graffiti-ridden wall.

The **VVV** are near the St Servaas Brug at Vissermaas 5 (Monday-Saturday 0900–2000, Sunday 1000–1230/1400–1630). As far as a bed for the night is concerned, there's nothing super-cheap in Maastricht apart from **Camping de Dousberg** – almost in Belgium on the western edge of town (bus 7 from the railway station or Markt and about a mile's walk). If you're not prepared to rough it, try the **pensions** near the station in WIJK, an appendage to the main town. The VVV have a list but here are some selected ones: *Pension Ummels*, Hoogbrugstraat 72A (f22.50), *Hogeboom*, Twennestraat 31(f25), *Vroemen*, St Martenslaan 1 (f27.50). Saturdays in Stationstraat there's always a small **flea market**.

Eating: *Lunchshop Margo* and *De Maretak* in Brusselsestraat are both cheap, the latter a macrobiotic restaurant with a changing daily menu at f8. Similar is *La Yapa*, Th. Schaepkenstraat 11 (in Wijk) – vegetarian for around the same price. For straight Dutch food, try *Stap-in*, on the river at Kesselskade 61 – from about f7.50.

Finally, **NBBS** are at Wicker-Brugstraat 25 and there's a **De Slegte** at Grote Staat 53. Look out too for the **Pink Pop Festival** – usually held in late May, north of Maastricht, at Geleen.

EAST OF MAASTRICHT

Set in the green wooded valley of the Geul, and with its picturesque castle ruins, **VALKENBURG** seems the ideal place for those wanting to escape the clogs and canals of the north. Unfortunately, like too many other Dutch towns, it's a victim of its location, and has become one of Holland's primary holiday resorts; coachfuls of tourists unload here throughout the summer.

The **Castle** overlooks the town from a neatly placed peak at the end of the main street, the f1.50 to get in only worth it for the view it gives you over Valkenburg and the forested slopes beyond. It was blown up in 1672 on the orders of William III, after he had retrieved it from its French occupiers. Repair and restoration began in 1921 and continue still, uncovering a series of underground passages that served as escape routes in times of siege. These are part of the **Fluwelen Grot**, which can be visited for f3 (no museumcards; f4 for Castle and Grot). Like St Pietersburg in Maastricht, the caves were formed by the constant quarrying of marl, used for building in this area, and are a damp, cold way to spend an hour – not much more than a subterranean art gallery, displaying mediocre charcoal drawings of local subjects. Of slightly more interest is a clandestine chapel that was used during the late 18th-century French occupation, and the signatures and silhouettes of American soldiers who wintered here in 1944.

HEERLEN, ten minutes further by train, is an ugly modern town, fragmented and sprawling, that would have little to recommend it if it were not for the excellent **Thermen Museum** (Tuesday-Saturday 1000–1700, Saturday/Sunday 1400–1700; f1.50). The discovery of a pillar in 1940 led to excavations which unearthed the preserved and complete baths of what was the Roman settlement of Coriovallum – then an important town on the Cologne-Boulogne trade route. These are now enclosed in an ideally suited, gleaming hi-tech building, with walkways and tapes in English. Finds are displayed in an adjacent room and include glasswork from Cologne, shards of pottery, tombstones and coins, all neatly labelled. To get to the museum, follow Saroleastraat as far as Raadhuisplein and turn right.

About fifteen minutes from Heerlen lies **KERKRADE**, an unbelievably dull town that only merits inclusion in this book because of the **Abdij van Rolduc**, with its fine 12th-century church. Though now entirely post-16th century, the abbey was originally built by Ailbert, a young priest who came here in 1104. Currently being restored, its choir displays a simply ornamented symmetry, with frescoes and a marvellous mosaic floor. The clover-leaf-shaped crypt has a darkened mystery, and contains the relics of Ailbert, brought here from Germany where he died. The carvings on the pillars down here are unique, probably the work of Italian craftsmen. The modern abbey is used for a variety of things – a seminary, conference centre and the **Mine Museum**, which describes mining through the ages in this area; appropriate enough in the shadow of the giant slag-heaps nearby.

OVER THE BORDERS: LIÈGE AND AACHEN

South Limburg's position – hemmed in by two other countries – makes quick raids across the border quite feasible if you're spending any time in Maastricht or the surrounding area. **LIÈGE** is the nearest large Belgian town, half an hour's train ride from Maastricht and f10.80 for a day return. It spreads formlessly out from the banks of the meandering Meuse, a grubby and modern industrial centre and collection of anonymous suburbs that encroach on the countryside around. That said, it's to some extent a centre for French-speaking Belgium; a university city with some good museums and churches, as well as quite a sparkling nightlife.

Most things you're likely to find of interest are on the left bank of the river, and this broadly divides into two parts – the old and new towns. The **Old Town** is to the north, clinging to the hill that runs steeply down to the river. Not, as you might think, one of the nicer parts of the city, it's instead rather scruffy and run-down. A **Tourist Office** at Feronstree 92 (Monday-Friday 0800–1800, Saturday 1000–1600, Sunday 0900–1400), has a free detailed map and comprehensive info on Liège's wide selection of museums, most of which are within walking distance. Among the best are those devoted specifically to aspects of the French-speaking population. Virtually next door to the Tourist Office is the **Museum of Walloon Art** (Tuesday-Saturday 1000–1230/1400–1700, Sunday 1000–1600; F20; free at weekends), which has a collection of Walloon work from the 16th to 20th century. Up the hill is the **Museum of Walloon Life** (same times and prices, which are fairly standard). And at the far end of Feronstree, surrounded by a glut of museums, is the church of **St Barthelemy**, a Romanesque structure that has been ruined inside by 18th-century additions and is really visited for just one thing: a gold baptismal font of 1108 that the Tourist Office hopefully describe as 'one of the seven wonders of Belgium'.

Place St Lambert is where the old and new towns meet. The **New Town** is very nearly devoid of anything of specific interest, the only exception being the **Cathedral of St Paul**, a splendid Gothic church that was promoted to cathedral status in 1803, after the previous one had been destroyed by the French a few years before.

Finally, if you're staying for any time, the area around Rue Routure, across the river and in the old working-class district of **Outremeuse**, is good for **restaurants** and has a lively atmosphere. The Tourist Office have lists of **rooms**.

In Germany, **AACHEN** is as close as Liège, but a little more expensive to reach at f17 for a day return. Despite that, if you're going to one or the other, this is the one to choose. When the ageing Charlemagne was looking for somewhere to retire to in 794, he plumped for Aachen – partly for strategic reasons and partly for its warm springs – and from here he ruled his empire and reflected on the spoils and successes of his life. He had an appropriately grand palace built, a gargantuan complex of which little is left – only the towers at each end of the town hall, and the octagonal chapel, now incorporated into the cathedral.

Badly bombed in the last war, much of the city has been rebuilt, and only the immediate centre is of real historic interest. The **Markt** is the focal point – a small square with a bronze statue of Charlemagne in the middle, around which often curl the sleeping forms of hippies and foot-loose travellers. On one corner is the **Tourist Office** (Monday-Friday 0730–1700, Saturday 1000–1200), who have free maps and lists of **rooms** and hotels, if you want to stay. Cheapest places – at around DM20 or less – are to be found in the spa suburb of Burtscheid, behind the railway station to the south; try *Erckenstrasse* or *Malmedyerstrasse*. There's also a **Youth Hostel** at Maria Theresa Allee 260 (buses 12/22 from Elisen-brunnen). **Food** tends to be cheaper than in Holland, and Pontstrasse, which runs north-west from the Markt, is the **student quarter** and the best place for budget eating.

The Gothic **Rathaus** or town hall (Monday-Friday 0800–1300/1400–1700, Saturday 1000–1300), fronts onto the Markt, its façade lined with the figures of fifty Holy Roman Emperors – thirty-one of them crowned in this city. Above the entrance, Charlemagne shares a niche with Christ and Pope Leo III, who dedicated the Palatinate chapel in 804. Built in the first half of the 14th century on the foundations of part of the palace, the town hall is these days a mix of attempts to restore its original Gothic form and the inevitable Baroque changes of later years. The glory of the building is the much-restored *Empire Hall*. In the corner stands a bronze Charlemagne which used to be in the square downstairs but was replaced with a copy in 1969 after it had been consistently maltreated. Five large frescoes give a romantic portrayal of episodes from Charlemagne's life, but your attention is more likely to be drawn by the Imperial crown jewels, shiningly displayed at one end – though again replicas; the originals are in Vienna.

Behind the Rathaus is **Katsch Hof**, across which the palace once extended, but now lined with ugly modern buildings. The **Cathedral** is at the far end, a complex and exuberant blend of spires, pinnacles and a central segmented dome. Inside it's a perfect compound of Carolingian, Gothic and 20th-century church architecture: even after the tales of Charlemagne's palace chapel in Aachen, you can't help being over-whelmed by its extraordinary symmetry, height and grandeur. Modelled on the Byzantine church of San Vitale at Ravenna, it has an 8-sided domed centre, surrounded by a 16–sided ambulatory, above which is a 2-storey gallery with 8 arcades of columns. The number eight is significant, representing perfection and harmony. The circumference of the octagon is 144 Carolingian feet – the cardinal number of the heavenly Jerusalem – and that of the outer polygon exactly twice that: an impeccable concord and order that is symbolic of heaven.

High and narrow, the Gothic choir seems almost entirely glass; completed as recently as thirty years ago, it reaches up nine long fingers to almost the full height. The shrine that contains the mortal remains of Charlemagne normally stands here, but was away for restoration when I was there, and his relics left enigmatically and anonymously in a plain sealed box.

Through the St Nicholas chapel is the **treasury** (Monday-Saturday 0900–1300/1400–1700, Sunday 1030–1300/1400–1700; DM3 and worth every pfennig). The collection includes the *Prosperpine Sarcophagus* of Charlemagne, in which the emperor reposed until 1165. The *Mariaschrein* dates from 1238 and contains the 'Four Relics of Aachen' – the gown of the Virgin, the swaddling clothes and loin cloth of Christ and the garb of John the Baptist; all brought here by Charlemagne and the subject of great medieval pilgrimages.

Walking roughly east from here are the **Elisenbrunnen** thermal drinking fountains, a small rotunda pervaded by the lingering smell of sulphur. And, whatever else you do, leave time for the nearby **Suermondt-Ludwig Museum** (Wilheminastrasse 18; Tuesday-Friday 1000–1700, Saturday/Sunday 1000–1300), an extraordinary collection of medieval sculpture. Its colossal range of pietàs, passions and Madonnas together convey a powerful impression of man's attempts to understand God through art and convention. An added bonus is a good group of 17th-century Dutch painters – Dou, Brouwer, Cuyp among them – and several rooms of 20th-century works.

TRAVEL DETAILS

Trains
Vlissingen–Amsterdam (1 an hour; 2 hours 40 mins), Vlissingen–Middelburg (2 an hour; 6 mins), Vlissingen–Roosendaal (2 an hour; 55 mins), Roosendaal–Antwerp (1 an hour; 1 hour 25 mins), Roosendaal–Breda (2 an hour; 18 mins), Breda–Eindhoven (2 an hour; 35 mins), Den Bosch–Eindhoven (2 an hour; 25 mins), Den Bosch–Nijmegen (4 an hour; 35 mins), Den Bosch–Amsterdam (2 an hour; 1 hour 5 mins), Eindhoven–Roermond (2 an hour; 30 mins), Eindhoven–Venlo (2 an hour; 35 mins), Venlo–Venray–Nijmegen (2 an hour; 18 mins, 55 mins), Sittard–Maastricht (2 an hour; 20 mins), Maastricht–Amsterdam (1 an hour; 2 hours 30 mins), Maastricht–Liège (1 an hour; 35 mins), Maastricht–Aachen (7 a day; 40 mins), Maastricht–Luxembourg (2 a day; 3 hours 30 mins), Maastricht–Valkenburg–Heerlen (2 an hour; 15 mins, 35 mins), Heerlen–Kerkrade (2 an hour; 15 mins).

Buses
Middelburg–Veere (ZWN Bus 52; 10 mins), Goes–Zierikzee (ZWN Bus 10; 25 mins), Rotterdam Zuidplein Metro–Zierikzee (ZWN Bus 133/136; 1 hour 25 mins), Venray–Overloon (ZO Bus 27/28; 25 mins; restricted service), Roermond–Thorn (VSL Bus 73; 40 mins).

Chapter seven

BELGIUM AND LUXEMBOURG

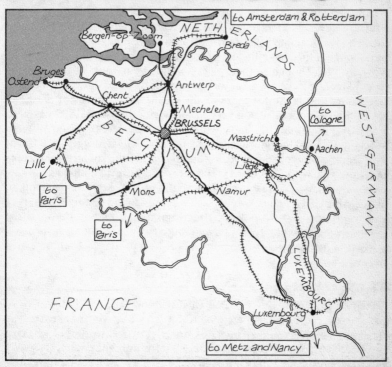

The modern country of **BELGIUM** only dates from 1830, when a revolution split the Northern and Southern Netherlands for good, after centuries of bitter dispute and disarray. Afterwards, French became the official language of the government and all the major institutions of the country and Flemish (Dutch) was consigned to the status of peasant tongue, despite the fact that a majority of the population were Flemings. Now the differences that were supposed to have been hammered out and resolved in 1830 have become polarised in today's Belgium, in a wrangle between the French-speakers of the south (*Walloons*) and the disaffected *Flemings* of the north. Though Belgium is officially bilingual, French is still the ruling tongue, and the Flemings feel they have been consistently passed over when it comes to the top positions of power in the country;

this in spite of the fact that they occupy some of the leading industrial centres and wealthiest cities. There's widespread feeling that while the Flemings do the work, the Walloons reap the benefits, and they are now demanding two separate governments under the umbrella of a national administration. Such is the deep divide here at the moment, they believe their demands will soon have to be met.

Brussels, capital more by virtue of its central position than for any real historic reason, is the symbol and centre of these clashes. It's really a Flemish city – situated just north of the invisible linguistic boundary – and though officially bilingual these days, French is the language of everyday life. Though a good place to start your tour, apart from the Grand Place, it lacks the great monuments of its more illustrious Flemish neighbours and is known more as the businesslike nucleus of the EEC, NATO and European diplomacy; a patchy city that since 1830 has been the victim of enthusiastic but often short-sighted development. **Antwerp** is Belgium's brighter and livelier second city, whilst **Bruges** and **Ghent** represent the superbly preserved medieval heart of the country – museums in themselves, with a glut of art treasures and historic buildings.

If it's scenery you're after, head south to the Ardennes and on to **LUXEMBOURG**, which, while it isn't exactly inundated by sights, is at least very beautiful to look at. Americans flying to Europe on cheap Icelandair tickets will arrive at Luxembourg city which, though expensive, is worth a day or two of your time before you disappear to more exotic climes.

Some practical points

Belgium's **train** network is comprehensive and efficient and while not particularly cheap, is far preferable to bus services, which are extremely localised. To give you some idea of prices: Brussels to Bruges will cost you F235, Brussels to Antwerp F130. Returns are, quite simply, double, and day returns don't exist; though there is such a thing as a *Beau Jour* ticket, which gives a 50 per cent reduction to some places and is available during the summer, Christmas, Easter, etc. If you intend to spend some time here, you can save by buying a *Tourrail* ticket, which gives unlimited travel throughout the country. There are three types: a sixteen-day ticket which is available all the year round and costs F2140 or tickets that are valid for any five or eight days within a period of sixteen – they cost F1690 and F1280 respectively and are on sale during the spring and summer months or at Christmas. Finally there's a *50 per cent reduction card,* which is valid for a month on all Belgian railways and entitles you, for F430, to an unlimited number of tickets at half-price. If you're travelling down to Luxembourg or up to Holland, the *Benelux Tourrail* pass is the best idea as it gives you rail freedom in all three Benelux countries (for details see p. 8). All of the above are available from any Belgian railway station or in advance from the YHA shop, 14 Southampton Street, London WC2.

Bikes are a good way to get around – distances are short and apart from the Ardennes the countryside is fairly flat. You can hire them for F125 a day (F95 if you're a rail passenger) from selected railway stations, and they have the built-in advantage that you can drop them at any station you like at the end of the day. If you're really hard up, **hitching** tends to be good, but don't forget it's illegal on motorways. For the more solvent, the going rate for **car-hire** is from around F750 a day, plus a charge per kilometre. Most of the big car rental firms can be found in the larger cities.

Accommodation is more of a problem: Belgian hotels tend to be expensive, with prices ranging from F350 for a single room and F550 for a double. If money is tight then hostels are a better bet, at around F200 for a dormitory bed. Most of the more touristy towns have a couple of these plus an official Youth Hostel, and campsites are usually cheap at about F30 pp.

Eating can also be a costly business, and it's best to stick to snacks, omelettes or the *Plat du Jour* – a standard meat and two veg combo that you get for about F150. In university cities you can normally use the student restaurant, which is heavily subsidised and by far the cheapest option.

Banks stay open Monday-Friday 0900–1530 and will change money in return for a large commission. If it's late, or a weekend, railway stations often have exchange offices that keep longer hours. Belgian currency is francs (F) and the current rate of exchange is around F80 to the pound.

BELGIUM

BRUSSELS

Present-day **Brussels** is a largely unsatisfactory patchwork of old and new, the result of ruthless and unthinking planning. Despite that, it has its attractions, and there's plenty to keep you occupied for at least a couple of days. It divides into **Upper and Lower Towns,** the former a thin strip of land to the south and east – infinitely grander, and spaciously planned along French lines with wide avenues and long clear vistas; traditionally the home of the government and bureaucracy of the country. The Lower Town is more mixed, varying from the poor working-class quarters to the south to the gabled Flemish opulence of the Grand Place.

Living

There are three railway stations in Brussels: Nord, Centrale and Midi. International trains tend to only stop at Nord and Midi, while domestic ones stop at all of them. The best place to get off is Gare Centrale, right in the city centre and just five minutes from the Grand Place. Getting around isn't difficult and Brussels has an exhaustive **public transport** system of buses, trams and metro. The flat fare is F30 on all these services but if you're here for any length of time, a ten-ride ticket is better value at F170. Alternatives are a 24-hour ticket for F110 or a special tourist pass for F100. All of these are available from the tourist office or metro stations. The **Tourist Office,** at rue de Marché aux Herbes 61 (daily 0900–2000), does a good city guide for F30 and will book you a room for a F75 fee. Far better, though, to go to **ACOTRA,** the student travel office just around the corner at rue de la Montagne 38, where they not only book rooms for nothing but also hand out free detailed maps.

Most of the **campsites** are a fair way out: the nearest one is **Wezembeek-Oppem,** about eight miles east of the city – buses NL/NS from the north station. Apart from that, the best place to stay is undoubtedly the **Sleep-Well,** rue de la Blanchisserie 27 (from F180 incl. breakfast). **CHAB** is slightly cheaper at F140, but further out – tram 62 from the north station. The **Youth Hostel** is at rue de St Esprit 2, next door to Notre Dame de la Chapelle. If none of these appeal to you, there are usually beds at the **university** from July to September – from F290 (metro Petillon).

Other than that, most cheap **hotels** are centred on the streets around the Gare du Midi, though this is a rough area you may want to avoid. If you do, *Hotel Berckmans,* rue Berckmans 12 (singles F385, doubles from F550, metro Place Louise) or *Pacific,* rue Ant. Dansaert (singles F360, doubles from F520) are both in far more salubrious parts of the city.

Likewise, the Gare du Midi is the best area for cheap **eating,** including one street – rue de l'Argonne – literally packed full of Greek restaurants, all offering a daily menu. If you don't like Greek food or this part of town, then try *Taverne Take 5,* rue d'Arenburg (around F100, spaghetti, omelettes, etc.), *Athena 3,* rue des Hirondelles (plats du jour from F100) or the *student restaurant* at rue Evers 2, off Boulevard Waterloo, where they do a menu for F80 (Monday-Friday 0900–1645). *Le Sans Nom,* rue des Eperonniers, isn't exactly cheap, but the food is good and they have a menu at F210.

The **rue des Bouchers** is where you'll find most action in the evening. The tiny streets here are normally thick with people late into the night, and there are loads of bars, restaurants, etc. *Brasserie Vossen,* just beyond here in rue Montagne aux Herbes-Potagères, is a good place to drink, popular with locals rather than tourists.

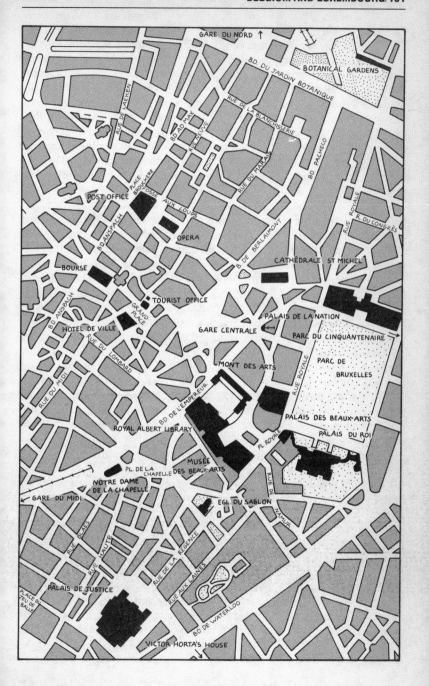

GARE DU NORD ↑

BOTANICAL GARDENS

BD. DU TARDIN BOTANIQUE

RUE DE LA BLANCHISSERIE

BD PACHECO

BD AD MAX

RUE DE LAEKEN

RUE NEUVE

RUE DU MARAIS

PLACE
BROUCKERE
DE BROUCKERE

POST OFFICE

BD ANSPACH

AUX LOUPS

RUE ROYALE

R DU CONGRÈS

OPERA

BD DE BERLAIMONT

CATHÉDRALE ST MICHEL

BOURSE

B. DE BERLAIMONT

BD ANSPACH

TOURIST OFFICE

GRAND PLACE

HOTEL DE VILLE

GARE CENTRALE

PALAIS DE LA NATION

PARC DU CINQUANTENAIRE

RUE DU LOMBARD

MONT DES ARTS

PARC DE BRUXELLES

RUE DU MIDI

BD DE L'EMPEREUR

RUE ROYALE

ROYAL ALBERT LIBRARY

PALAIS DES BEAUX-ARTS

PALAIS DU ROI

PL. ROYALE

MUSÉE
DES BEAUX-ARTS

PL. DE LA
CHAPELLE

NOTRE DAME
DE LA CHAPELLE

RUE DE NAMUR

GARE DU MIDI

EGL. DU SABLON

RUE BLAES

RUE HAUTE

RUE DE LA REGENCE

RUE AUX LAINES

PALAIS DE JUSTICE

PLACE DU
JEU DE
BALLE

BD DE WATERLOO

VICTOR HORTA'S HOUSE

The lower town

The **Grand Place** is where everybody heads first, and without it Brussels would be a good deal quieter – and poorer. Probably the best preserved square in Europe, it's a rectangular retreat from the modern city, exhibiting a civic pride that is at first a little unreal. Counts Egmont and Hoorn, who couldn't bring themselves to be disloyal to Philip II, were beheaded here in 1568, while the Duke of Alva looked on from the **Maison du Roi** – on the north side of the square and now a 19th-century rebuilding of a number of Gothic predecessors. It normally houses the **Musée Communal** (Monday-Friday 1000–1200/1300–1700, Saturday/Sunday 1000–1200; F20, free on Sunday), the local historical museum, but was closed for renovation when I was there, though I suspect it may be open by now. The **Hôtel de Ville** faces it from the other side, a notable Gothic survivor that stands out against the Italianate splendour surrounding it; soaring skywards rather than weighted down by cumbersome ornamented gables and pediments. The front part is the oldest, built over an eighty-year period and finished in the late 15th century. The spire, light, like connecting loose skeins, dates from 1454, and is topped with the archangel Michael, patron saint of the city. Inside, it's a succession of pristine 18th- and 19th-century restorations, and though you can wander around freely in July and August, the rest of the time you're confined to guided tours (Monday 0900–1300, Tuesday-Friday 0900–1700, Sunday 1000–1300/1400–1600; F20).

Heavily bombarded by the French in 1695, almost all of the rest of the square was constructed immediately after that date. The **Guild Houses** went up at the turn of the century – Baroque visions of the multifarious Brussels guilds, and samples of their wealth and power. The most magnificent ones are either side of the town hall, and it was under their flamboyant gables that Verlaine shot his protégé Rimbaud one night in 1873, after a particularly violent and very drunken quarrel.

Walking south, you come eventually to the church of **Notre Dame de la Chapelle,** a small and unpretentious Gothic church, built between 1210 and 1300. Its major claim to fame is that it contains the tomb of Pieter Bruegel the Elder in one of the chapels of the south aisle. He is reputed to have lived and died nearby at rue Haute 132, and his house is now a small museum. When I was there it was undergoing some fairly extensive repairs, but it should be finished by now and will be open – Tuesday, Thursday, Saturday 1400–1800, in the summer months.

Rue Haute and rue Blaes make up the central axis of the Quartier Marolles, traditionally the poor working-class and immigrant district of Brussels. Things are cheaper here (bars, restaurants, etc.) and even if you're travelling on a really tight budget you should be able to afford something at the **Place de Jeu de Balle Flea Market** which, unlike its trendier equivalents in Paris or London, is the genuine article: it looks as if people have just emptied their homes of all unwanted junk and piled it up in the square to sell. You'll find mountains of clothes, furniture, shoes, books and anything else you're willing to rummage for (summer – open every day; winter – Saturday/Sunday only).

The upper town

The **Cathedral** (Monday-Saturday 0730–1900, Sunday 1400–1900) occupies the edge of the steep slope down to the lower town, commanding the buildings below with its towering west front. It was begun in 1220 and is dedicated jointly to St Michel and St Gudule, patron and patroness of Brussels. Severely damaged during the Reformation and the French shelling a century later, it was Napoleon who took the first steps to restoring it. A major restoration is in progress, due to finish in 1985. The choir is the earliest example of Gothic in the Netherlands, flanked by two large chapels and with some fine stained glass from a mixture of periods; best of all is a 16th-century panegyric to the Hapsburgs, showing Maximilian, Charles V and Philip II and their consorts. Otherwise it's a fairly simple Gothic structure: churches have never been top priority in Brussels, it seems, and there aren't really any of note. This one was only made a cathedral in 1961, more for its size and position than anything else.

The rue Royale and rue de la Régence form the regal backbone of the upper town, on which the Place Royale is a statuesque and dignified midpoint. From here the ground drops away to the **Mont des Arts** – a still-developing agglomeration of buildings devoted to the arts in all their various forms. Back at the top of the hill, the Palais de la Nation, home of the Belgian parliament, faces the long-fronted **Palais du Roi** across the shady elegance of the Parc de Bruxelles. No longer the home of the royal family – their city residence is just outside Brussels, in Laeken – you can visit the Palais du Roi during the summer; and the **Hôtel Belle-Vue** next door is open all the year round, with sundry collections relating to the Belgian royals.

The **Musée Royal des Beaux Arts** (Tuesday-Sunday 1000–1700, galleries close for lunch) is just off the Place Royale, in a heavy neo-Classical edifice by Balat. It's divided into three routes, of which the *Blue Route* is the most rewarding – devoted to 15th- and 16th-century Flemish painters. Highlights include some good portraits by van der Weyden, the detailed elongated figures of Bouts, and work by van der Goes and Memling. In one room Cranach demonstrates amply his skill in painting the human body, and in another Aertsen and Beuckelaer hit you with some superabundant kitchen scenes. Bosch is a little sparse, the most complete collection of his work being in Madrid's Prado, and Bruegel suffers the same fate – you have to go to Vienna to see his best work. The *Fall of the Rebel Angels* is here though, and shows just how much

Bruegel owed to Bosch, to whom the painting was attributed until the discovery of Bruegel's signature beneath the frame.

The Red Route is just two rooms of 17th- and 18th-century works, mainly from the studio of Rubens; which means canvases by Jordaens, Van Dijk and Rubens himself. Jordaens's paintings stand out: vigorous and erotic, more a celebration of the sensual than anything else.

A separate modern museum is currently under construction behind the main building, and until that opens 19th- and 20th-century works are kept under the *Yellow Route*. This is mainly modern Belgian painters – the impressionistic Ensor, the Expressionist Permeke and the sculptor Meunier, though most of his work is in a museum solely devoted to him, in his house in Ixelles (a suburb of Brussels: Meunier's house is reachable by bus 38 from the Gare du Nord, or trams 23, 32, 90, 93, 94. The museum is open Monday, Wednesday, Friday, Saturday 0900–1200/1400–1700). Magritte and Delvaux provide a Surrealist conclusion.

The rue de la Régence offers a terminating prospect of the colossal **Palais de Justice,** a great Graeco-Roman wedding cake that cowers the poor Marolles quarter below; a gigantic reminder no doubt, of the power of Belgian justice. Built by Poelart in 1883 to commemorate 50 years of independence, it's a mammoth building, larger than St Peter's in Rome and more impressive for its size than beauty.

Other museums

Brussels is endowed with masses of museums and for me the **Horta Museum** is one of the best (Tuesday-Sunday 1400–1700; F25). On the southern edge of town at rue Américaine 25, it's a fair step from the centre (take bus 54 or tram 93) but worth it for one of the finest fin-de-siècle interiors you'll see anywhere. Victor Horta was the Belgian architect who spearheaded Art Nouveau in the Low Countries, and this is his house – a paradise for fans of the ironwork, stained glass and furniture of the period; total design right down to the doorknobs. Nearby, at rue Paul Emile Janson 6, is the **Tassel House,** generally acknowledged as the first Art Nouveau house – built by Horta in 1893 and utterly original in its use of exposed ironwork and the unity of its plan and decoration. Important buildings followed, right up to the turn of the century but, sadly, few of these remain and most of Horta's work in Brussels belongs to his later, almost reactionary, phase, when the graceful curves and iron are gone, replaced by the conservatism of old age. Two years before his death, Horta destroyed all his early drawings, rejecting totally the achievements of his early years.

The **Palais des Beaux Arts,** in rue Ravenstein, is an example of his later work: a drab grey structure that houses a theatre, concert-hall, numerous exhibitions and the excellent **Musée du Cinema** which, as well as displays on the history of film, shows old movies between 1730 and 2230 every evening. A mere F30 entitles you to two hours' viewing.

West of town in the Parc du Cinquanténaire, the **Royal Art and History Museum** (Tuesday-Friday 0930–1230/1330–1700, Saturday/Sunday 1000–1700) is more orthodox, with a mediocre collection of Egyptian, Greek and Roman antiquities, together with ecclesiastical articles from nearer home. The **Royal Army Museum** is virtually next door, and traces Belgian military history from 1789 to the present day with an uninspired lot of uniforms and weapons in a series of overcrowded rooms.

The **Atomium,** north of town at the national exhibition centre, is a remnant of the Expo' 58 world fair. It's a 120m high aluminium representation of an iron atom with escalators linking the spheres that are the nine electrons, the bottom three of which are used for a permanent exhibition on the peaceful use of nuclear energy. At F80 a go I'd say save your money, but it's really a question of taste. Bus 89 or trams 18, 81 or 103.

Finally, the **Royal Albert Library** on the Mont des Arts has a number of small permanent exhibitions which may be of interest if you've half an hour to spare. They're on amazingly diverse subjects from books to coins to musical manuscripts to engravings, to name but a few. Most are open weekdays 0900–1700.

Facts and things

Books   English books are available from *Smith's,* at Boulevard Adolphe Max 71.

Car Hire   *ABC* (rue Anderlecht 133); *Avis* (rue Américaine 145), *Europcar* (rue de l'Abbaye 20), *Hertz* (boulevard M. Lemonnier 8), *Inter Rent* (Pachecolaan 9).

Change   If you're stuck, there are offices at the Gare du Midi and Gare du Nord that will change money – 0700–2300 daily.

Embassies   American (boulevard dé Régent 27), Australian (Avenue des Arts 52), British (rue Joseph II 28), Canadian (rue de Loxum 6), Irish (rue du Luxembourg 19).

Gay   What gay scene there is in Brussels tends to be confined to the centre of town. *La Cage* (rue des Bouchers 71) is one of the most popular bars, and *Le Duquesnoy,* the other side of the Grand Place at rue Duquesnoy 12, is another. *Why Not* is a gay disco, rue des Riches Claires 7. For information and advice on gay life in Brussels and the whole of Belgium, contact *ADEHO,* rue de la Sablonnière 17.

Hitching   If you're going north, take tram 52 from Place Rogier to the end of the line and pick up the E10. For Ostend and the ferry, you should get bus 85 from the Rue des Halles, near the Bourse. For the E40 and Namur and Luxembourg: metro stop Demey. For the E10 going south to France: bus 50 to the terminus.

Infor-Jeunes, Rue de Marché aux Herbes 27 (Monday-Friday 1200–1800)   Information and advice for young people on health, jobs, courses and accommodation. The notice-board is useful for contacts.

Markets   The best is the *Place de Jeu de Balle Flea Market,* every day in summer and weekends in winter. There's a flower market every day in the Grand Place, and a bird market there on Sunday mornings. The Place du Grand Sablon is very much the elegant part of town and the centre of Brussels's antique and fine art trade – weekend art and antique market.

Parks   The Parc de Bruxelles is the most central, and it was here that the first skirmishes took place between Belgian patriots and Dutch troops in 1830. It offered a fairly rugged landscape then, until Zinner laid it out in symmetrical French style in 1835. The Parc du Cinquanténaire is further east – metro Mérode. It is exactly what it claims to be – created in 1880 to celebrate fifty years of Belgian independence. The Forest of Soignes offers a more natural beauty – a vast beech forest south east of town, and reachable by bus 95 from Place St Jean.

Post Office   The main post office is in the *Centre Monnaie* building, open 0900–1700. There's a 24–hour one at the Gare du Midi.

Shopping   Rue Neuve is the principal shopping street, leading north up to Place Rogier and Brussels's unbelievably seedy red light district. Place and avenue Louise are the places for chintzy and expensive boutiques, and boulevard Waterloo has a varied array of different stores.

SOS-jeunes   Rue de la Blanchisserie 27, offers friendly 24–hour help for most kinds of crises.

Student Travel   *ACOTRA* have offices at rue de la Montagne 38 and at the airport. *TEJ* are at rue Traversière 8 (Monday-Saturday 0900–1900).

Telephone   Telephone boxes take 5-franc coins; ones which display a series of international hats are, believe it or not, for international calls. You can also call home from boulevard de l'Impératrice 17, next to the Sabena building – daily 0800–2200.

Women   There's a women's restaurant – *Vendredi 13* – at Impasse de la Fidélité 6 and next door a small and friendly bar, *The Black Swan. Virago,* in rue des Villers, is a women's centre that comes highly recommended and, if you want something a bit more lively, *Madam,* Galerie du Roi 25, is a flash disco bar.

ANTWERP

Antwerp fans out carelessly from the east bank of the Scheldt, its centre a rough polygon of the enclosing boulevards and river. Most people prefer it to Brussels: it's smaller, uncomplicated and more of a homogeneous whole, with a denser concentration of churches of interest and a varied selection of distinguished museums – redolent of an auspicious

BELGIUM AND LUXEMBOURG/157

past. The differences are like those of The Hague and Amsterdam: one the duller location of business and political affairs while the other is a lively cultural centre, more colourful, with a spirited nightlife.

In the **Grote Markt** stands the **Brabo** fountain – a haphazard pile of rocks surmounted by a bronze Brabo flinging the hand of the giant Antigonus into the sea. Legend says that this giant extracted tolls from all the Scheldt shipping, cutting off the arms of those who refused to pay. He was eventually beaten by the valiant Brabo, who tore off his hand and threw it into the sea, giving rise to the name of the city, which means literally 'hand-throw'. There are more realistic theories to explain the city's name, and the legend is a heroic adaptation of the facts. There is an old Antwerp saying that 'Antwerp has to thank God for the Scheldt and the Scheldt for all the rest', and there's no doubt that the freeing of this supremely important waterway, by buying the rights of the landowners who exacted tolls on its traffic, expanded the volume of trade considerably, and Antwerp prospered well into the 16th century.

The **Guild Houses** lean inwards like grandiose spectres, mostly 16th-century and the afterglow of the city's Renaissance lustre. They are overshadowed though, by the **Stadhuis,** completed in 1566 to a design by Cornelis Floris and a formative architectural work (Monday 0900–1200, Tuesday/Saturday 1200–1500, other days 0900–1500; F5 and F10 for the guide). The pagoda-like roof gives it a faintly oriental appearance, but apart from the central gable it's really quite plain, with a long pilastered façade of Doric and Ionic columns. These are short and rather shallow, and with the windows, lend a simple elegance, in contrast to the purely decorative gable (there is no roof behind it), which was added as an up-to-date alternative to a tower, which would have been considered old-fashioned at the time. The niches at the top add to the self-congratulatory aspect of the building: beneath the Virgin Mary are Justice and Wisdom which, if they symbolise anything at all, it's the Antwerp burghers patting each other on the back in typical Renaissance fashion. Entry to the town hall is by a side door on the right, and you first come to the staircase of the high main hall. This central area used to be an open courtyard and was only covered in the late 19th century, which accounts for the monumental gallery on all four sides. Paintings take the place of windows, and represent aspects of commerce and the arts – a balance which Antwerp is conscious of and anxious to preserve in everything. Among the other rooms you can see are the Leys Room, named after the painter who decorated it with the present frescoes in the 1860s, and the Wedding Room, which has a chimney-piece from the original town hall, decorated with two caryatids by Floris himself, who was also a master sculptor.

Nearby, the river has been clearly separated from the town since Napoleon razed the muddle of houses here and constructed proper quaysides.

Your view of the fast-moving Scheldt is always obscured by the sheds which stretch the length of Antwerp, and you can't help thinking it would have been better left as it was. The **Steen fortress** juts out commandingly from all this, claiming its right as the building from which the rest of the town spread. The first fortification is known to have been here as early as the 9th century, though the oldest parts of the present one date back to the 14th. Restored by Charles V and later serving as a prison, the castle became the symbol of people's worst fears under the bloody rule of Alva. Since 1952 it has had a more innocuous role as home of the **National Maritime Museum** (daily 1000–1700) which, in a series of cramped rooms, has some magnificent models of ships and other nautical items.

A few steps away is the **Vleeshuis** (Tuesday-Sunday 1000–1700), the old butchers' hall and a large gabled building that has been likened to streaky bacon, with its alternating layers of brick and stone-work. These days it's a museum with a strong though mixed collection of applied arts, in particular a good set of 17th- to 19th-century musical instruments.

This part of Antwerp was destroyed by war-time bombing and was open-space until a few years ago. Recently restored in a fake vernacular style, it's in pristine pink contrast to the dilapidated **red-light** area beyond, which begins as you approach Antwerp's tough dockland and is a sequence of grubby, grotty little streets with sporadic tattoo parlours and a lot of bored and cynical faces at windows. If Amsterdam's red lights are spectacular, Antwerp's are just sad. **Falconplein** is the solid working-class district where a Slavonic minority have set up their textile shops. East down Klapdorp and Paardenmarkt cheap bars and restaurants abound, on what is the edge of the student quarter and an unusually self-contained little community.

On St Paulusstraat an arch leads through to the precincts of the **St Pauluskerk** (May-September, Tuesday-Saturday 0900–1200/1400–1700, October-April, Tuesday-Saturday 0900–1200), a fine and dignified very late Gothic church of 1571. If you see only a couple of Antwerp's churches, this should be one of them for its exceptional wood carving and host of art treasures. The confessionals and intricately carved choir stalls with their snake-like, almost arabesque pillars were done by P. Verbrugghen the elder in the mid-17th century. Rubens's *Dispute on the Holy Sacrament,* an early work of 1609, hangs in an altar by the same man. A long series of paintings lines the north aisle, and includes works by Rubens, Van Dijk and Jordaens, though they're not at their best in the gloomy church light. Outside is the **Calvaryberg,** an artificial grotto of 1697–1747 that clings to the buttresses of the south transept, eerily adorned with statues of Christ and other figures, and supposed to symbolise His suffering on the cross. Writing in the 19th century, Charles Tennant described it as 'exhibiting a more striking instance of religious fanaticism than good taste', and he wasn't far wrong.

The **Onze Lieve Vrouwe Cathedral** (Monday-Friday 1200–1700, Saturday 1200–1500, Sunday 1300–1600; F20) stands at the very centre of town, marked from everywhere by its spire feeling its way elegantly heavenwards. Long a source of fascination to travellers, William Beckford (18th century) 'longed to ascend it that instant, to stretch myself out upon its summit and calculate, from so sublime an elevation, the influence of the planets'. When the tower was finished in 1518, Antwerp's cathedral was the largest church in the Netherlands – appropriate enough for what was then the rich trading capital of the country. Restoration work has been in progress since 1969, repairing the roof and the nave. Work on the choir has only just started and it's unlikely to be finished for another fifteen years at least, so it will be quite some time before you can see the place in its entirety. The triple-aisled nave in itself is breathtaking, if only because of the sense of space which is quite unlike any other church; a feeling that is enhanced by the way the restoration has left the cathedral clean, open, bare and a little antiseptic. A fire of 1533, the Calvinist Fury of 1566 and the fact that the church became Protestant later that century have ensured that no Gothic decoration remains, and you visit it now more for the subsequent Baroque embellishments, notably three early paintings by Rubens which for the moment hang in the nave. The *Descent from the Cross* is without doubt the most beautiful of these works, painted soon after Rubens's return from Italy and distinctive in its restrained and moving realism, derived from Caravaggio. Christ languishes in the centre in glowing white, helpless and surrounded by mourners or figures who are tenderly struggling to lower him. As was normal, with commissions pouring in from everywhere, students in Rubens's studio worked on the painting, among them the young Van Dijk, who repaired the face of the Virgin and the arm of Mary Magdalen. His work was so masterful that the great man is supposed to have declared it an improvement on his own. In the central aisle of the nave hangs the *Assumption,* definitely a more Baroque painting and one of several Rubens did on the subject.

Rubens – and Antwerp's museums

Rubens has left an indelible mark on this city, a stamp much more worthy of him than his statue on Groenplaats suggests – it now fulfils the unhappy function of toilet for Antwerp's pigeons. Arguably the greatest northern Baroque painter, and certainly Antwerp's most celebrated, his **house,** at Wapper 9 (daily 1000–1700), was only acquired by the town in 1937, by which time it was little more than a shell. Skilfully restored, it opened as a museum in 1946. It's not so much a house as a mansion, splitting into two parts: on the left the more traditional, gabled Flemish house

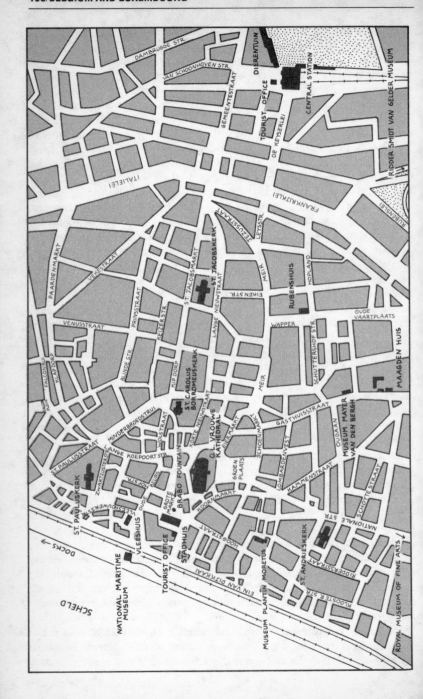

and on the right the classical Italian studio where Rubens worked, taught, showed his finished canvases and entertained the artistic and cultural elite of Europe. He had an enviably successful career, spending the first eight years of the 17th century studying the Renaissance masters in Italy, and settling here in 1608. Soon after, he painted the Antwerp Cathedral series and his fame spread, both as a painter and diplomat, working for Charles I in England, and receiving commissions from all over Europe. Unfortunately, there are only one or two of his more undistinguished paintings here, and nothing like the works of other artists he collected avidly throughout his life – most of which have been dispersed in other galleries. The restoration of the rooms is convincing though, and the garden is laid out in its former 17th-century order, just how it appears in the *Walk in the Garden,* now in Munich. The Baroque portico is also somehow familiar, principally from Rubens's Medici series, now in the Louvre.

He died in 1640 and was buried in the **St Jacobskerk** (Monday-Saturday 1000–1200/1400–1700), very much the church of the Antwerp nobles, and a Gothic building that was begun in 1491 but not finished until 1659: a date that means much of its Gothic splendour was hidden by an over-decorous Baroque interior. Its soaring heights are broken and flattened by the heavy black altars. Payment of F20 will admit you to the choir, or at least the chapelled ambulatory, where the apsidal **Rubens Chapel** remembers the painter. The large altar was the gift of Hélène Fourment, Rubens's second wife, and shows one of his last works: *Our Lady surrounded by Saints*, in which he painted himself as St George, his wives as Martha and Mary, and his father as St Jerome, as if he knew this was to be his epitaph. Indeed, he had asked that if he were to have a burial chapel, he would like it adorned with nothing more than a painting of the Virgin Mary with Jesus in her arms, encircled by various saints.

Rombout's *Mystical Marriage of St Catherine* is to the left of the chapel, and Jordaens's vigorous *Christ by the Sea of Tiberias* hangs in the first chapel on the right.

The **Royal Museum of Fine Arts** (Tuesday-Sunday 1000–1700) occupies an immense neo-Classical edifice at the southern end of the town. It's normally free but if there's an exhibition you may have to pay – it depends on the exhibition. Otherwise, downstairs has relatively modern works, and upstairs a well-displayed collection of paintings from Flemish Primitives to 17th-century masters. Everything is a little mixed up, making it difficult to plan a chronological route, but a lighting-up plan in the first room gives you some idea where each painter is, if you want to see something special.

The early Flemish section isn't as complete as it could be – so much has been scattered in galleries throughout the world – but all the major painters are well represented; van Eyck, van der Weyden and Memling especially so. Quintin Massys's *Lamentation* triptych is the most memorable thing here, a profound and moving work, commissioned for Antwerp Cathedral in 1508 and regarded by many as his most successful painting.

Rubens has two large rooms to himself, such a concentration of his work making his genius obvious and unquestionable. One very large canvas stands out above all: the *Adoration of the Magi*, a beautifully free and very human work, painted in 1624. Rubens apparently finished it in a fortnight, no doubt with the help of his studio, the major figures of which – Van Dijk and Jordaens – are represented in the rooms that follow; beyond which there's a small group of Dutch paintings. Both Adriaen Brouwer and David Teniers did raucous scenes of peasant life, and they fittingly share the same room. Born in Flanders, apprenticed to Frans Hals in Haarlem and very much influenced by Bruegel, Brouwer bridges the gap between Flemish and Dutch art. When he was imprisoned in 1633, the prison baker, Joos van Craesbeek, became his pupil, and his pictures are here too, sometimes excelling even Brouwer in their violence.

The **Plantin-Moretus Museum** (daily 1000–1700) is housed in the mansion of the great Antwerp printing family that began with Christopher Plantin who came here in 1548. Originally a bookbinder, he was mugged one night in 1555 and had to give up all heavy work, turning to printing for a living and later becoming printer to Philip II. The house is worth seeing for itself, but the museum has a variety of attractions ranging from fine arts to a succession of interiors that provide an insight into how Plantin and his offspring conducted their business. There are Rubens portraits which give an early record of the dynastic family, printing workshops with five presses still in working order and a beautiful collection of ancient books, including a Gutenburg Bible that Plantin obtained in 1514, when he was preparing his five-language Biblia Polyglotta.

The **Maagdenhuis**, Lange Gasthuisstraat 33 (Monday-Friday 0830–1630), literally 'maidens' house', was a girls' orphanage in times gone by, but is now occupied by the local social security offices. Most of its prodigious collection of paintings has found its way to the Royal Museum, but a few remain, displayed in three ground-floor rooms and the chapel: among them works by Van Dijk and Jordaens, and including a touching *Portrait of an Orphan Girl* by Cornelis de Vos.

Probably the best of the smaller Antwerp museums is the **Mayer van den Burgh** (Tuesday-Sunday 1000–1700) at Lange Gasthuisstraat 19, consisting of the private art collection of the wealthy merchant of the same name. In a reconstruction of a 16th-century town-house, there are works by Massys, Mostaert and Aertsen, to name only a few, but pride of place goes to Bruegel's *Dulle Griet* or 'Mad Meg': one of his most Boschesque paintings, in which a woman, loaded down with possessions, stalks the gates of hell – a surrealist landscape of monsters and pervasive horror. The title refers to the archetypal shrewish woman who, according to Flemish proverb 'could plunder in front of hell and remain unscathed'.

The **Ridder Smidt van Gelder Museum** is out of the centre of town at Belgielei 91 (Tuesday-Sunday 1000–1700), another collection donated to the city by an aristocratic patron. An absurdly opulent assortment of paintings, furniture and porcelain in an 18th-century mansion, its extravagance soon gets wearing, and there's nothing to keep you here for long.

Getting around and finding a place to stay

Antwerp has two **railway stations,** Berchem and Centraal. International trains stop at Berchem (except those from Paris and Amsterdam) and the rest at Centraal Station, in the heart of the Jewish quarter of the city. There's a small sub-**Tourist Office** next door on Koning Astridplein (Monday-Friday 0830–2000, Saturday 0900–1900, Sunday 0900–1700) and the main one is in the centre of town at Suikerrui 19 (Monday-Friday 0830–1900, Saturday/Sunday 0900–1700). They have a detailed map for F10 and lists of rooms, etc. **Getting around** is no problem – the centre of Antwerp isn't large and is easily walkable. If you prefer to ride, F25 is the flat fare on buses and trams and you can buy an eight-ride ticket for F113, available from the station. If you're just staying for a day or two, then the best bet is a *Tourist Card,* which you can get from the Tourist Office: valid for one day F70, two days F120.

Camping Vogelzang is on the southern side of town (bus 17 from the station and there's a **Youth Hostel** nearby in Eric Sasselaan (bus 27). The next cheapest alternative is **dormitory rooms** from F200 at *International Youth and Student Home,* Volksstraat 58, near the Royal Museum, or *New International Youth Pension* at Provinciestraat 256, behind the station. Most cheap **hotels** are near the station: try *Old Tom,* De Keyserlei 53 (singles F560, doubles F715) or *Florida,* De Keyserlei 59 (singles F430, doubles F585).

You'll find inexpensive places to **eat** in the student streets around Prinsstraat and St Jacobsmarkt. The *University restaurant* in Koningstraat does a F60 meal (daily 1115–1330/1800–1930), *Bistrot de Jezuiet,* on the corner of Venusstraat and Blindestraat, has dishes for around F100, and *Eethuis Buikskerond* does a good variety of stuff from F75.

There are one or two good **bars** in Hoogstraat and around Hendrik Conscience Plein. *De Muze* is lively and very hip (jazz on Thursdays), as is *De Volle Maan,* on Koornmarkt.

Extras . . . and essentials
Books   English books are available from *Standaard,* Huidevetterstraat 57.
Car Hire   *Avis* (Ankerui 20), *Europcar* (Oude Vaartplaats 16), *Hertz* (St Jacobsmarkt).

Consulates   American (Rubens Centre, Nationalestraat 5), British (Fran-rijklei 27).

Exhibitions   Temporary exhibitions of work by contemporary Belgian artists at *ICC* (International Cultureel Centrum), Mier 50.

Gay   Most gay bars are situated behind the station in Van Schoonhoven-straat and Dambruggestraat. For information, there's *GOC*, Dambrugge-straat 204.

Markets   On Vrijdagmarkt there's a Wednesday and Friday morning *second-hand goods* auction – usually good for real bargains if your Flemish is up to it. *General and bric-à-brac* market – Sunday mornings on Oude Vaartplaats. During the summer there are Saturday *antique markets* (Lijnwaadmarkt) and *art markets* (Dageraadplaats).

Main Post Office   Groenplaats (Monday-Friday 0900–1800).

Student Travel   *ACOTRA*, Pieter van Hobokenstraat 20.

Student Antics   Look out for the riotous processions in October, when the students take to the streets to initiate the latest first-year intake.

Telephone   International calls at Jezusstraat 1 (0800–2000 daily).

Women   For contacts and information try *Vrouwencafe Chatterbox*, Vrijdagmarkt 5.

BRUGES

'Somewhere within the dingy casing lay the ancient city', wrote Graham Greene of **Bruges,** 'like a notorious jewel, too stared at, talked of, trafficked over'. Perhaps so, but despite its enormous popularity Bruges has kept its tourist industry under well-ordered control – if you are exploited here it's deftly done and gently felt, though it's best to come out of season to find the placid serenity for which the town's famous. In the small streets that wind and wander with the intricacy of the lace patterns sold here are some gorgeous medieval buildings, and the **Groen-inge** and **Memling Museums** both have great collections of Flemish art. A central *Sleep-In* makes Bruges a cheap place to stay, so all in all there's no excuse for failing to have a look at one of the most beautiful towns of the Low Countries.

Bruges had a violent past: the first of many horrific incidents happened in 1302 when the town revolted against French rule and massacred the garrison; for good measure they also executed anyone who wouldn't pronounce the Flemish *schild en vriend* (shield and friend) to their satis-faction. In the 17th century the town was known as *Bruges-la-morte* because of the frequent and bloody sieges that followed its decline as a great trading centre. At its height Bruges was a showcase for the products of the Hanseatic League, a union of mostly German towns that protected its interests from piracy, and had the most important market in northern Europe. Venetian merchants sold oriental fabrics and spices, and the metals of central Europe, Russian furs, English wool and North African fruits all found their way to the town. Medieval banking houses made fortunes, and the Dukes of Burgundy held opulent court, patronising the artists now known as the Flemish Primitives.

Following this 'Golden Age' Bruges declined and Antwerp rose in fortune, but the town has retained its medieval characteristics, mainly because it escaped damage in both world wars. As you might expect, centre of the town is the **Markt,** a square-cum-car-park towered over by the ostentatiously over-tall **Belfry** (daily 0930–1200/1400–1800; F30), built in the 13th century when the town was at its richest and most extravagant. It's well worth the climb to the top, especially in the late afternoon when the warm colours of the town are at their deepest. The eastern side of the Markt is fronted by the acceptable neo-Gothic Government Palace and Post Office, but the **Burg** off Breidelstraat has a better group of buildings, of which the **Chapel of the Holy Blood** is most interesting: the drops of blood are supposedly those washed from the body of Christ by Joseph of Arimathea, by tradition brought here from Jerusalem in 1150. They're venerated each Friday in the **Upper Chapel,** (0830–1145/1500–1600, chapel also open during the week) whose interior is spoiled by excessively rich 19th-century decoration. Simpler and much more atmospheric is the shadowy, crypt-like **Lower Chapel,** built in Romanesque style to house a relic of St Basil. In spite of modern scepticism, reverence for the Holy Blood remains strong: on Ascension Day (12 May) the phial containing the Blood is carried through the town in a colourful but solemn procession.

Next door to the chapels is the **Stadhuis:** freshly refaced following repair to the damage of the 18th-century French occupation, its **Gothic Hall** of 1400 drips pendant arches like decorated stalactites. The only reason to visit the **Bruges Vrije Museum** adjacent (Monday-Friday 1400–1730, Sunday 0930–1200/1400–1700; F5) is to see Lancelot Blondeel's elaborate **chimney-piece.** Commissioned by Charles V's sister Margaret of Austria, it's a paean of praise to the Emperor – a little thank you for the absolute power he granted her to rule the Low Countries in the 16th century.

Dijver, near the Burg, has Bruges's four main museums, for which you can buy a reduced combination ticket (F140) from the first you visit. The **Groeninge Museum** (daily 0930–1800; F50) houses the town's collection of Flemish art, including works by the Flemish Primitives, painters of the late 14th and 15th centuries. **Van Eyck** was the most important of these artists, and his *Madonna of Canon van der Paele* is the gallery's most popular painting. Glowing and richly analytic, three figures surround the Madonna: the kneeling Canon, his cavalierish patron saint, St George, and St Donatian, to whom he is being presented. Though the work is full of symbolic minutiae it's the luminous, fastidious detail that impresses:

to those who saw it in the 15th century the portraiture must have seemed miraculous, the Virgin as real as the palpably human Canon. In St George's armour you can just make out the reflections of a man, presumably van Eyck himself, observing the scene, a similar statement of presence to the mirror reflection in his famous *Arnolfini Marriage* in London. As well as this there's van Eyck's small portrait of his wife and work by van der Weyden, van der Goes and Gerard David, plus a coarsely-executed *Last Judgment* from the studio of Bosch. The later and modern paintings aren't exactly engaging but look out for Jean Delville's weird *De Godmens*, a repulsively fascinating picture of writhing bodies striving (I think) for Christ's salvation.

At the end of Dijver on Mariastraat is the St Jans Hospitaal, a 600-year-old building that was used as an infirmary until the 19th century. Inside the finely-proportioned Great Hall is the **Memling Museum** (daily 0900–1230/1400–1800; F50), a small but important collection of works by **Hans Memling,** who lived and worked in Bruges for most of his life. He painted the *Mystical Marriage of St Catherine* for the Hospital between 1475 and 1479 and it is his masterpiece; gently formal symmetry in the Eyckian realist tradition, graceful and warmly coloured. Also here is his *Reliquary of St Ursula,* an unusual and lovely piece, a miniature Gothic church depicting the story of St Ursula and the 11,000 virgins. Memling accepted the theory that the number of virgins had been erroneously multiplied by a thousand somewhere along the historical line, and his six panels show Ursula making her pilgrimage to Rome, only to be massacred by pagans in Cologne. It's the mass of incidental detail that makes the reliquary so enchanting – the tiny ships, figures and churches in the background carefully depicting the late medieval world.

The **Arentshuis Museum** (daily 0930–1200/1400–1800; F50) has a dull display of paintings, plates, pots and pewter, and is only worth visiting if you're interested in the work of Frank Brangwyn, an unfashionable English artist born in Bruges who donated his work to the town. More enjoyable, though for its interior rather than its collection, the **Gruuthuse Museum** (daily 0900–1200/1400–1800; F50) was once a palace and has an unusual private chapel overlooking the adjoining **Onze Lieve Vrouwe Church,** whose bleak spire is the tallest in Holland and Belgium. Despite its many paintings the church has little to endear it: even the delicate *Madonna and Child* by Michelangelo seems out of place here. Brought from Tuscany by a Flemish merchant living in Bruges, it was the only work to leave Italy during the artist's lifetime and probably had an important influence on the painters working here at the beginning of the 16th century. There's a charge of F25 to enter the choir and see the tombs of Charles the Bold and Mary of Burgundy.

South of the Onze Lieve Vrouwe Church signs direct you to the

Begijnhof, a wide court of tall elms surrounded by formal little white-fronted houses. The quaintness of the Benedictine sisters, who wear a costume unaltered since the 15th century, makes the small **Museum of Begijn Life** popular and crowded, but the tranquil area around the lake is worth the short walk from the centre.

In its undecorated interior the **St Salvator Cathedral** (Monday/Tuesday, Thursday-Saturday 1000–1200/1400–1700, Sunday 1500–1700; F20) is similar to the Onze Lieve Vrouwe Church, though its graceful Gothic proportions are much more appealing. A small museum contains the church's treasures, reliquaries, ornaments and paintings by Bruges artists. Though not the grandest, perhaps the most likeable of the town's churches is on Balstraat, an area of low, toytown houses east of the centre. A copy of the Holy Sepulchre in Jerusalem, the **Jerusalem Kerk** (Monday-Saturday 0900–1200/1400–1800, Sunday 1100–1200/1400–1800; free, ring bell next door to enter) was built by the Adornes family in the 15th century. Anselm Adornes, son of the church's founder, was executed in Scotland for spying but his heart was returned to Bruges and buried here. You can see his portrait in the windows of the church, a building still privately owned by his descendants. Apart from tourists searching for the Lace Centre on Balstraat this part of Bruges escapes most visitors. Like much of the town it's really best for the ambiance of the well-preserved streets rather than anything specific, but while you're here have a look at **St Walburge's Church;** a dazzling white interior, immaculately restored.

Practical points

Bruges's **Tourist Office,** below the belfry in the Markt, will give you the best free map of the town. They're open Monday-Friday 0900–1900, Saturday/Sunday 0930–1230/1400–1900 and offer exchange facilities. Travel within the town is only really practical on foot or by **bike,** hireable from the train station (F125 per day, F95 with a valid rail ticket). It takes a few days to see Bruges and the best place to stay is the *Snuffel Sleep-In* at Ezelstraat 49 (F210 per night, 3 bus from train station). It's central, clean and has a café serving cheap substantial food and dangerously strong beer. A launderette next door completes the list of just about everything you need. Alternatives are *Van Acker* at Barrierstraat 13 (F300) or the **Youth Hostel** at Bar. Ruzettel 143 (F250). Two **campsites:** *St Michiel* at Tillegemstraat 55 can be reached by a 7 bus, but *Lac Loppem* at Lac 10 is accessible only by car.

Good for accommodation, Bruges isn't the best place for cheap **eating.** Other than the usual fast-food chains you'll be hard pushed to find anything but expensive tourist-geared places. The *Snuffel*'s evening meals are best value at F80–F160. Finally, here's an arbitrary selection of bars: *'t Mozarthuis* at Hidevunsplein 1 has classical music; *Oud Huis Achiel* *van Acker*, St Annarei 23 an antique interior; *Untitled* and *Bauhaus* at Langestraat 135 and 137 music and food. Also popular are *Chagall*, and *Cactus*, at St Amandstraat 40 and 13.

GHENT

Ghent is a frustrating place: even today its 15th-century glory is not hard to appreciate – the medieval buildings keep much of their splendour – but near impossible to explore. For the moment you have to content yourself with outside views of its fine churches and Guild Houses since most are closed for one reason or another.

Surrounded by bleak docks and industry, Ghent's centre lies between the Koornmarkt and St Baafsplein, with its best building, the mainly Gothic **St Baaf's Cathedral,** squeezed in the eastern corner (Monday-Saturday 0930–1200/1400–1800, Sunday 1300–1800). St Baaf's tidy nave, begun in the 15th century, is supported by tall, slender columns that give the whole interior a cheerful sense of lightness, though the 17th-century marble screens rather spoil the effect of the darker choir. In a small ambulatory chapel is St Baaf's, and Ghent's, greatest treasure – a seminal painting that is the real reason for a visit to the town. Since the discovery of a Latin verse on its frame in the 19th century, there's been heated discussion on who actually painted the **altarpiece** known as *The Adoration of the Mystic Lamb*: the inscription reads that Hubert van Eyck 'than whom none was greater' began and Jan van Eyck 'second in art' completed the work, but as almost nothing of Hubert is known, some art historians doubt his existence. Reputedly a resident of Ghent, Hubert was perhaps invented by the townspeople jealous of Jan's pre-eminence in their old rival Bruges. We don't know, but what is certain is that in their new manipulation of the technique of oil painting the brothers were able to capture a needle-sharp realism that must have seemed revolutionary to their contemporaries.

The altarpiece is a complex work and an explanation of its symbolism and complexities would (indeed has) filled volumes. The cover screens have a lovely Annunciation scene, the archangel Gabriel's wings reaching up to the timbered ceiling of a 15th-century Flemish house, with the streets of a town, perhaps Bruges or Ghent itself, visible through the windows. In a brilliant coup of lighting the frames of the shutters throw their shadows into the room, increasing the spectacle of reality. Below, the donor and his wife piously kneel alongside statues of the saints.

When the shutters are opened – this would have happened on special occasions like feast days – the altarpiece is stunning. On the upper level sit the Omnipotent, the Virgin and John the Baptist in gleaming radiant clarity, with, to the left, a marvellous group of singing angels who strain to read their music. (Van Mander, writing in the 16th century, thought they were so artfully painted you could discern the different pitches of their voices.) In the lower panel the Lamb, symbol of Christ's redemption of sins, is approached by bishops, saintly virgins, and Old and New Testament figures in a heavenly paradise that Kenneth Clark described as 'the first evolved landscape in European painting'. The Kingdom of Heaven is seen as a sort of idealised Low Countries – look closely and you can see the cathedrals of Bruges, Utrecht and Maastricht, surrounded by fastidiously detailed flora.

Tucked away in the small chapel, it's remarkable the altarpiece survived at all: Emperor Joseph II so disapproved of Adam and Eve's nudity that he had clothed versions painted (they're in the church near the western entrance) and in 1934 someone stole the *Just Judges* panel; it was never found so a copy was made. A few years later the whole altarpiece was stolen, this time by the occupying German forces who hid it down an Austrian salt mine. It'll cost you F15 to see the altarpiece – and you'd be mad to miss it.

After St Baaf's it's a little disappointing that all the old buildings on the square and Emile Braunplein adjacent are closed: the **Lakenhalle** now contains a restaurant and an audio-visual history of the town, but there's no admission to the old **Belfry** next to it. The **Castle of Gerhard the Devil** sounds promising and looks forbidding, but it houses the state archives and is closed to the public. Ghent's **Tourist Office** (Monday-Friday 0900–1230/1330–1700) is installed in the basement of the **Stadhuis,** whose north façade is a mass of flamboyant Gothic decoration, while the later eastern side has the stern severity of post-Reformation Calvinism.

Dodging the trams of Koornmarkt you reach the St Michelsburg bridge and Ghent's best view of its oldest port: **Graslei,** on the eastern side, has the squat, gabled guild and warehouses of the town's boatmen and grainweighers, and **Koornlei** opposite, more sedate buildings of the 18th century. North of Graslei the **Gravensteen** or castle of the counts (daily, 0900–1715; F10) seems straight out of a Bosch painting: its dark walls and angular turrets were built in 1180 to frighten the unruly citizens into behaving themselves and, perhaps not surprisingly, succeeded. A self-explanatory numbered tour includes the Oubliettes (with a couple of remaining skeletons) and an illustrated torture museum.

Of Ghent's dozen museums, three are worth a visit: the **Museum of Fine Arts** at Nicolaas de Liemaekereplein 3 (0900–1200/1400–1700; closed Monday; free), has some good Flemish school paintings and Hieronymus Bosch's *Carrying of the Cross,* showing Christ mocked by some of the most grotesque and deformed characters Bosch has ever painted. His smaller, less well-known *St Jerome at Prayer* is here too. The **Folklore Museum** at Kraanlei 65 (daily 0900–1200/1330–1730; closed Monday; F20) is a chain of period rooms depicting life and work at the turn of the century, prettily housed in a former almshouse. Finally, the

Museum of Antiquities at Godshuizenlaan 2 (daily 1000–1200/
1330–1430; closed Monday; free) has nothing rare or remarkable but
the old abbey buildings are some of the prettiest in Ghent.

Practical details
Ghent's **pensions** are small and not cheap: *Du Progress* at Koornmarkt
9 has a few single rooms at F275, doubles at F750 per room, and *'t
Postje*, usefully near the train station at Pr. Clementinalaan 136 offers
service without a smile and singles at F330, doubles F570. A better bet
from mid-July till mid-September are the university **Student Rooms,** F275
if you're under 25, F350 otherwise. Enquire at *Home Vermeylen,* Stal
Hof 6 (near Overpoortstraat). The **Youth Hostel** nearby in St Pietersplein
has dormitory rooms for F220 and the nearest **campsite** is in Ghent itself
at Zuiderlaan 12.

It's also from the *university* facilities in Overpoortstraat that you'll find
the cheapest **food:** lunch here is F100 and dinner F80 (Monday-Thursday
only). There's a cheap vegetarian restaurant, *Sou-En* at Hoogpoortstraat
30 (Monday-Friday, 1200–1400, 1800–2100) and the *Café Krieze,*
conveniently next door, has a good range of cheap beers.

LUXEMBOURG

The city of **LUXEMBOURG** occupies a plateau high above the winding
valleys of the Alzette and Pétrusse: a series of slate roofs, turrets and spires
reaching out from a common verdant centre. Both rivers are absurdly tiny
for the sheer gorges they have cut, and what tourist literature calls 'the
green heart of the city' is either given over to parks or small cultivated
plots, interspersed with villages known as 'suburbs'. The bustling city
above is divided into Old and New, either side of the Pétrusse valley.

You visit Luxembourg less for its sights than for its spectacular
location, and nearly everything of interest is confined to the Old Town:
not as ancient as you might expect, as most of the medieval city was
destroyed in a gunpowder explosion of 1554. The centre of Luxembourg
life is the **Place d'Armes,** where you'll find a number of cafés charging
unreasonably high prices, and the **Tourist Office** (Monday-Friday
0900–1300/1400–2000, Saturday 0900–1300/1400–1900, Sunday
1000–1200/1400–1800). Beware – Luxembourg is expensive, and if
you're on any kind of budget you won't be able to afford more than a
day or two here. The city is really Switzerland moved north, with the
chintzy shops, banking sector and tax concessions that all mean your
money will disappear at a terrifying rate. The Luxembourgeois affect the

appropriate air of sophistication to go with all this. Communication isn't difficult: French is the official language but German is spoken almost as much, while the older natives converse in a weird dialect of low-German incomprehensible to most people. You can spend Belgian or Luxembourg francs — basically the same thing but with a different sovereign on the front.

For cheap **accommodation** you'll have to venture across the ravine into the seedier New Town. Most places are around the railway station, but here's a selection anyway: *Hotel Atlas,* 30 rue de Fort Neipperg, *Hotel Carlton,* 9 rue de Strasbourg, *Hotel Windsor,* 7 rue de Strasbourg, *Hotel Weber,* 50 rue Zithe. These will normally set you back about F500 for a single, and from around F700 for a double. Alternatively, there's a **Youth Hostel**, scenically situated at rue du Fort Olisy 2, or **Camping Grunewald** — north of town on the road to Echternacht, bus 20 from the Cathedral. **Eating** and **drinking** are similarly dear and often it's best to exist on bread and cheese, and alcohol from the supermarket — wine is cheap at around F50 a bottle, and beer ridiculously so, at about F25 a litre. Less pricey restaurants include *Giorgio,* rue de Nord 11 (pizzas from F140), *Target,* rue des Bains 17 (self-service — hamburgers, etc. from F120), *Loch Ness,* rue Notre Dame 13 (chicken, hamburgers, etc. from F120).

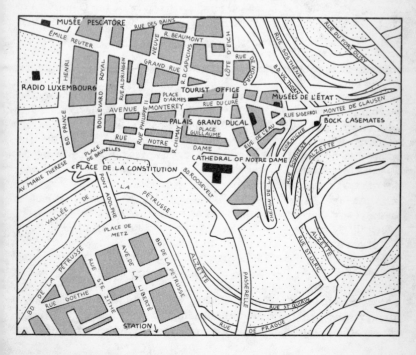

The oldest quarter of town is called **Bock,** in a long loop of the snaking Alzette where, in 963, Count Siegfried decided to build the fortress that was the beginning of the modern town. An ideal defensive position, it was subsequently expanded on by just about every major power, making Luxembourg into one of the most strongly defended cities in Europe. The streets here cling to the side of the valley, overlooking the huddles of black slate below. The fortifications were destroyed in 1867, but the **Bock Casemates** – defensive positions carved out of the rock – remain since it was impossible to demolish them without doing the same to the whole of this part of town. They were used as bomb shelters in the last war, and it's possible to visit them now. You are given a leaflet and have to make your own way. The views are good but otherwise it's not especially interesting, and I wouldn't bother going unless your idea of fun is trudging around in 200-year-old damp and draughty corridors (daily 1000–1800; F30).

Nearby, in the Marché aux Poissons, are the **Musées de l'Etat** (Tuesday-Sunday 1000–1200/1400–1800; free), two museums in one, and so enormous and confusingly laid out that it's best to decide on what you want to see first, as otherwise you'll spend hours wandering aimlessly. The History and Art section takes up one building, and breaks down as follows: *ground floor* – archaeological finds from the Gallo-Roman and Merovingian eras; *1st floor* – the military history of the country; *2nd floor* – contemporary Luxembourgeois painters; *3rd floor* – visual arts again, mainly Italian and Flemish primitives and nothing particularly distinguished, except *Charity* by Cranach. The *annexe* holds Applied Arts (only open afternoons), which includes furniture, ceramics and period interiors.

The only other gallery in town is the **Musée Pescatore** (Monday, Wednesday, Friday 1500–1900, Saturday/Sunday 1000–1200/1500–1900; F20), near Radio Luxembourg in the park. This is small, has few items of interest, and you expect more from what is after all the 'municipal museum of painting', wondering what the Luxembourgeois do when they want a shot of culture. The museum concentrates on *Dutch, Flemish* and *French* painters from the 17th to the 19th century, but apart from the odd canvas by Teniers, Dou and Courbet, there's nothing to keep you here longer than half an hour. Labelling is at best extremely poor, attempting to force you to buy the catalogue at F100 – don't bother.

Back in the centre of town is the **Palais Grand Ducal,** which the Luxembourg royals adopted as their residence in the 19th century, but only keep for state occasions these days, having moved out to somewhere a little less public. It was built originally as the town hall – a replacement for a previous Gothic structure that had perished in the earlier explosion – and has a Moorish Renaissance façade, turretted, with pilasters and arabesques, attached to an extension of 1743. Visitors are kept to July and August, and there's no escaping the guided tour, which can actually be quite interesting, though whether it's worth F80 or not is debatable. You have to buy a ticket in advance from the Tourist Office (English tours are at 1600 on Monday/Tuesday/Thursday/Friday).

It's a short walk from here to the **Cathedral of Notre Dame**, a perplexing church that is an unsatisfactory mingling of different styles. Finished in 1618, its only notable features are a beautiful carved Rococo rood screen, and the graceful, slender black spires which dominate Luxembourg's puckered skyline.

Travel information and other essentials

Buses and Taxis   Buses cost F20 a ride, however far you go. Better value is a ten-journey ticket for F140. Taxis are expensive and don't cruise: you can find them at the station, on the Place d'Armes, or on most other main squares.

Books   English books from *P. Ernster,* rue du Fosse 27 or *Paul Bruck,* Grand Rue 22.

Car Hire   *Avis* (rue Duchscher 13), *Europcar* (boulevard Prince Henri 33), *Hertz* (avenue de la Liberté 25), *Inter Rent* (rue de Thionville 88).

Change   Outside banking hours, you can change money at the railway station.

Embassies   American (E. Servais 22), British (boulevard Royal 28), Irish (route d'Arlon 28).

Flea Market   Saturday mornings, Place Guillaume.

Gay Life   Luxembourg has a lively and sociable gay scene scattered all over town. *Chez Mike* is *the* bar, Av. Emile Reuter, and *Mini-Hilton,* up on Montée de Clausen, comes with a strong recommendation, despite the name.

Hitching   Those hitching south into France should take bus 6 from the post office as far as rue de Thionville. To Brussels: take bus 7 out to the route d'Arlon.

23 June   is the Luxembourg national day and everyone takes to the streets. In the capital the atmosphere is festive, with a torchlight parade, fireworks and illuminations.

Post Office and Telephone   The main post office is in rue Aldringen and is open 0700–2045 – you can make international calls from there. There's a 24-hour post office in the Place de la Gare.

Women   Try the women's bar *Au Petit Fada* at rue de Hollerich 24.

There are train connections to most major European cities: information and tickets from **TEJ Student Travel**, rue Aldringen 21. However, if you have time on your hands it's a good idea to see something of the Luxembourg countryside, as it *is* very beautiful. For this you had best get a season ticket of some kind: F146 gives unlimited travel on trains and buses throughout the country for one day, and F413 entitles you to the same for any five days within a period of fifteen. The **National Tourist Office**, in the Air Terminal building in Place de la Gare, has plenty of maps, lists and glossy info (July-September 1900–1930, otherwise, daily 0900–1200/1400–1830), and I'd strongly recommend trips up to **Vianden** and **Echternach** at least.

TRAVEL DETAILS

Trains

Brussels–Ostend (1 an hour; 1 hour 20 mins), Brussels–Bruges, (2 an hour; 1 hour), Brussels–Ghent (2 an hour; 30 mins), Brussels–Antwerp (3 an hour; 40 mins), Brussels–Paris (7 a day; 3 hours), Brussels–Amsterdam (1 an hour; 3 hours), Brussels–Namur (1 an hour; 50 mins), Brussels–Liège (1 an hour; 1 hour 20 mins), Brussels–Luxembourg (roughly 1 an hour; 2 hours 30 mins), Brussels–London (5 a day; 10 hours), Bruges–Ghent (3 an hour; 30 mins), Bruges–Zeebrugge (1 an hour; 15 mins), Bruges–Ostend (4 an hour; 15 mins), Bruges–Antwerp (1 an hour; 1 hour 10 mins), Luxembourg–Brussels (1 an hour; 2 hours 30 mins), Luxembourg–Amsterdam (11 a day; 7 hours via Maastricht, 6 hours via Brussels), Luxembourg–Maastricht (5 a day; 4 hours), Luxembourg–Trier/Koblenz (7 a day; 40 mins, 2 hours), Luxembourg–Cologne (8 a day; 3 hours 20 mins; change at Koblenz), Luxembourg–Hamburg (7 a day; 7 hours 30 mins; change at Koblenz), Luxembourg–Copenhagen (4 a day; 13 hours; change at Koblenz), Luxembourg–Munich (5 a day; 7 hours; change at Koblenz), Luxembourg–Metz/Strasbourg (9 a day; 1 hour, 2 hours 30 mins), Luxembourg–Paris (12 a day; 4 hours), Luxembourg–Nice (3 a day; 13 hours; change at Metz), Luxembourg–Basle/Milan (5 a day; 4 hours, 10 hours).

Buses

Bruges–Ghent (Bus 58A; 1 hour 40 mins), Bruges–Breskins – for Vlissingen ferry (Dutch bus no. 2; 1 an hour; 1 hour).

Part three
CONTEXTS

DE·NEDERLANDS

THE NETHERLANDS: A HISTORY

*What's now known as the Netherlands
didn't reach its present delimitations until
1830. Until then its borders were conti-
nually being redrawn following battles,
treaties and alliances, and what follows
is as much a history of the Low Countries
as the emergent Dutch nation. The term
'Holland' refers to the province – not the
country – throughout.*

Beginnings

When Caesar began the conquest of
Gaul in 57 BC he found three tribes living
in what are now the Netherlands, the
mainly Celtic **Belgae**, and the Germanic
Batavi and **Frisians**. These are the first
people recorded living in an area that
was dangerously exposed to flooding
and, to the north, little more than a
collection of sandbanks and marshes.
Few traces remain of the earlier, prehis-
toric inhabitants: in Friesland and Groningen mounds known as *terpen* were
raised as habitations above the marshy
low-lying ground, and in Drenthe
Neolithic tombs, *hunebedds*, stretch
scattered across a bleak ridge.

Though his troops were massively
outnumbered, Caesar's tactical skills
subdued the tribes. The **Roman occupation** continued for 500 years until the
troops had to withdraw to protect the
crumbling power of the southern empire.
All that's left of their presence are the
beautiful baths at Heerlen in Limburg,
one of the main colonial settlements. As
the Romans withdrew, two groups of
Franks pushed south and west into the
area, those from what is now Germany
into the north, the Romanised Franks to
the south, creating the basic division of
languages that would evolve, respectively, into Dutch and French. After
AD 400 Christianity began to spread
slowly through the Low Countries, initially under SS Boniface and Servaas in
the south and Willibrord, first bishop of
Utrecht. By 800, the year in which the
Frankish king **Charlemagne** was elected
Holy Roman Emperor, the pagan Frisians and Saxons had been converted.
The strength and stability of Charlemagne's court at Aachen spread to the
Low Countries, bringing a flurry of building of superb Romanesque churches
like Maastricht's St Servaas. Following
Charlemagne's death the area that's

now the Netherlands was repeatedly
divided and partitioned among his
successors, and by the 10th century was
under the control of **French kings** and
German emperors. These various
feudal lords brought a stability to the
region, aiding the growth of towns by
granting charters which gave a degree
of autonomy in exchange for taxes, and
military and labour services to the lord.
With the confidence of a civic charter,
towns began to grow and by the 13th
century most of what are now the country's major towns had their independence. To the south, Bruges and Ghent
were quickly developing into wealthy
cloth producers, starting a chain of
prosperity that would lead to Amsterdam's Golden Age 400 years later.

Burgundian rule

By the late 14th century the political
situation in the Low Countries is fairly
clear: five lords controlled the Provinces,
paying only nominal homage to their
French or German overlords. In 1419
Philip the Good of Burgundy succeeded to the countship of Flanders and
by a series of adroit political moves
gained control over Holland, Zeeland,
Brabant and Limburg, and Antwerp,
Namur and Luxembourg to the south. He
consolidated his power by establishing
a strong central administration in Bruges
and revoking the privileges granted in
the towns' charters. During his reign
Bruges became the emporium for the
Hanseatic League, a mainly German
association of towns who acted as a
trading group and protected their interests from piracy. The wealth of the town
was near fabulous, and the rich court
patronised the early and seminal Nederlandish painters like van Eyck and
Memling, whose works can still be seen
in the Flanders towns. When Philip died
Bruges's prosperity began to die too,
and **Antwerp** succeeded the town as
Europe's chief market.

After a brief reign Charles, Philip's
successor, was killed and the French
seized the opportunity to take back
Arras and Burgundy. Before the northern
provinces would agree to fight the
French they kidnapped Charles's
daughter, Mary, and forced her to sign
a charter that more than restored the

civic privileges removed by her grand-father Philip. In 1477 Mary married the archduke Maximilian of Austria, and Burgundian power transferred to the **Habsburgs**.

Mary was killed in a fall when riding (her tomb and that of her father are in the Onze Lieve Vrouwe Kerk in Bruges). Maximilian continued to rule until 1494 when he became Holy Roman Emperor, eventually succeeded by his grandson **Charles V**, who in turn became Holy Roman Emperor and King of Spain. Though the Netherlands were part of his possessions, Charles delegated much of his power there, wary of the separate identity of the various provinces. But whatever his display of authority, a spiritual trend was emerging that would question not only the rights of the Emperor but the power of the Church itself.

The rise of the Reformation

Around the beginning of the 16th century the invention of typography allowed the mass printing of cheap Bibles. Religion was no longer the exclusive property of the Church, and humanists like **Erasmus of Rotterdam** centralised the idealised human, seeing man as the crowning of creation rather than the sinful creature of the Fall. The superstition and ceremony of the Church was attacked throughout Europe and in 1517 **Luther** produced his ninety-five theses against indulgences, rejecting among other things Christ's presence in the sacrament of the Eucharist and denying the Church's monopoly on the interpretation of the Bible. His works and Bible translations were printed in the Netherlands and his ideas gained a following in a group known as the Sacramentarians. They, and other reforming groups branded as **Lutheran** by the Church, were persecuted and escaped the towns to form fugitive communes where the doctrines of another reformer, **Calvin**, became popular. Luther stated that the Church's political power was subservient to the state's; Calvin that the supreme authority was the Church. When the fanatical Catholic bigot **Philip II** succeeded his father in 1555 the scene was set for a massive confrontation.

The revolt of the Netherlands

On his father's abdication, Philip left the Netherlands under the control of his sister Margaret and removed his troops, but installed Jesuit priests to combat the Protestantism rising among the working people. In 1561 he reorganised the Church and created fourteen new bishoprics, a move that was construed as a wresting of power from civil authority, and an attempt to import the persecution of the Inquisition. Protestantism and Protestant sympathies spread to the nobility, who petitioned Philip for moderation of anti-Protestant edicts – and were dismissed out of hand. In 1565 a harvest failure caused a winter famine among the mainly Calvinist workers, and in many towns throughout the country they ran riot in the churches, sacking them of their wealth and destroying their rich decoration in a violent display of iconoclasm. The ferocity of this outbreak shocked the higher orders into renewed support for Spain, and Margaret regained the allegiance of most nobles. Most, because the Calvinists had had the support of the country's greatest landowner, Prince William of Orange-Nassau, known as **William the Silent** (William the Taciturn is probably a better translation). Of Germanic descent, he was raised a Catholic but the excesses and rigidity of Philip had caused him to side with the Protestant movement. A firm believer in individual freedom and religious tolerance, in the face of political despotism William became – and for the Dutch remains – a symbol of liberty. After the uprising had revitalised the pro-Spanish aristocracy he prudently slipped away to his estates in Germany.

The Netherlands under Alva

Philip II saw himself as responsible to God for the salvation of his subjects and therefore obliged to protect them from the heresy of Protestantism. He appointed the **Duke of Alva**, with an army of 10,000 men, to enter the Netherlands and suppress this heresy absolutely. Alva's first act was to set up the Council of Blood, which tried and condemned 12,000 of those who had taken part in the rebellion the year before. The policy briefly worked: when William attempted an invasion from Germany in 1568 the towns, garrisoned by the Spanish, offered no support. William waited and conceived other means of defeating Alva. In April 1572 a band of privateers entered Brielle on the Maas and captured it from the Spanish. They were *Waterguezen* or sea-beggars, one of the commando units commissioned by William and operating, initially, from England. Though most of the towns' councils were comprised of Catholic nobility, they despised Alva's presence, and let the Watergeuzen into the towns. Once in they were as ruthless as the Spanish themselves, often torturing and murdering Catholics to gain control. Gain control they did: by June all the province of Holland was in the hands of the rebels, and William was able to take control of his troops from Delft. Alva and his son Frederick fought back, taking Gelder, Overijssel and the towns of Zutphen and Naarden, and in June 1573 Haarlem, massacring the Calvinist ministers and most of the garrison. But the people retaliated: utilising their superior naval power the dykes were cut and the Spanish forces, unpaid and sensing the strength of the opposition, were recalled.

Philip replaced Alva with Luis de Resquins, who initially had some success in the south, where a compromise with Spanish rule was more easily forthcoming. But William's triumphant relief of Leiden in 1574 increased the pride of the rebel forces and when a few months later de Resquins died, his unpaid troops mutinied. Though Spain held several towns, William's troops momentarily controlled the country. The various forces signed the **Pacification of Ghent** in 1576, agreeing freedom of religious belief, but differences between Protestant north and Catholic south were unreconcilable: another army arrived from Spain and the south returned to Spanish-dominated Catholicism, beginning a separation that would lead, after many changes, to the modern country of Belgium. In 1579 seven provinces (Holland, Zeeland, Utrecht, Groningen, Friesland, Overijssel and Gelderland) signed the **Union of Utrecht**, an alliance against Spain that was the first unification of the provinces as an identifiable country. The agreement stipulated freedom of belief in the provinces – important since the struggle against Spain wasn't simply a religious one: many Catholics disliked the Spanish occupation and William did not wish to alienate this possible source of support. Though this liberalism didn't extent to the freedom of worship, a blind eye was turned to the celebration of Mass if it were done privately and inconspicuously, giving rise to the 'hidden churches' found throughout the country.

The United Provinces

In order to follow the developments of the 16th and 17th centuries it's necessary to have an idea of the organisation of **The United Provinces**. Holland, comprising today's North and South Holland, was far and away the dominant province economically and politically. The provinces maintained a decentralised independence, but as far as the United Provinces as a whole were concerned, what Holland said, went.

The assembly of the provinces was known as the States General, and met at The Hague; it had no domestic legislative authority, and could only carry out foreign policy by unanimous decision. The position of the *stadholder* was the most important in each province, roughly equivalent to that of governor. The *Council Pensionary* was another major post and in both cases the man who held the title in Holland was a powerful statesman.

In 1584 a French Catholic tricked his way into William's court in Delft and shot him, his family receiving the reward Philip II had promised for such an assassination. As William's son **Maurice** was just 17, control of the United Provinces was handed to **Johan van Oldenbarneveldt**, later Council Pensionary of Holland. Things were going badly in the fight against the Spanish: Nijmegen and Antwerp had fallen and Henry III of France refused help even with the offer of sovereignty. In desperation the United Provinces turned to Elizabeth I of England, who offered the Earl of Leicester as governor general. He was accepted but completely mishandled the situation, alienating the Dutch into the bargain. Oldenbarneveldt, Maurice and William Louis took over and had great success in routing the Spanish from much of the country. By 1609 the English had defeated the Spanish Armada and Philip II was dead; a twelve-year truce was signed and the United Provinces were consolidated.

The early 17th century: internal discord and further fighting

In the breathing space created by the truce, the long-standing differences between Maurice and Oldenbarneveldt polarised. An obscure argument within the Calvinist church on predestination proved the catalyst of Oldenbarneveldt's downfall. The quarrel, between two Leiden theologians, began in 1612: Armenius argued that God gave man the choice of accepting or rejecting faith; Gomarus, his opponent, that predestination was absolute – to the degree that God chooses who will be saved and who damned with man powerless in the decision. This row between the two groups (known respectively as Remonstrants and counter-Remonstrants) became closely linked to the political and social divisions of the early 17th century. When a synod was arranged at Dordrecht to resolve the matter the State of Holland, led by Oldenbarneveldt, refused to attend. He and the State supported the provincial independence favoured by Remonstrant sympathisers, whereas Maurice sided with the orthodox counter-Remonstrants who favoured a strong central authority. The counter-Remonstrants won at Dordrecht: Maurice, with his troops behind him, quickly overcame his opponents and had Oldenbarneveldt arrested. In May 1619 he was executed in The Hague 'for having conspired to dismember the states of the Netherlands and greatly troubled God's church'.

With the end of the twelve-year truce fighting with Spain once more broke out. Initially successful, the Spanish were, however, weakened by their war with France, and under fresh attack from Maurice's successor, his brother Frederick Henry, suffered a series of defeats on sea and land. By 1645 the Spanish were broken and three years later were forced to sign the **Peace of Westphalia**, ending hostilities and closing the Scheldt estuary, an action designed to destroy the trade and prosperity of Antwerp. The commercial expansion and pre-eminence of Amsterdam was assured, and the Golden Age began.

The golden age
The brilliance of **Amsterdam**'s explosion on the European scene is as difficult to underestimate as it is to detail. The size of its merchant fleet had long been considerable, bringing masses of Baltic grain into Europe. Even the determined Spaniards had been unable to undermine Dutch maritime superiority, and following the effective removal of Antwerp as a competitor Amsterdam

became the emporium for the products of north and south Europe and the new colonies in the East and West Indies. Amsterdam didn't only prosper from its market – her own ships carried the produce, a cargo trade that greatly increased the city's wealth. Dutch banking and investment brought further prosperity, and by the mid-17th century Amsterdam's wealth was spectacular. The Calvinist bourgeoisie indulged themselves gently in fine canal houses, and commissioned reflections of themselves in group portraits. Civic pride burgeoned and if some were hungry, few starved, with the poor cared for in municipal almshouses. The arts flourished and religious tolerance stretched even to the traditional scapegoats, the Jews, who quickly became enterprising merchants.

Though **The House of Orange** had established its royal credentials with the marriage of Frederick Henry's son William II to Mary of England, the conflict between central authority under the Orange rulers and provincial autonomy again arose. On William II's death the state of Holland used the fact that his heir was still an infant to force through measures abolishing the position of Stadholder, thereby reducing the powers of the Orangists and increasing those of the states, chiefly Holland itself.

Holland's foremost figure in these years was **Johan de Witt**, Council Pensionary to the state. He guided the country through wars with England and Sweden, concluding a triple alliance between the two countries and the United Provinces in 1678. This didn't succeed, however, and when France and England marched on the Provinces two years later, the republic was in trouble. The previous victories had been at sea and the army, weak and disorganised, could not withstand an attack. The country turned to **William III of Orange** for leadership and Johan de Witt was brutally murdered by a mob of Orangist sympathisers in The Hague. By 1678 William had defeated the French and made peace with the English – and was rewarded (along with his wife Mary) with the English crown ten years later.

The 18th century – decline and invasion
Though the French had been beaten, their leader Louis XIV retained designs on the United Provinces. When his

grandson succeeded to the Spanish throne and control of the Spanish Netherlands (Brabant, Flanders and Antwerp), Louis forced him to hand the latter over to French control. The United Provinces, England and Austria formed an alliance against the French and so began the **Wars of the Spanish Succession**, a haphazard campaign that dragged on till 1713 and the treaty of Utrecht. The fighting drained the country's riches and a slow decline in wealth began, furthered by a mood of unadventurous conservatism that was a reaction against the lucrative financial speculation of the previous century. No longer under foreign threat, the internal fighting between the Orangists and the pro-French ruling families (who called themselves 'patriots') worsened in the latter half of the century and by 1787 the last few years of the United Provinces saw near-civil war. In 1795 the French, aided by the Patriots, invaded, setting up the **Batavian Republic** and dissolving the United Provinces and their power framework. Effectively under French control, the Dutch were unenthusiastically at war with England, and in 1806 Napoleon appointed his brother Louis King of the Netherlands in an attempt to create a commercial gulf between the country and England. Louis, however, wasn't willing to allow the Netherlands to become a simple satellite of France; he ignored Napoleon's directives and after just four years of rule was forced to abdicate. The country became part of the French Empire controlled from Paris, and for three gloomy years suffered military repression and heavy taxation to finance Napoleon's campaigns. Following his disastrous retreat from Moscow, the Orangist faction once more surfaced to exploit weakening French control of the country. In 1813 Frederick William, son of the exiled William V, returned to the county and eight months later was crowned king **William I**. A strong-willed man, he spent much of his life trying to unite North and South Netherlands, an ambition that failed because of the North's attempted domination of the South. The South revolted against his plans and in 1830 the **kingdom of Belgium** was proclaimed, completing a slow process of separation that had begun 300 years earlier.

The kingdom of the Netherlands: 1830 to the present day
A final attempt at invasion of Belgium in 1839 gave William most of Limburg, ending the centuries of changes of border and territory. In this new stability the country prospered, canal building opening Rotterdam and Amsterdam to the North Sea. The political climate was outstandingly liberal, influenced by cabinet leader **J. R. Thorbecke**. A farsighted reformer, he furthered the openminded liberalism that is now part of the national identity.

At the outbreak of the **Great War** the Netherlands remained neutral, but suffered privations as a result of the Allied blockade of ports through which Germany might be supplied. Similar attempts to remain neutral in the **Second World War** soon failed: the Germans invaded on 10 May 1940, destroying Rotterdam four days later. The Dutch were quickly overwhelmed, Queen Wilhelmina fled to London, and retaliation against the Nazis was continued by the Resistance. Instrumental in destroying German supplies and munitions, they also helped many downed airmen to escape back to England. A heavy price was paid for their opposition; 13,000 resistance fighters were killed in the war years. Tragically, Amsterdam's old Jewish community, swollen by those who had fled the persecution of the 1930s, was obliterated, leaving only the deserted Jodenhoek and the diary of a young girl as testament to the horrors.

Liberation began in autumn 1944 with **Operation Market Garden**: this was a British plan to create a corridor stretching from Eindhoven to Arnhem, gaining control of the three main rivers, isolating occupying forces to the west and pushing into Germany. It was a dangerous gamble, but if successful would hasten the end of hostilities. On 17 September the 1st Airborne Division parachuted into Oosterbeek, a small village near the northern vanguard of the operation, **Arnhem**. German opposition was much stronger than expected, and after heavy fighting the Allied forces could only take the northern end of the fateful bridge. Support from Nijmegen became increasingly difficult, and after four days of fighting the battalion defending the bridge, reduced to just a hundred men, gave up. The rest of the division, decimated by casualties, pulled back to Oosterbeek a few days later. In Arnhem at least Operation Market Garden had been a military disaster, and the city would not be relieved until the arrival of the Canadians five months later, shortly before the general surrender of the occupying forces on 5 April 1945.

The post-war years were spent patching up the damage of occupation. Rotterdam was rapidly and imaginatively rebuilt, and the dykes blown in the war to slow the German advance repaired. Two events mar the late 1940s and early 1950s: the former Dutch colonies of Java and Sumatra, taken by the Japanese at the outbreak of the war, were now run by a nationalist Republican government in Java that refused to recognise Dutch sovereignty. Following the failure of talks on Dutch control the troops were sent in; world opposition to this was strong and after much condemnation and pressure the Dutch reluctantly handed over their colonies. Back at home, tragedy struck on 1 February 1953 when an unusually high tide was pushed over Zeeland's sea defences by a westerly wind, flooding 40,000 acres of land and drowning over eighteen hundred people. The response was to secure the area with the **Delta project**, closing off the western part of

the Scheldt and Maas estuaries with massive sea dykes. A brilliant and graceful piece of engineering, the main dyke at Hellevoetsluis was opened in 1970. Elsewhere rebuilding continued; in Amsterdam all the land projected for use by the year 2000 in 1947 was in fact used up by the 'garden cities' of the dormitory suburbs by 1970, and the polder towns also expanded. But growth wasn't only physical: the social consciousness and radicalism of the 1960s reached Amsterdam early, and the word of the psychedelic revolution was quick to catch on. It was quick to fade too, replaced by the cynicism of the seventies. Today, the country is lumbered with a system of proportional representation that while intent on giving everyone a fair say, does little to change anything, and politics and politicking seems a bland compromise between the three main parties, the Protestant-Catholic CDA coalition, the Liberal VVD and the Socialist PvdA.

Perhaps the possible arrival of cruise in a few years' time will galvanise the fragmented lesser parties and capture the minds of the people, but at the moment, despite the effects of the recession, the Netherlands remains comfortably complacent.

THE SIXTIES AND AFTER: PROVOS, SQUATTERS AND RIOTS

The sixties were swinging, the summer of '65 was warm and a group of young people were making it a weekly ritual to gather around a statue in the centre of Amsterdam to watch a remarkable performer, one-time window-cleaner and magician extraordinaire, **Jasper Grootveld**. Grootveld had won notoriety a couple of years earlier by painting K for *kanker* (cancer) on cigarette advertising hoardings throughout the city. Later he had set up an 'anti-smoking temple' and proclaimed the statue of the *Lieverdje* ('Lovable Rascal') on the Spui the symbol of 'tomorrow's addicted consumer' because it had been donated to the city by a big cigarette manufacturer. But Grootveld was not the only interesting character around town, Roel van Duyn, philosophy student at Amsterdam University and initiator of a New Left

movement, the **Provos**, started joining Grootveld's magic happenings. . . . But who would have dreamed that this peaceful scene would spark off a chain of rebellion that would influence events in the Netherlands for the next 20 years?

The number of 'real' Provos never exceeded about twenty-five but their actions appealed to a large number of young people, attracted by the 'happenings' staged on Amsterdam's streets by this core of politically motivated activists. They had no coherent structure: they emerged into public consciousness through one common aim – bringing points of political or social conflict to public attention by spectacular means. More than anything, the Provos were masters of publicity and pursued their 'games' (their connotation) with a spirit of fun rather than grim political fanaticism.

They reflected very much the swinging sixties attitude of young people all over the Western world.

In July 1965, the police intervened at the Saturday night happening on the Spui for the first time and set a pattern for future confrontations – they had already confiscated the first and second issues of the Provos' magazine in which their initiator Roel van Duyn published the group's manifesto and in which their policies later appeared under the title 'The White Plans'. These included the white bicycle plan which proposed that the City Council ban all cars in the city centre and supply instead 20,000 bicycles (painted white) for general public use.

There were regular incidents throughout 1964 and 1965 involving a variety of Provo protests, but it was the action taken on 10 March 1966, the wedding day of Princess Beatrix and Claus von Amsberg, that provoked the most serious police confrontation. Smoke bombs were thrown at the wedding procession and fights with the police broke out throughout the city.

The following month, April 1966, Provo Hans Tuynman was arrested for handing a policeman a leaflet protesting against the police. The Provos and their supporters were furious and street demonstrations followed with further arrests being made. On 11 May, Tuynman was sentenced to three months' imprisonment and there were more protests.

Through all this conflict, the Provos were winning increased public support – reflected in the municipal elections of 1966 when they received over 13,000 votes – 2½ per cent of the total and enough for a seat on the Council.

But this achievement didn't mean the end of the Provos' street actions. Indeed, the next event they were involved in was the most violent of the 1960s. It started with a demonstration by construction workers in Amsterdam on 13 June, during which one worker suddenly died. The workers assumed he had been killed by police who were patrolling the demo (such was the general anti-police feeling) and the following day they staged a strike and marched through the city together with thousands of supporters, including the Provos who by now were regarded as the champions of the public versus the police. The worker had actually died of a heart attack but the

mood had been set and there were clashes between police and rioters for four days. A month later, The Hague government ordered the dismissal of Amsterdam's Police Chief and, a year later, that of the Mayor.

But by May 1967 the Provos' inspiration was waning and at a final gathering in Vondelpark on the 13th, they announced they would disband although they still had a member on the City Council.

The next phase of the Provo phenomenon was the creation of the 'Oranje Free State', an alternative society set up by van Duyn in 1970 in the form of a mock government with its own 'ministries' and 'policies'. The new movement, the **Kabouters** (named after a helpful gnome in Dutch folklore), was successful if short-lived. They adopted some of the more reasonable 'white policies' of the Provos and went as far as winning seats in six municipalities including five in Amsterdam. But by the end of 1971 the Kabouter movement and its brave new world faded amid disputes over methods.

As the Provos' and Kabouters' movements gradually disappeared, many of their members joined neighbourhood committees which were emerging as active opponents of certain council plans in Amsterdam. By far the most violently opposed plan was that to build a metro running through the **Nieuwmarkt**. The initial idea was conceived in 1968 and consisted of a plan to build a four-line network at an estimated f250 million. By 1973, the cost had risen to a phenomenal f1500 million – for just one line connecting the newly constructed suburb of Bijlmermeer to Amsterdam's Centraal Station.

It was actually the Council's policy to cope with the ever-growing problem of housing by moving residents to these suburbs that enraged Amsterdammers who felt their city was being sold to big businesses and their homes converted to banks and offices. The opponents of the metro plan objected to the number of houses that would have to be demolished and believed it was merely a prestige development of no real use to the public.

Official clearance of the Nieuwmarkt area was scheduled for February 1975 but confrontation between police and protesters began in the previous

December. Many residents of the condemned houses refused to move and further violent clashes were inevitable. The worst action came on 24 March 1975, a day that became known as Blue Monday. The police began early in the morning and their tactics were heavy. Tear-gas grenades were fired through windows smashed by water cannons. Then came armoured cars ramming down front doors and the police were in, arresting occupants (residents and supporters) who threw paint cans and powder bombs in retaliation. The fighting went on late into the night with thousands of demonstrators joining in. At the end of the day, 30 people had been wounded, including 19 policemen, and 47 arrested; 450 complaints were filed against the police. A couple of weeks later came another big clash, but this time the demonstrators used different tactics, merely forming human barricades in front of the houses to be cleared. The police charged, armed with truncheons. It was an easy clearance. But the protesters had made their point too and after the clearance they showed their spirit of rebellion by holding parties on the rubble-strewn site. Despite continuing opposition, the metro was eventually opened in October 1980.

Meanwhile the ever-increasing problem of housing in Amsterdam was seeing the emergence of a new movement – the **squatters**. Although the Dutch Squatters Movement is said to have been born on 5 May 1970, which was declared the first National Squatters' Day, it was not until the late 1970s, early '80s that they became a force to be reckoned with.

At first the Squatters Movement was just a hazy shape on the edges of society, consisting mainly of completely autonomous neighbourhood committees which operated independently. There was little sense of unity until joint actions in defending a handful of symbolic squats in Amsterdam. These shaped the development of the Squatters Movement, today a strong political force with its own spokespeople and weekly newspaper, *Bluf!* which has now printed over a hundred issues.

To bring this transition into focus, one must examine the events surrounding four key squats – the *Grote Keyser,* the *Vondelstraat,* the *Lucky Luyk,* and *Wyers* – and the national squatting day of

action on 30 April 1980, the day Queen Beatrix was crowned.

The Grote Keyser in Keizersgracht is a listed building of considerable importance to Amsterdam. It was squatted in November 1978 and an eviction attempt was made at the end of 1979 but was unsuccessful – for the first time squatters throughout the city had combined to defend 'their' building. Eventually the Council bought the Grote Keyser for f1.8 million and negotiations with the squatters who remain in the building are still going on.

The eviction of the Vondelstraat squat in Amsterdam's most prestigious neighbourhood close by the Rijksmuseum, is perhaps the most famous squatting event in the Netherlands. Three days after the empty office premises were squatted in March 1980, police tanks were ordered in to remove the squatters. About a thousand police took part and the resulting riots spread through surrounding streets and reached Amsterdam's most popular tourist spot, the Leidseplein. The battle raged the whole day and 50 people were wounded. The squatters were evicted but it was not long before they re-occupied – they're still in the building today. The significance of the Vondelstraat squat is not only that it remains in the hands of the squatters but that the eviction and ensuing riots cost the Council a considerable amount of money – and the squatters decided to use this as a tactic to make future evictions too expensive for the authorities. The squatters were starting the move towards policy-forming. . . .

The next major event involved not a specific squat but protest actions on the day Queen Beatrix was crowned, 30 April 1980. Squatters throughout the Netherlands decided to stage protest action against what they considered the huge amount of money being spent on festivities and the reputed f84 million spent in the rebuilding of her residence in The Hague. They decided to squat a total of 200 buildings in 27 cities in Holland. Half of these token squats were cleared on the same day and it was one of these clearances that sparked off the first battle in Amsterdam. Then in the early afternoon, a protest demonstration set off to march through the city to the Dam Square where the crowning ceremony was taking place. Confrontation with the police began almost immediately on Waterlooplein, and from then on the city was in complete chaos. The squatters' ranks were swelled by other protesters who were angry at the public expenditure at a time when Amsterdam City Council were claiming they could not afford to build homes in the city. Public festivities came to an abrupt end as fighting broke out in city streets and continued until midnight. Tear gas enveloped the city while baton-armed Special Squad Police made relentless charges and many revellers were caught up with the rebels as police cordoned off areas of the city.

By 1982 the Squatting Movement was reaching its peak. After the success of the Vondelstraat squat in 1980, hundreds of premises were being squatted every week and there were an estimated 10,000 squatters in Amsterdam. The eviction of squatters from the Lucky Luyk, a villa on the Jan Luykenstraat, was the most violent and most expensive (damage ran into millions of guilders) the city has known to date.

The Lucky Luyk was originally squatted in April 1980 after standing empty for a few years. In October 1980 squatters were forcibly evicted twice by the *knokploegen* – groups of 'heavies' hired by property owners to protect their investments. Two months later the owners of Lucky Luyk won a court case for the official eviction of the building. At this stage, Amsterdam City Council stepped in to avoid the violence that was certain to accompany such an action. In September they bought the villa for f350,000 – giving the owner an easy f73,000 profit. The squatters were not happy but agreed to leave the building if it were used for young people's housing. On 11 October 1982, two days before a negotiating meeting between the Council and the squatters, twelve policemen from the Special Squad broke into the Lucky Luyk through the roof and arrested the five occupants – a surprise attack that enraged squatters all over the country and resulted in sympathy actions in many cities including Utrecht, Nijmegen and Arnhem.

It did not take long for riots to start in Amsterdam and they raged for three days with more than 170 arrests. Supporters of the Lucky Luyk, which included many non-squatters, built barricades, wrecked cars, destroyed property and set fire to a tram while police retaliated with tear gas and water cannons. The city's Mayor declared unprecedented emergency measures permitting police to arrest anyone suspected of disrupting public order.

The squatters learnt a lesson – the authorities had now had enough and were prepared to evict at any price. The Council were also learning and were discovering easier ways of eviction.

Squatters needed to develop a new tactic of defence. They hit on politics, and found a new case to defend – Wyers. Wyers, a one-time distribution centre for a textile firm, was squatted in October 1981 by about a hundred squatters from different groups all over the city. They were soon informed that *Hollandse Beton Maatschapij,* one of Holland's largest building companies, had obtained planning permission to build luxury apartments and shops on the site.

However, trouble was postponed on this occasion because HBM decided the market was not right for their financial investment and scrapped their plan. But in the spring of 1982 they applied for planning permission again, this time to build a hotel on behalf of Holiday Inn. Their initial application was turned down but an amended plan was approved by the Council in June 1983. An eviction order was presented to the Wyers inhabitants but the squatters, now employing new political tactics, found legal loopholes within the eviction order and the whole thing was delayed.

They were also busy preparing an alternative plan to present to the Council which involved using the building as a kind of combined cultural-living complex with art studios, rehearsal rooms, small businesses, theatre and art gallery as well as living space. This constructive alternative has won the support of many people and even the Council consider it a viable idea. Consequently, they have offered the Wyers' community an alternative site for their plan but this has been rejected by the squatters who say it is too far from the city centre, unsuitable for their purposes and too expensive. Dialogue between the Council and squatters continues but eviction now seems certain. All that remains to be seen is what tactics the squatters will use this time – because they certainly don't intend to surrender without a fight.

The Provos won for Amsterdam (not without casualties) the reputation of being a politically progressive city. Dedicated to fighting the system from the outside, they achieved something unexpected – they broke through and found themselves on the inside, and lost their reason for existence. And the squatters? Are they here to stay? Is their growing public support and respectability vital to their survival or a step towards integration into society making this movement as inevitably temporary as the Provos? And what comes next?

Wyers: a postscript

Sadly, Wyers was cleared by police on 14 February 1984 and it looks now as if the Holiday Inn plan is set to go ahead, despite the fact that there's obviously no need for a new luxury hotel in the city centre – most of the present ones are frequently half empty. The eviction was carried out swiftly and with relative ease; the squatters had decided beforehand not to resist and instead linked arms and waited for the police onslaught. Minor disturbances lasted most of the day but by late evening the city was calm. Time will tell whether this means the end of the Amsterdam squatting movement; we can only hope not. As banners proclaimed after the eviction; 'You can demolish Wyers but you will never destroy the ideas behind Wyers.' Let's hope that they're right.

DUTCH ART: A BRIEF GUIDE

It's important to point out that this, of necessity, is the very scantiest of introductions to the subject, and is only supposed to serve as a quick reference on your way around galleries. For more in-depth and academic studies, see the 'Books' listings, p. 13.

Until the 16th century much the most artistically productive part of what was then one country was Flanders in modern Belgium, and the work of painters there provided the solid realist footing on which Dutch painting developed. For this reason we've begun with the **early Flemish painters.** Their works are pretty thin on the ground in Holland, and even in Belgium most collections are not as complete as they might be – many of them ending up the property of the ruling Habsburgs and disappearing off to Spain, where they have remained. Nevertheless, Ghent's van Eyck *triptych* is an absolute must if you're down that way, Bruges has a museum solely devoted to Memling and the city galleries of Antwerp and Brussels have passable collections of most of the major masters.

Jan van Eyck (1385–1441) is generally regarded as the father of Netherlandish painting, and has even been credited with the invention of oil painting, though it seems more likely that he perfected a new technique by thinning his paint with the recently discovered turpentine, thus making it more fluid and more flexible. His most famous work is the Ghent altar-piece, supposedly, though debatably, painted with the help of his lesser-known brother Hubert. Revolutionary in its realism and detail, the altar-piece, like the rest of van Eyck's work, displays a new regard for elements of landscape and portraiture. Following on from van Eyck are the **Master of Flemalle** (**Robert Campin**) (1378–1444) and **Rogier van der Weyden** (1400–64), the former believed by some to be Rogier's teacher, while others simply regard the Master's output as early works by van der Weyden. Campin's paintings are closely akin to van Eyck, but Rogier shows a more emotional and religious intensity, rejecting, to some extent, van Eyck's unsentimental detachment. **Dieric Bouts** (1415–75), recognisable by his stiff, rather elongated figures, was clearly influenced by van der Weyden. Van Mander, the first Dutch art historian, counts him as a Dutch painter as he was born in Haarlem, but he was most active in Louvain and so must be considered in the Flemish tradition. **Hugo van der Goes** (d. 1482) was the next Ghent master after van Eyck, though the time gap deems he couldn't have been his student. Most famous for the *Portinari altar-piece* in Florence's Uffizi, he continued the realist tradition and, after a short career painting and travelling, died insane. **Hans Memling** (1440–94) is popularly believed to have been a pupil of van der Weyden. Active in Bruges throughout his life, he is best remembered for the serene and pastoral charm of his pictures. **Hieronymus Bosch** (1450–1516), on the other hand, is best known for the macabre and twisted visions of tortured people and grotesque beasts of his religious allegories. Bosch's approach must have been a major factor in the work of **Pieter Bruegel the Elder** (1525–69), who divided his time between gruesome allegory and pleasant, though innovative, interpretations of religious subjects in terms of his own landscape and people.

While all this was going on **Geertgen tot Sint Jans** (d.1490) (Little Gerard of the Brotherhood of St John), the strangely naive student of **Albert van Ouwater**, had been working in **Haarlem,** initiating an artistic tradition in that city that would hold good right through the 17th century. **Jan Mostaert** (1475–1555) took over after Geertgen's death, and continued to develop a style that was diverging more and more from that of the southern provinces. **Lucas van Leyden** (1489–1533) was the first painter to ring real changes in northern painting. Born in Leiden and the pupil of **Cornelis Engelbrechtsz,** his bright colours and narrative style were refreshingly new at the time, and introduced a novel dynamism into what had up till then been staid treatment of devotional subjects. Van Mander claimed **Jan van Scorel** (1495–1562) was a better painter and complained of Lucas's dandyish ways, though this was probably just sour grapes as van Scorel was a Haarlem painter and it was van Mander's avowed aim to publicise that city as the Dutch artistic capital. That said, van Scorel's effect should not be underestimated. By this time, the influence of Italy was all-important and every painter was supposed to travel there to view the works of Michelangelo, Raphael *et al.,* which embodied the cardinal painting virtues. Van Scorel was the first to Italianise the previously independent tradition of the north, when the Bishop of Utrecht ascended to the papacy as Hadrian VI and took the artist with him as court painter. Hadrian died soon after, and van Scorel returned north, taking back a number of half-digested Italian ideas and doctoring them with his native tradition. **Maerten van Heemskerck** (1498–1574) learned the Italian style from him before heading off to Italy himself in 1532. He stayed there five years before returning to Holland and settling in – where else – Haarlem.

The Golden Age

One of the few chroniclers of the art of the Low Countries, van Mander's *Schilderboek* of 1604 was modelled on Vasari's *Lives of the Italian Painters,* and puts into perspective for the first time Flemish and Dutch traditions up to the 17th century, as well as specifying the rules of fine painting. He was an artist too, but one who seems to have spent more time writing than painting and examples of his work are rare. More prolific were his contemporaries, **Cornelius Cornelisz van Haarlem** (1562–1638), who refined the Mannerist creed espoused by van Mander in elegant depictions of Biblical and mythical themes, and **Hendrick Goltzius** (1558–1616), a skilled engraver in the same style and an integral member of van Mander's Haarlem academy. With **Mannerism,** the subject became subordinate to the way it was painted: Biblical stories became a vehicle whereby artists could apply their skills in painting the human body, landscapes or plenteous displays of food. All this served to break the stranglehold that religion had had on art until then, and make legitimate a whole range of everyday things as subjects for the painter. In Holland this was compounded by the Reformation: the austere Calvinism that had replaced the Catholic faith in the northern provinces had no use for images or symbols of devotion in its churches, which had been stripped bare of almost any form of ornamentation. Painters had lost their greatest patron and now had to cater for the ordinary public – as the Dordrecht artist, van Hoogstraten, remarked in 1678: 'the best careers in the churches no longer exist.' Artists also no longer felt the need to go to Italy, and the real giants of the 17th century – Hals, Rembrandt, Vermeer – stayed in Holland all their lives. Thus began the greatest age of Dutch art, when painting was split into different categories – genre, portrait, landscape, etc. – and painters tended (with some notable exceptions) to confine themselves to one field throughout their working lives.

Some artists – Rembrandt for one – continued to portray classic subjects, but in a new way that was totally at odds with the Mannerists' stylish flights of imagination. **Abraham Bloemaert** (1564–1651), painting in Utrecht, is the link: though a solid Mannerist all through his career, he encouraged his pupils to adopt the more fashionable realism of Caravaggio – yet another Italian import. **Gerard van Honthorst** (1590–1656), **Hendrick Terbrugghen** (1588–1629) and **Dirck van Baburen** (1590–1624) all studied under him and made up the nucleus of the influential **Utrecht School:** a group of painters active in Utrecht in the early 17th century who followed Caravaggio almost to the point of slavishness. Honthorst was perhaps their leading light: he learned his craft from Bloemaert and in Rome where he was nicknamed Gerardo delle Notti for his ingenious handling of artificial light – a skill that in his later paintings would become more of a clever trick than anything else. Though undoubtedly a supremely competent artist, Honthorst remains somewhat discredited among critics today. Terbrugghen's reputation seems to have aged rather better: he soon forgot Caravaggio and developed a style of his own, his lighter, later work being the biggest influence on the young Vermeer. Baburen is the least considered member of the group and few of his paintings survive. However, after the obligatory jaunt to Rome, he shared a studio with Terbrugghen and produced some fairly original work; work which was again a partial influence on Vermeer.

Rembrandt was by far the most original history painter of the 17th century, and he painted religious scenes throughout his life. The poet and statesman Constantin Huygens procured him his greatest commission in the 1630s – a series of five paintings of the Passion, beautifully composed and uncompromisingly realistic. Later, Rembrandt got fewer and fewer commissions, since his treatment of Biblical and historical subjects was far less dramatic than his contemporaries'. While the more conventional Jordaens, Honthorst and Caesar van Everdingen were busy decorating the Huis ten Bosch for Frederick Henry, he was having his monumental *Conspiracy of Claudius Civilis* (painted for the new Amsterdam town hall) rejected – no one knows why, but it was probably because it was too real, too pagan an interpretation of what was an important symbolic event in Dutch history. **Aert van Gelder** (1645–1727) was Rembrandt's last pupil and he painted in the style of his aged master, producing shimmering Biblical scenes well into the 18th century.

Genre painting

A term first coined in the 18th century, **genre** refers to scenes from everyday life: a type of painting that, with the decline of the church as patron, had become popular in Holland by the mid-17th century, and produced a spate of painters solely devoted to producing genre work. Though some were simply unidealised portrayals of common scenes, others were moral entreaties to the viewer, and by means of symbols or carefully disguised details, they had a didactic purpose. **Hendrik Terbrugghen** and **Gerard Honthorst** spent more time painting religious subjects, but they also adapted the realism and strong chiaroscuro they had learnt from Caravaggio to a number of low-life tableaux. **Frans Hals** too is better known as a portraitist, but he did some early genre paintings, no doubt influencing his pupil, **Adriaen Brouwer** (1605–38), whose riotous tavern scenes were well-received in their day and collected by, among others, Rubens and Rembrandt. Brouwer spent only a couple of years in Haarlem under Hals before returning to his native Flanders to lead a dissolute existence, and influence the younger **David Teniers. Adriaen van Ostade** (1610–85), on the other hand, stayed there most of his life, painting skilful groups of peasants and tavern brawls, though his acceptance by the establishment in later life led him to water down the uncompromising realism he had learnt from Brouwer. He was teacher to his brother **Isaak** (1621–49), who before his early death produced a large number of open-air peasant scenes; subtle combinations of genre and landscape work.

E. V. Lucas dubbed Teniers, Brouwer and Ostade as 'coarse and boorish' beside **Jan Steen** (1625–79), who with Vermeer is probably the most admired Dutch genre painter. You can see what he had in mind: Steen's paintings offer the same Rabelaisian peasantry in full fling, but they go their debauched way in broad daylight, and nowhere do you see the filthy rogues in shadowy hovels favoured by Brouwer and Ostade. Steen is both more humorous and more moralistic, and he at once identifies with the hedonistic mob and reproaches them. Many of his pictures are illustrations of well-known proverbs of the time – popular epithets on the evils of drink or the transience of human existence that were supposed to teach as well as entertain.

Gerrit Dou (1613–75) was Rembrandt's Leiden contemporary and one of his first pupils – though it's difficult to detect any trace of the master's influence in his work. Dou instead initiated a style of his own: tiny, minutely detailed and beautifully finished views of a kind of ordinary life that was decidedly more genteel than Brouwer's. More admired for his painstaking attention to detail than for any special inventiveness he would, so they say, sit in his studio for hours waiting for the dust to settle before he could start work. Among his students were **Frans van Mieris** (1635–81), who continued the highly finished technique in small, intimate portrayals of the middle classes, and **Gabriel Metsu** (1629–67) – perhaps Dou's greatest pupil and another meticulous recorder of the Dutch bourgeoisie. His pictures often convey a blatant moral message if you can read the symbols. **Nicholas Maes** (1634–93) of Dordrecht was another of Rembrandt's many protégés, though a much later one than Dou: his early paintings were almost entirely genre, beautifully and sensitively executed but again with the little moral hints. In later life he devoted himself almost exclusively to a refined style of portrait work he had picked up in France.

As a native of Zwolle, **Gerard Ter Borch** (1617–81) found himself far from all these Leiden/Rembrandt connections, and despite several trips abroad to most of the artistic capitals of Europe, he remained very much a provincial painter all his life, depicting Holland's merchant class at play and becoming renowned for his curious doll-like figures and enormous dexterity in painting the textures of different cloths.

Ter Borch's ordered domestic scenes lead neatly on to Vermeer and **De Hooch** (1629–after 1684), whose simple depictions of everyday life with no trace of sentimentality or, refreshingly, moral commentary, represent this kind of painting at its height. De Hooch's favourite trick was to paint darkened rooms with an open door leading through to a sunlit courtyard; a trick that, with his favourite rusty red colour, make his work easy to identify and, at its best, exquisite. His later pictures would go on to reflect the encroaching decadence of the Dutch republic as his rooms become more richly decorated, his arrangements more contrived and his subjects far less homely. **Jan Vermeer** (1632–75) too was a master at depicting the play of natural light on indoor surfaces, and it's for this and the curious peace and intimacy of his pictures that he's best known. Again, a recorder of the better-heeled Dutch households, but like De Hooch without the moral tone, he is generally regarded – with Hals and Rembrandt – as one of the big three Dutch painters, though he was also, it seems, a slow worker and only about forty small paintings can be attributed to him with any certainty. Living all his life in his native **Delft**, Vermeer is the archetypal 17th-century Dutch painter – rejecting all the pomp and ostentation of the High Renaissance and instead quietly recording his contemporaries at home; painting for a public that demanded no more than that.

Portraits

Naturally, the ruling bourgeoisie of Holland's flourishing mercantile society wanted to put their own success on record too, so it's little wonder that portraiture was the best way for a young painter to make a living. **Michiel Jansz Miereveld** (1567–1641) was the first real portraitist of the Dutch republic, court painter to Frederick Henry in The Hague, but his stiff and rather conservative figures were soon superseded by the more spontaneous renderings of **Frans Hals** (1585–1666). Hals is perhaps best known for his 'Corporation-Pieces' – portraits of the Dutch civil guards that had been formed in most larger towns while the threat of invasion by the Spanish was still imminent. These large group pieces demanded a superlative effort of technique, as the painter had to give equal prominence to all subscribers while not just making them a collection of individual portraits. Hals achieved this remarkably, with innovative lighting effects and the subtle arrangement of his sitters, all put together in a fluid and dynamic composition. As well as these

Hals did many individual portraits, making his ability to capture fleeting and telling expressions his trademark. His pictures of children are particularly sensitive, though they sometimes border on the sentimental and many people prefer his later work, darker and more akin to Rembrandt. The best collection of Hals's work is in the Haarlem museum named after him, but most Dutch galleries, not least the Rijksmuseum, have good examples.

Jan Cornelisz Verspronck (1597–1662) and **Bartholomeus van der Helst** (1613–70) were the other great Haarlem portraitists after Frans Hals, Verspronck recognisable by the smooth, shiny glow he always gives to his sitters' faces. Van der Helst left Haarlem when he was young, to begin a solidly successful career as portrait painter to Amsterdam's burghers. His competent but unadventurous style owes little to Hals, but it was certainly more popular, and influenced a number of later painters – all of whom no doubt decided that while not very inventive, it was a lot more profitable to paint like this.

The reputation of **Rembrandt van Rijn** (1606–69) is still relatively young – 19th-century connoisseurs preferred Gerrit Dou – but he is now justly regarded as one of the greatest and most versatile painters of all time: while others confined themselves mainly to one pictorial category, Rembrandt's talents transcended them all. Born in Leiden, the son of a miller, he was apprenticed at an early age to **Jacob van Swanenburgh,** a then quite important local artist. At the time he shared a studio with **Jan Lievens** who, while he showed equivalent early promise, is now relatively forgotten. Rembrandt went up to Amsterdam to study under the fashionable **Pieter Lastman,** and from then on went from strength to strength, painting commissions for the Amsterdam elite and becoming an accepted member of the very highest society. Constantin Huygens acted as his agent, obtaining by means of his connections all of Rembrandt's more lucrative jobs. In 1634 he married Saskia van Ulenborch, daughter of the burgomaster of Leeuwarden and quite a catch for the still relatively humble Rembrandt. The artist's *self-portraits* at this time show the confident face of the career boy – on top of things and quite sure of where he's going. Rembrandt was the only 17th-century painter to submit himself regularly to this kind of pictorial examination and, because he painted them with the freedom of not having to work to a commission and gratify someone else's ego, they reveal their subject with a brutal realism quite unmatched in the portraiture of the time, even Rembrandt's own.

Rembrandt would not always be the darling of the Amsterdam smart set, but his fall from grace was still some way off when he painted the *Night Watch* – a group portrait popularly associated with the artist's decline in favour. Even though Rembrandt's fluent arrangement of his subjects was totally original at the time, there's nothing to say that the military company who commissioned the painting were anything but pleased with the result. More likely is the fact that the conservative Amsterdam burghers were not quite ready for his revolutionary genius which manifested itself in later years in obscurely lit pieces with a psychological insight he had previously reserved for paintings of himself. His patrons were certainly not enthusiastic enough about his art to support his taste for collecting paintings and his expensive house on Jodenbreestraat. In 1656 possibly the most brilliant artist the city would ever know was declared bankrupt, eventually dying thirteen years later, as his last self-portraits show, a broken and embittered old man. Most Dutch galleries have a Rembrandt or two, but you'll find the best collections in Amsterdam's Rijksmuseum or The Hague's Mauritshuis.

Throughout his career Rembrandt maintained a large studio, and his influence coloured the next generation of Dutch painters. Some – Dou, Maes – have already been mentioned and were more famous for their genre work. Others turned to portraiture.

Govert Flinck (1615–60) was perhaps Rembrandt's most faithful follower, ironically being given the job of decorating Amsterdam's new town hall after his teacher had been passed over. He died at a tragically young age before he could execute his designs, and Rembrandt was one of several artists commissioned to execute them. **Ferdinand Bol**'s work (1616–80) was so heavily influenced by Rembrandt that for a long time art historians couldn't tell the two apart. His later portraits are more individual but just how committed to painting he was is best shown by the fact that he gave it up in 1669, after marrying a rich widow. Most of the pitifully little extant work of **Carel Fabritius** (1622–54) was portraiture, but he too died young before he could properly realise his great promise as the most gifted of all Rembrandt's students. Generally regarded as the teacher of Vermeer, he forms a link between the two masters in that while adopting Rembrandt's technique, he reversed his practice of painting figures against a dark background, prefiguring the lighting and colouring of the Delft painter.

Landscape painters
Bruegel's paintings had paved the way for a new tradition of landscape painting in the 17th century, in their first-hand reproduction of native surroundings. **Gillis van Coninxloo** (1544–1607) imbued this with elements of fantasy, painting the richly wooded views he had seen on his travels around Europe as backdrops to his Biblical scenes. Probably the two most important early 17th-century landscape painters were **Hercule Seghers** (1590–1638) and **Esias van de Velde** (1591–1632). Seghers was apprenticed to Coninxloo and continued the style of forested and mountainous landscapes, some real, others not. His work is rare but it is believed to have been a considerable influence on the landscape work of Rembrandt. Van de Velde's quaint and unpretentious scenes show the first real affinity with the Dutch countryside but, though his influence was great, his mastery as a painter was soon well overtaken by his young pupil **Jan van Goyen** (1596–1656), a remarkable painter who belongs to the so-called 'tonal phase' of Dutch landscape painting. Van Goyen's early pictures were highly coloured and close to his teacher, but it didn't take him long to develop his markedly personal touch – using different tones of greens, browns and greys, and giving everything a characteristic shimmering haze. His paintings are, above all, of nature, and if he includes figures it's just for the sake of scale. Neglected until a little over a century ago, his fluid and rapid brushwork became more accepted as the Impressionists rose in stature.

A native of Haarlem, **Salomon van Ruysdael** (1600–70) was also directly affected by van de Velde and his works were for ages consistently confused with those of van Goyen – simple but atmospheric landscapes, not terribly adventurous. More esteemed is his nephew, **Jacob van Ruisdael** (1628–82) (the difference in spelling is consistent on all the fully signed pictures), who is generally considered the greatest of all Dutch landscapists. He heralded a more realistic phase, with fastidiously observed views of quiet flatlands dominated by stormy skies around his native Haarlem; pictures that were to influence European painters' impressions of nature right up to the 19th century – Constable certainly acknowledged a debt to him. His foremost pupil was **Meindert Hobbema** (1638–1709), whose *Avenue at Middelharnis* has a little place in everyone's knowledge of Dutch art, however scant. He followed Ruisdael faithfully, sometimes even painting the same views. Another artist whose reputation has declined in recent years, he gave up painting in later life for a more stable career in the wine trade.

Nicholas Berchem (1620–83) and **Jan Both** (1618–52) were the 'Italianisers' of Dutch landscapes. They studied in Rome and were there influenced by Claude, taking back to Holland rich, golden views of the world, full of steep gorges and hills, picturesque ruins and romantic wandering shepherds. **Allart van Everdingen** (1621–75) had much the same sort of approach, but his romanticism stemmed from his travels in Scandinavia which, after his return to Holland, he reproduced in all its mountainous glory.

Albert Cuyp (1620–91) stayed in Dordrecht all his life, painting what was probably the favourite city skyline of Dutch landscapists. He inherited the warm tones of the Italianisers, and his pictures are always suffused with a deep, golden glow.

One or two **more specialist 17th century painters** can also be included in this section. **Paulus Potter** (1625–54) is rated as the best painter of **domestic animals** ever. He produced a fair amount of work in his short life, all of animals, and he's best known for his lovingly executed pictures of cows and horses.

The accurate rendering of **architec-**

tural interiors became a specialist field with the work of **Pieter Saenredam** (1597–1665). Indisputably a great painter in his own right, he is easily recognised by his finely realised paintings of the inside of Dutch churches, which were admirably suited in their cool, light plainness. **Emmanuel de Witte** (1616–92) continued in the same vein, though his churches lack the spartan crispness of Saenredam's. **Gerrit Berckheyede** (1638–98) worked in Haarlem soon after but kept himself to the outside of buildings. Probably the least imaginative of all Dutch painters, he spent most of his time producing variations on the same scenes around town.

Still-life also became a thriving category of its own in the 17th century. Most common were 'Vanitas' groups – objects gathered together to remind the viewer of the transience of human life and the meaninglessness of all worldly pursuits – often a skull would be joined by a book, a pipe or a goblet, and some half-eaten food. Again, two Haarlem painters dominated this field: **Pieter Claesz** (1598–1660) and **Willem Heda** (1594–1680), who confined themselves almost entirely to these carefully arranged groups.

The 18th and 19th centuries: from Troost to Van Gogh

The inevitable results of Holland's boom years were what Kenneth Clark called 'defensive smugness and sentimentality', and by the time the first quarter of the 1700s was over, the creativity of the previous century had given way to what were to be years of little inspiration. The delicate cabinet-pieces of Dou and co. led to unnecessarily finnicky still-lifes and minute studies of flowers, as well as the finely finished portraiture and religious scenes of **Adriaen van der Werff** (1659–1722). **Gerard de Lairesse** (1640–1711) spent most of his time decorating the splendid civic buildings and palaces that were going up all over the place lest anyone should forget the glory of the Dutch republic; and like the buildings his style and influences were French. **Jacob de Wit** (1695–1754) continued where Lairesse left off, gaining more commissions in churches as Catholicism was allowed out of the closet.

Amidst all the decadence came **Cornelis Troost** (1697–1750), the only painter of any renown who, while he didn't produce anything really new, painted competent portraits and some neat and faintly satirical pieces that have since earned him the title of 'The Dutch Hogarth'. Cosy interiors continued to prove popular and the Haarlem painter, **Wybrand Hendricks** (1744–1831), satisfied demand with numerous proficient examples.

The 19th century began badly but once underway improved dramatically. **Johan Barthold Jongkind** (1819–91) was the first great artist to emerge, painting landscapes and seascapes that were to influence Monet and the early Impressionists; he spent most of his life in France and was exhibited in Paris with the Barbizon painters, though he owed less to them than to the 17th-century landscapes of Van Goyen *et al.*

Jongkind's work led logically on to the art of the **Hague School** – a group of painters based in that city between 1870 and 1900 who tried to re-establish a characteristically Dutch national school of painting. They did atmospheric studies of the dunes and polderlands around their native city – nature pictures that are characterised by grey, rain-laden skies, windswept seas and silvery flat beaches, all breathing pure sentiment and nostalgia. **J. H. Weissenbruch** (1824–1903) was in many ways a founder member, and he specialised in low, flat beach scenes dotted with stranded boats. **H. W. Mesdag** (1831–1915) – a banker turned artist late in life – concentrated on much the same things, but with more skill than imagination. **Jacob Maris** (1837–99) was perhaps the most typically 'Hague school' painter, with his rural and sea scenes, heavily covered by grey chasing skies. His brother, **Matthijs** (1839–1917), on the other hand, is probably the least predictable, ultimately getting fed up with his colleagues' straight observation and going to London to design windows. The youngest of the three artist brothers, **Willem** (1844–1910), is best known for his small, unpretentious studies of nature.

Anton Mauve (1838–88) did soft pastelly landscapes and was an early teacher of Van Gogh. Profoundly influenced by the French Barbizon painters – Corot, Millet *et al.* – he went to Hilversum in 1885 to set up his own group, which became known as the 'Dutch Barbizon'. **Jozef Israels** (1824–1911) has often been likened to Millet but he has more in common with the Impressionists, and his best pictures are sad, melancholy portraits and interiors. Lastly, **Johan Bosboom**'s (1817–91) church interiors sum up the nostalgia of the Hague School – shadowy, and populated by figures in 17th-century dress, they seem to yearn for Holland's Golden Age.

One of the most important of all modern painters, **Vincent Van Gogh** (1853–90) lived out most of his relatively short painting career in France. After countless studies of peasant life in his native North Brabant – studies which culminated in the sombre *Potato Eaters* – he went to live in Paris with his art-dealer brother Theo. There, under the influence of the Impressionists, his palette began to lighten, following the pointillist work of Seurat and 'trying to render intense colour and not a grey harmony'. However, his surroundings, rather than the theorising of the Impressionists, were to lead to real stylistic changes, and after quarrelling with his brother for two years he went south to Arles, to 'the land of blue tones and gay colours', where, struck by the harsh Mediterranean light, his characteristic style began to develop. After a disastrous attempt to live with Gauguin, and the much-publicised episode when he cut off part of his ear and presented it to a woman in a nearby brothel, he was committed to an asylum at St Remy, where he produced some of his most famous canvases – strongly coloured and with the paint thickly, almost frantically applied. There are superb collections of his work in both Arnhem and Amsterdam.

Jan Toorop (1858–1928) was very much an intellectual artist and, like Van Gogh, he went through multiple artistic changes, radically adapting his technique from a fairly conventional pointillism, through a tired expressionism, to later symbolist work that had an Art Nouveau feel. **G. H. Breitner** (1857–1923) was a better painter and one who refined his style rather than changed it. His almost snapshot impressions of his beloved Amsterdam figure among his best work and provide a hopeful start to the new century.

The 20th century: the search for a style
Artists at the beginning of the 20th century were faced with an immediate problem – what constituted a work of art? – a question that they would strive to answer via the myriad movements and trends that characterise the first half of this century, most of which found their way to the Netherlands at one time or another. After a trip to Paris, **Jan Sluyters** (1881–1957) brought back the concept of Fauvism and **Leo Gestel** (1881–1941) was an early pioneer of Cubism. **Piet Mondriaan** (1872–1944) developed the realism he had learnt from the Hague School painters – via Cubism, which he criticised for being too cowardly to depart totally from reality – into a complete abstraction of form, which he called **neo-plasticism.** This consisted of horizontal and vertical lines, the three primary colours and white, black and grey; freeing the work of art from the vagaries of personal perception and making it possible to obtain 'a true vision of reality' – an idea no doubt the result of Mondriaan's mystical belief that all the universe emanated from one source. It was a wish to re-create this perfect harmony that was at the centre of **De Stijl**: a movement set up around the magazine of the same name and one of the most important, and certainly the most 'Dutch', contributions to modern European art. It entailed all mediums – forging new notions in every aspect of design, from painting to interiors to architecture. **Theo van Doesburg** (1883–1931) was a co-founder and its major theorist. His work is similar to Mondriaan's except for the noticeable absence of the thick black borders. Van Doesburg also introduced diagonals into his work, calling his paintings 'contra-compositions' which, he said, were both more dynamic and more in touch with 20th-century life. **Bart van der Leck** (1876–1958) was the third member of the circle – identifiable by his white canvases covered by seemingly randomly placed, interlocking coloured triangles.

Mondriaan split with De Stijl in 1925, going on to attain new extremes of clarity and soberness. Despite that, his final period was perhaps his most exuberant, his visit to New York in the 1940s producing untypically mottled works like *Victory Boogie Woogie* – so named because of the artist's love of jazz. The best all-round collection of his work is in The Hague's Gemeente Museum.

During and after De Stijl, a number of other movements flourished, though they had a lot less impact and their influence was largely confined to Holland. The expressionist **Bergen School** was probably the most localised of all, apart from **Charley Toorop** (1891–1955), daughter of Jan, who developed a glaring but strangely sensitive realism of her own. **De Ploeg** (The Plough), centred on Groningen, was headed by **Jan Wiegers** (1893–1959) and influenced by Kirchner and the German Expressionists. Wiegers set out to capture the uninviting landscapes around his native town, producing violently coloured canvases that hark back to Van Gogh. Another group, known as the **Magic Realists**, surfaced in the 1930s, painting quasi-surrealist scenes that, according to their leading light, **Carel Willinck** (b. 1900) reveal 'a world stranger and more dreadful in its haughty impenetrability than the most terrifying nightmare'.

Post-war Dutch art began with **COBRA** – a loose grouping of like-minded painters from Holland, Belgium and Denmark, forming their label from the initial letters of their respective capitals. Their first exhibition was at Amsterdam's Stedelijk Museum in 1949, and it provoked a huge uproar at the time. **Karel Appel** (b. 1921) was at the centre of it all: his brutal abstract expressionist pieces with paint plastered on inches thick were, he maintained, necessary for the age; indeed inevitable reflections of it. As he remarked: 'I paint like a barbarian in a barbarous age.'

Of contemporary Dutch painters, the **Stedelijk Museum** in Amsterdam has the best collection. Look out for the abstract work of **Edgar Fernhout** and **Ad Dekkers,** and the multi-medium productions of **Jan Dibbets.**

A-Z OF ARCHITECTS AND SCULPTORS

MARI ANDRIESSEN (b. 1897) Certainly the most familiar of Dutch sculptresses, her work enjoyed a boom in post-war years with the demand for modern war memorials and imaginative municipal planning. Her most famous work is *The Docker* in Amsterdam, but you can expect to see most town centres adorned with at least one piece of her sculpture.

HENDRIK PETRUS BERLAGE (1856–1934) The father of modern Dutch architecture, his first important building was Amsterdam's *Beurs*: an eclectic work which paved the way for all subsequent architectural trends. He was also involved in town planning – he designed the layout of *Amsterdam-Zuid*. His last major work – The Hague's *Gemeente Museum* – is one of his least typical, more akin to Dudok in style.

JACOB VAN CAMPEN (1595–1657) The leading architect in Holland at the height of the Golden Age, and the main exponent of the plain Palladian style that predominated then. His buildings influenced generations of architects to come, and they certainly shaped the work of his contemporaries. Major works – *Amsterdam Town Hall (Royal Palace)* and *The Mauritshuis* in The Hague.

P. J. H. CUYPERS (1827–1921) *The* 19th-century Dutch architect, and the one most responsible for the Gothic revival in the Low Countries. His most famous buildings are the monumental neo-Renaissance *Centraal Station* and *Rijksmuseum* in Amsterdam but, a staunch Catholic, he was also responsible for countless neo-Gothic churches all over the country – among the best those in Leeuwarden and Hilversum. His son, Joseph, continued his father's work, most imposingly in the mighty *Cathedral of St Bavo* in Haarlem.

WILLEM MARINUS DUDOK (1884–1974) Municipal architect in Hilversum, his 'pièce de résistance' was the *town hall* there, which enjoyed world-wide acclaim and influence. His style is characterised by plenty of exposed brick, thin bands of windows and a general interlocking rectangle pattern.

CORNELIS FLORIS (1514–75) Architect and sculptor, and prime initiator of the northern Renaissance in *Antwerp Town Hall*.

HEMONY BROTHERS 17th-century makers of carillons, which you either love or hate. Churches and public buildings all over Holland have examples made by these men, many still in working order.

VICTOR HORTA (1861–1947) Commonly recognised as the creator of the first real Art Nouveau buildings in his *Hotel Tassel* in Brussels. Sadly, his later work was the last word in convention.

ROMBOUT KELDERMANS (1460–1531) Most renowned of Belgian master masons of the Gothic era; buildings include the towers of the *Bruges, Brussels* and *Louvain town halls.*

LIEVEN DE KEY (1560–1627) First architect of the Dutch Renaissance and probably the most distinctive and inventive one too. Haarlem's municipal architect, his showy and playful decoration has left a mark on today's city.

HENDRIK DE KEYSER (1565–1621) De Key's more celebrated and certainly more restrained contemporary. As Amsterdam municipal architect he was responsible for the first Protestant churches of that city, adapting them, with a centralised plan, to the nature of the new religion.

MICHAEL DE KLERK (1884–1923) The leading member of the Expressionist Amsterdam school, and distinctive in his free and expressive use of brickwork. Projects include the *Eigen Haard* estate in Amsterdam, and numerous buildings in Berlage's Amsterdam-Zuid district.

P. L. KRAMER (1881–1961) De Klerk's right-hand man in Amsterdam. His main project was the *De Dageraad* estate.

J. M. VAN DER MEIJ (1878–1949) Worked in the office of Edouard Cuypers, nephew of P. J., and produced Amsterdam's most prominent and elaborate Expressionist masterpiece in the *Scheepvarthuis* on Prins Hendrik Kade.

J. J. P. OUD (1890–1963) With Rietveld, the architectural branch of De Stijl. Stylistically, his buildings rejected the previous fancifulness of the Expressionists and instead strove for the sharpness and clarity associated with De Stijl.

JOSEPH POELAERT (1817–79) Foremost 19th-century Belgian architect, best known for his over-the-top, almost vulgar experiments in neo-classicism like the *Palais de Justice* in Brussels.

PIETER POST (1608–69) Van Campen's side-kick on the Amsterdam Town Hall and most loyal follower in later years, producing sober and unpretentious classical structures. The *Huis ten Bosch* near The Hague is his most acclaimed work.

ARTUS QUELLIN (1609–68) South Netherlands sculptor who worked on the Amsterdam town hall.

GERRIT RIETVELD (1888–1964) Integral member of De Stijl and most celebrated for the *Schroder House* in Utrecht and his chair, which was the ultimate in the rational, but not very functional De Stijl design. Later works include the *Van Gogh Museum* in Amsterdam.

ROTGER OF COLOGNE A member of the famous Parler family of medieval German masons. His uncle worked on Prague Cathedral and he himself was largely responsible for the *Cathedral of Cologne* and a number of *Dutch churches,* notably those of Kampen.

ARENT VAN S'GRAVENSANDE Yet another faithful disciple of van Campen. Municipal architect in Leiden and responsible for a number of buildings there, among them the *Lakenhal* and the domed *Marekerk* – the city's first Protestant church.

DANIEL STALPAERT Amsterdam municipal architect who executed the scheme for the enlargement of the city in the 17th century.

HENRY VAN DE VELDE (1863–1957) Belgian Art Nouveau architect, and very much influenced by the Arts and Crafts movement in England. As well as Brussels, he did a number of buildings in Germany, indirectly instigating, via Gropius, the Bauhaus. His best work in Holland is unquestionably the *Kroller-Müller Museum,* near Arnhem.

ROMBOUT VERHULST (1625–96) Sculptor who worked with Quellin on the Amsterdam town hall, and in various parts of the Netherlands.

P. AND J. VINGBOOMS 17th-century Dutch architects producing, in the wake of van Campen, grand but restrained town-houses with classic pilastered façades.

HANS VREDEMANE VRIES (1527–1606) Painter and graphic artist whose pattern books were a big influence on northern Renaissance architects.

JAN BAPTIST XAVERY 18th-century sculptor from Antwerp who settled in The Hague; best work in Haarlem's *Church of St Bavo.*

TWO DUTCH WRITERS: JAN WOLKERS AND SIMON CARMIGGELT

*One of Holland's more controversial contemporary writers, **JAN WOLKERS** has been likened to everything from 'a crude rancorous little man with a sadistic mind' to 'a sensitive Christian individual'. His debut was* Serpentina's Petticoat, *a collection of short stories that took the Dutch literary establishment by storm; so much so that copies were either sent back to him smeared with human excrement or covered in lipstick kisses. Certainly, critics have never sat on the fence where he's concerned, and over the years he's become accustomed to diverse reactions, courting outrage with an irreverent glee. An accomplished sculptor too, his work can be seen outside Amsterdam's central post office and in the Stedelijk Museum. The story below is from* Serpentina's Petticoat *and was translated by Adrienne Dixon; first published in English in* The Paper, *April 1983.*

VIVISECTION

I don't hear a thing. Not the creaking of his joints at the one hundred knee bends that normally wakes me up every morning, inexplicably, because it is not noisy. But maybe he utters strange shouts only until there is a movement under the sheet. I think of the pale skin of his thighs under which the muscles slide back and forth each time, as if snakes as thick as wrists are making frantic efforts to wriggle out of a linen sack, to escape. There is still no sound. The sheet covers my face and where it touches my forehead and nose it clings to my skin which is moist with sweat. Maybe he is smoothing out the creases in his civil defence uniform which he draped over the dresser last night so it looked as if there was a soldier without a body in the attic. To frighten the life out of me. Under it, the strange boots with their rows of gleaming buckles like an army of beetles fleeing from a picked-clean carcass. Beside the feet, the laces run away across the floor like desperate streams of black blood. But the calves of the boots are curved outward. The right trouser leg still sticks inside the boot but the left one has slipped out and hangs down hollow.

I see his fine Italian-fascist profile before me again, at the parade. The way he walked, rigid and straight among the others who trudged along half asleep. His left arm swinging stiffly back and forth, his right hand clenched white around the rifle strap. And you could hear them laughing and jeering and calling out to him. But inside you, it cheered, it sent a fist into your throat, it echoed inside your head.

And then the yellow streetcar begins to buzz in my head, the little yellow streetcar from Leiden to The Hague in which I will ride to the laboratory today. Only one stop. I could just as easily walk along the rusty gravel by the side of the rails. Past the house of professor Van Bever who, with that drooping grey moustache of his, will probably be smiling again like an unreal walrus among the hollyhocks by the garage in which his old-fashioned Rolls Royce is locked away like a big gleaming spider. He will put up his hand and call out in his husky voice: 'Hello there, little nature lover!'

And then the dark fir trees and the deep, secret ditch. But you can see that better from the rear platform of the streetcar, for along the bank there is a screen of reeds.

Then suddenly the hum of the streetcar is outside my head, above the roof, in the air which rocks back and forth under the rolling waves of sound amid which a crackle of dull pops can be heard, as of fireworks.

With a jerk I pull the sheet from my head and sit up in bed. It is half dark in the little attic room. My brother is standing on a chair and his body fills the opening of the slanted skylight. He is standing on tiptoe, his head hangs outside in the swelling thrum. His uniform is still draped across the dresser but as the lower doors have been opened, the legs of the riding breeches have swung away almost horizontally to the left and right, as if the ankles are being forcibly pulled sideways. It makes me think of the assassin of William the Silent. The boots have toppled over, on the floor in front of them there lie, on a cloth, a revolver, a rusty bayonet and an opened box of grease. I get out of bed, go up to my brother and nudge him gently in the

back.
– What is going on, I ask anxiously, starting to shiver in the spring-morning chill which comes flowing in through the window past his body.

He pulls his head in and jumps light-footedly backward from the chair. Then he looks at me gravely.

– We're at war, he says, they are dropping parachutists over the airfield. His face is pale and tense, only his jaw muscles tremble.

I climb up on the chair and hoist myself up by the galvanised window frame. I place my feet on a rail at the back of the chair.

The sky is filled with charcoal-coloured aircraft, square and rigid like charred coffins with their lids laid cross-wise over the front. In the distance, above the trees, hover tiny umbels each with a dark little figure hanging beneath, as if from an invisible point in heaven the fluffy head of a gigantic dandelion is being blown bare.

mirror

As I step down from the chair, with effort, my soles aching from the sharp chair-back, my brother is standing in his uniform in front of the large mirror which is set at an angle against the wall so as not to fall over. He is holding his arms stiffly against his sides and stares himself hard in the face, as if he has become an enemy who must stand up against the reflection in the mirror. His fatigue cap presses his dark curls low upon his forehead.

Suddenly I am assailed by an immense fear which takes shape in an explosion above the house. The roof seems to be heaving up and down. There is a chinking of glass and small objects fall from the crossbeams. The mirror quivers like a pond into which a stone has been thrown. I let out a piercing scream while I press my hands tightly against my stomach. Before my eyes the image of my brother disintegrates in the trembling glass. Horizontal streaks shoot across it and fill up with clear water. His pale face is squeezed flat by his black curls and bulges out sideways as in a distorting mirror. The mirror is a vertical battlefield in which guns and the wheels of tanks have all but wiped out a soldier. My brother has remained motionless. In the mirror he slowly recovers himself. From the glass

he stares at me sombrely. Then he turns on his heels, puts his arm around my shoulder, and we go out of the room together. As he lets me walk down the stairs in front of him he leaves his hand resting on my shoulder.

While I go into the bathroom my brother continues his way down the stairs. He treads softly. I can hear from the creaking of the wood that by stretching his arms he is letting the banisters take a large part of his weight. I know why. He is going to leave without saying goodbye to anyone. He knows he is not going to come back. Saying goodbye for ever you can only do by simply leaving. At the bottom of the stairs he stops for a moment. Then I hear the sigh of the glass swing door and the click of his metal heel-plates on the marble floor of the hall. I go to the wash stand and open the faucet. Then I look at my face in the mirror. It looks strange and contorted. Down my cheeks there run tears that seem to come out of my eyes without any effort on my part, without me crying. I bend deep down over the sink and let the cold water pour over my head until I have no feeling left in it and my skull seems filled with ice.

Downstairs in the passage I come across my mother. She has got the breakfast cloth in her hand and I follow her into the dining room.

– What a terrible day, and I meant to go and see grandma, she says with a sigh.

She does not mention the war at all. She unfolds the breakfast cloth and throws it over the round table. For a moment it stays up in a dome, because of the air that is trapped underneath. Then it collapses like the parachute of a landing soldier. As she smooths out the folds she asks where Peter is.

– He has just gone out, I say. In his uniform, I add hesitantly. Mother hurries out of the room. I know she is rushing to the front door, but the streets will be appallingly empty in both directions. Only the echo of his hurried steps will still be caught in the chilly shade of the early morning street. She will stare with eyes wild with fear at the empty space where he has turned the corner, trying to call back his silhouette from among the green of the shrubs, to fill the emptiness.

Only now do I notice from the coolness around me that the sunroom doors are open. From somewhere high up in the air there comes the rattle of machine guns. My father is kneeling on the terrace, his back turned toward me. He holds his hands clasped in front of his breast, his head lifted up. As I draw nearer and stand in the open door, I hear him praying: 'Strike them down from thy heaven like flies, O God of Abraham, Isaac and Jacob. Do not abandon thy people, destroy those that hate thee. Let the horizon burn in the fire of thy wrath.'

bomber

I follow my father's gaze. High up in the sky a slender fighter plane with a double tail is circling around a heavy bomber. And there constantly sounds a dry tick-a-tick, as if a typist is tapping quick, short sentences on a typewriter. Suddenly the bomber takes a plunge, drawing an exclamation mark of black smoke toward the earth. My father stands up and rubs his knees. As he walks past me into the house he looks at me absent-mindedly, with eyes in which the Burning Bush is still smouldering.

I walk into the back yard and jump up on the coal bin. Across a beam set into the masonry, over which the carpets are hung on Fridays, I climb onto the flat roof of the shed and lie headlong on the tar-and-gravel surface. Before me lies the corpse of a slow-worm. Carefully I press against the skin with a match stick, but I cannot yet poke through it. Its belly has already turned into a yellowish blue but I shall have to be patient for a few weeks or so before the rotting flesh will come away from the skeleton. The head, with the dull little eyes sunken deep in their sockets, looks crafty and peaceful, like a death announcement.

It suddenly strikes me that he only now looks like his Latin name, the way he lies there, fragile and a little dented: *Angius fragilis*. All animals get their Latin names when they are I dead, I muse. A centipede becomes a *Polydesmus,* a crested grebe a *Podiceps cristatus.* What is the Latin name of a human being? *Homo sapiens.* A name that smells of damp dust and old elder bush. I can do nothing for my brother, nothing. My father, yes, if he were to go on praying all day long. But his knees get sore before five minutes are up. I hide my face in the crook of my arm and press my eyes tightly against my sleeve to hold

back the tears. But my shirt becomes wet and my eyelids begin to smart. In the sunroom I hear my mother sobbing loudly with long drawn-out wails which my father punctuates with words that are meant to be comforting but that grow twisted with anguish.

I crawl backward on all fours, making sure that my head does not peep out above the edge of the roof. When my shoe touches the gutter at the far end of the roof, I slowly get to my feet. Through the young foliage of the apple trees I see my parents standing in the open doorway of the sunroom. My father has put his arms around my mother. Her face is red, his is dark and frowning. They gaze helplessly up at the sky. Holding on to the edge of the gutter I slowly let myself slide down along the stuccoed wall. For a moment I remain suspended, with stretched arms. Then I let myself drop into the weeds below with bended knees and walk through the alley into the street.

I walk simply on the sleepers between the rails. The yellow streetcar won't be running anyway today. There is fighting right up to the Haagse Schouw, a soldier told me at the streetcar stop. The sky is so blue that the sun is burning a hole in it. Only in the distance over the dunes there hovers a deceptive *fata morgana* of dark, growling insects and spirals of smoke. The rails, flashing white, stretch into the polder like two huge metal antennae scanning the danger. To the left rise the gloomy laboratory buildings, their walls festooned with hesitant trails of ivy, in a vain attempt to conceal their grimness.

Will doctor Van Stroom be there? What if the war has made him forget our agreement, what if he doesn't remember he promised me two white rats and a guinea-pig?

laboratory

I step across the low privet hedge separating the streetcar rails from the road and walk past the porter's lodge, which is empty, into the laboratory grounds.

Last year, in the summer vacation, I came here every day. I was allowed to feed the white mice, for a whole week. Ghastly creatures they were. If one of them had but the slightest injury the others were immediately attracted by the scent of blood. He'd be eaten alive. When his hind quarters had been nibbled bare, red and soggy like the discarded core of a stewed pear, he was still squeaking shrilly, his little front paws quivering. When he had been completely eaten up I put all the mice that were guilty of cannibalism in a large saucepan, stuck the gas tube into it and put the lid on it. The remaining gap between saucepan and lid, caused by the gas tube hanging over the side, I closed off with a damp cloth. Then I turned on the gas. For a while nothing happened, but then I heard muffled plops against the lid. They were leaping about frenziedly in a wild rhythm. After a time it began to grow fainter and then I heard nothing more. I turned the gas off and pulled the tube out of the pan. Cautiously I lifted the lid. There they lay, peacefully, their front paws clenched into tiny fists. Tears welled up in my eyes. I had taken revenge, but on whom? They were defenceless little mice. I took a paper bag and, picking them up one by one by their tails, carefully let them slide into it. Then I took a spade and went outside. The paper bag felt as if it had a warm soft roll in it. Under an old rhododendron bush I dug a hole. I put the bag into it and covered it up with earth. I flattened the churned-up ground and wrote S.O.S. on it with the handle of the spade.

The second turn on the left it was, and then the building on my right Physiology Laboratory, it says on a board beside the half-open door. I enter and walk through the small, white-tiled lobby, up some steps and into the large hall where the animals are operated on by clumsy students. I remember a big white rat being doped with ether under a glass bell. He sat up on his hind legs like a polar bear about to perform a trick. Then he tumbled head over heels a couple of times and fell down. A moment later he was lying on the table, his belly slit open. A student cut something out of his extruding intestines with a pair of scissors and deposited a tiny bloody morsel on a glass slide. Then he picked up the rat and tossed him into the zinc waste bin. When I looked into the bin later on, the rat was crawling about on the bottom. His intestines were hanging outside his body like a sidecar.

But today the hall is deserted. White coats are lying on the floor like mounds of dirty snow. So there have been students here. I also notice that there is a window open. I go to it, past rows of glass cupboards full of instruments and tables covered with bottles containing organs of small animals in spirits. Below the window is the door to the funeral chapel. Patients who die in the nearby hospital are taken there. In front of the door stands a furniture truck of which the doors half way down the side are open. A wide plank has been placed in position from the floor of the truck to the chapel entrance. There are students clustering around it, but I see no sign of doctor Van Stroom. A man appears in the open truck door. Although for the rest in civilian clothes, he is wearing a long military overcoat, which is hanging open. On his sleeve is a white band with a small red cross on it.

– Are you ready for them yet, Pete, he calls out to someone who is presumably inside the chapel.

– Okay, let's have them, a voice calls back.

The man vanishes inside the truck and returns a moment later, stopping as he drags something behind him over the floor. Then he pushes a soldier on to the plank. I stare at him transfixed and hold my breath in terror. He is dead, I think, he is stiff and hard.

He doesn't move. His boots are short and black and he is wearing a strange helmet which curves down an inch or two just in front of the ears, making him look like a monkey. The man in the chapel grabs hold of the boots and pulls the soldier inside. The red cross man has meanwhile shoved another soldier onto the plank.

– That one's parachute didn't open, he says to the students, who are watching speechlessly. We had to dig him up out of the mud.

What lies there resembles more than anything a clayey potato. It is barely more than three feet long. There is no sign of any arms, the head is pressed down between the shoulders. The smashed teeth gleam in the bloody patch where the mouth has been. The light blue eyes lie like stranded jellyfish on the muddy cheeks which have been pushed up to the eyebrows. The man in the chapel pulls the shapeless clump of flesh toward him with a hook. I turn away from the window, I dare not stay and watch any longer. I know that my brother is in that truck, cold and stiff, perhaps maimed.

I have been walking about all day. On the Hofdijk nobody stopped me from walking straight past the artillery which had taken up its position there and was sending shells whistling across to the airfield. They had also put a gun on the spot where the rich man was buried. Right next to his grave. Only the gleaming barrel poked out of the bushes. Just as if they had pointed the slender granite pillar, under which he lies, at an angle of forty-five degrees and were about to launch his skeleton into space, literally to sow death and destruction. But then the little dog that died of grief on his grave would have gone up as well. And he couldn't help it, he's an animal.

lights

But in the end I take the road back home. It is getting dark. People are standing in doorways talking to each other in muted voices. There are no lights burning anywhere, and the streetlights won't be lit either. In my mind there is the thought that I shall have to sleep on my own tonight and from now on every night. I shall throw away all the birds' nests and birds' skulls. And also the rabbit's skull with the long yellow front teeth. I shall have to wedge a match stick or a piece of cardboard between the two lower doors of the dresser to stop them from swinging open of their own accord. I wonder whether my mother and father know yet that my brother is dead? I dare not tell them.

The side door is locked. I cannot sneak up to my room, unnoticed. I put my hand into my pocket and switch on the little flashlight I bought today with the money I had intended to buy a grass snake with. The light shines faintly through the fabric of my pants. But I don't take the flashlight out of my pocket because there is no light burning anywhere. Slowly I walk back into the street. Our house looks gloomy and deserted, with wide-eyed black windows. Without making a sound I step across the low fence into the front yard. In the gleaming side window of the bay my silhouette approaches the house. I stop by the window, stick the flashlight into my mouth and switch it on again. A red coal fire starts to glow behind my cheeks. It makes my face look all the more hollow and thin. Then, through the reflection of the red glow, I suddenly see

my mother sitting behind the window. She has swivelled the armchair around and sits facing the street. She has fallen asleep. Her face, puffy and pale, melts into the darkness of the room. Her arms are lying on the armrests of the chair. I switch the flashlight off and take it out of my mouth. As I walk to the door I wipe the little glass ball, which has become wet with spittle, dry in the palm of my hand.

SIMON CARMIGGELT *is a Dutch literary institution. Seventy years of age, for nigh on forty of them he has contributed a regular column to* Het Parool, *the Amsterdam daily he helped found as a war-time anti-German newssheet. He writes under the pen-name 'Kronkel' (twist or kink), short pieces that are concise comments on everyday life, mixing wry anecdote with razor-sharp observation. As the author himself says: 'I write about people, what makes them tick, what they do, what they say.' It's a much imitated form, and annual anthologies are perpetual best-sellers. Carmiggelt has produced something like 9,000 of his 'Kronkels' in all and three are reprinted below from a book called* I'm Just Kidding, *translated by Elizabeth Willems-Treeman and first published in English in 1972.*

CORNER

In a café in the Albert Cuypstraat, where the open-air market pulses with sounds and colour, I ran into my friend Ben.

'Did you know Joop Groenteman?' he asked.

'You mean the one who sold fruit?' I replied.

'Yes. You heard about his death?'

I nodded. A fishmonger had told me.

'It's a shame,' said Ben. 'A real loss for the market. He had a nice stall – always polished his fruit. And he had that typical Amsterdam sense of humour that seems to be disappearing. He'd say "Hi" to big people and "lo" to little ones. If somebody wanted to buy two apples, he'd ask where the party was. No one was allowed to pick and choose his fruit. Joop handed it out from behind the plank. Somebody asked him once if he had a plastic bag, and he said, "I got false teeth. Ain't that bad enough?" He never lost his touch, not even in the hospital.'

'Did you go see him there?' I inquired.

'Yes, several times,' Ben said. 'Once his bed was empty. On the pillow lay a note: "Back in two hours. Put whatever you brought on the bed." He had to go on a diet because he was too fat. They weighed him every day. One morning he tied a portable radio around his waist with a rope, put his bathrobe on over it, and got on the scale. To the nurse's alarm he'd suddenly gained eight pounds. That was his idea of fun in the hospital. During one visit I asked him when he'd get out. He said, "Oh, someday soon, either through the front door or the back." '

Ben smiled sadly.

'He died rather unexpectedly,' he resumed. 'There was an enormous crowd at his funeral. I was touched by the sight of all his friends from the market standing round the grave with their hats on and each one of them shovelling three spadesful of earth on his coffin. Oh well, he at least attained the goal of his life.'

'What goal?' I asked.

'The same one every open-air merchant has,' Ben answered. 'A place on a corner. If you're on a corner, you sell more. But it's awfully hard to get a corner place.'

'Joop managed it, though?'

'Yes – but not in the Albert Cuyp,' said Ben. 'That corner place was a sort of obsession to him. He knew his chance was practically nil. So then he decided that if he couldn't get one while he was alive, he'd make sure of it when he died. Every time the collector for the burial insurance came along, he'd say, "Remember, I want a corner grave." But when he did die, there wasn't a single corner to be had. Well, that's not quite right. It just happened that there was one corner with a stone to the memory of someone who had died in the furnaces of a concentration camp. Nobody was really buried there. And the cemetery people gave permission to have the stone placed somewhere else and to let Joop have that plot. So he finally got what he wanted. A place on the corner.'

FAREWELL

My mother died as she had always hoped she would: gentle death called for her at night while she slept in her own bed in her own house. She had lived there thirty-nine years, first with her family, and after the war alone. All our

attempts to persuade her to move to a rest-home were frustrated by her steadfast refusal.

'I'm not going to live with all those old women,' she said to me. She was then over eighty. We could observe the marks of this age upon her when we entered the room on the first floor where she spent her last years, but after talking a quarter of an hour her face became young, probably because she laughed so much. Her humour could not be destroyed, although life did its best.

I remember how merrily she told us, not long ago, about an arrangement she had made with a friend who lived next door – a widow in her late seventies. The friend had said, 'You're all alone all day. Give me your key and I'll drop in every morning to see how you are.'

'Very well,' my mother had replied, 'but you're also alone every day, so you give me your key, or I won't give you mine.'

The exchange was made. When Mother heard her neighbour opening the door in the morning, she always called down from upstairs, 'No, I'm not dead yet.'

But on that Friday morning she could no longer give this reassurance. She had gone to sleep for ever – without having been ill, without becoming senile, without suffering, and without ever having had to be dependent on anyone. The evening before she had enjoyed herself immensely watching a play on television. And on her calendar for Friday she'd written, 'Go to hairdresser,' for we were coming to visit her on Saturday, and she wanted to look her best for us.

I have happy memories of our visits to her because they were always so much fun. She'd tell us everything that had happened to her recently, and that was a great deal, for her life was busy and her schedule full through her very last day. Good weather or bad, she travelled about The Hague by bus or tram. She refused to take a taxi, no matter how much I pleaded with her.

'If I listened to you,' she'd say, 'I'd end up in the poor-house.'

As a matter of principle, she never telephoned me.

'If you're interested in me,' she decreed, 'it's up to you to call.' When I did so and inquired how she was, she always answered 'I'm fine,' although she had all sorts of infirmities. But she refused to whimper about them.

A couple of years ago she had to go to a hospital to have her gall-bladder removed. I heard of it quite by chance from an acquaintance, because my mother had told me nothing. When I entered her hospital room that evening, she said in astonishment, 'Have you found me already?'

She had not expected it. That was the fundamental principle by which she lived: she wished to expect nothing from others and to build upon her own strength alone. Swift death had allowed her to stick to it till her last breath. There was but one little blemish: she died on my wife's birthday, so that the party for our grandchildren, with cakes and decoration, had to be cancelled at the last moment. Mother would have blamed herself harshly, for her love for little children was inexhaustible.

Day after day my wife and I have said to each other, 'She could not have longed for a more perfect death.' And that is true. But the memories of her courageous life still well up unavoidably.

When my granddaughter – five years old and every inch a woman – heard that her great-grandmother had died, she flew straight to the essence by asking piteously, 'Oh are all her things by themselves now? All her pans and her dishes – are they all alone?'

'Yes,' I said.

MAN

My six-year-old granddaughter Klaartje and her five-year-old cousin David were walking home with me, for they were going to eat with us. Two-year-old Ijsbrand had also wanted to come along for the walk, but I had refused, cheerfully yet firmly. He is too much for me. If he breaks loose and takes off, his speed is so great that I can't possibly catch him. In addition, he has surprising habits that I am unable to cope with.

The last time I was at his house he was playing very intently on the floor with toy automobiles. Suddenly he let his britches drop, squatted down, ejected a substantial glob, pulled up his pants, and walked briskly to the toy-chest. He returned with some sections of fence belonging to the railway set, put them around his achievement, and set up a police car to guard the lot. When his mother, despite these security measures, wanted to begin a cleaning-up operation, he shouted 'That's mine!'

Such things don't happen to me with David and Klaartje. They're a congenial pair, for they have wedding plans. The chronological fact that he's a year younger than the bride doesn't sit so well with David, to be sure. He compensates for it, however, with the biological fact that he is a man and can therefore do everything better than a woman.

When Klaartje, during our walk, suddenly exclaims, 'Did you hear that, Grandfather – I burped!', David counters, in as blasé a tone as possible, 'I burp all the time. I fart all the time, too.'

'Well, well.'

A little girl, hand in hand with her mother, approaches us. She smiles and says when she's close by, 'Hello, David.'

'Hello, Miriam,' he replies.

'I'm not Miriam – I'm Gale,' the child says and walks on in a bit of a pique.

'Does she go to your school?' I ask.

David nods. Then he says, 'I know so many girls – that's why I always get their names wrong.'

A man in overalls emerges from a house; in his arms he is carrying a black dog, which he takes to a delivery van parked near by.

Klaartje says to him tenderly, 'Where's the little dog going?'

'Him? In the soup, for supper,' says the man, disappearing into the van.

'Oh . . .' murmurs Klaartje, deeply shocked.

But David asks, 'Why is that dog going in the soup?'

'Oh, I don't think he is,' I answer.

'But that man said he was.'

'He was just joking.'

'Why was he joking?'

'Oh, just because,' I say. 'I think he wanted to be funny.'

'I don't think it's funny at all,' declares David. And there's something in that.

By this time we're close to my house. Klaartje suddenly begins dancing about in a manner whose significance I recognise.

'Do you *have* to?' I ask.

'Yes, yes!' she exclaims.

'Run as hard as you can, then. Grandmother will let you in.'

She flies away over the municipal grass.

Watching her go, David says, 'A peewie is easier.'

And, to demonstrate, he pulls it out and proceeds to water a near-by tree. Then, with something of sympathy in his tone, he adds, 'She can't do this.'

LANGUAGE

Dutch is a Germanic language – the word itself is a corruption of 'Deutsch', a label inaccurately given by English sailors in the 17th century. It's unlikely you'll need to speak anything other than English in Amsterdam: the Dutch have a seemingly natural talent for languages and your own attempts at their language may be met with amusement. Out of the capital things aren't quite so cosmopolitan, but even so the following words and phrases should be all you'll need to get by. You'll find a detailed Food glossary on p. 7. Of the available phrase-books, *Travellers Dutch* (Pan £1.25) is a useful companion, and to continue your studies have a look at *Colloquial Dutch* (RKP £3.95).

Pronunciation is much like English, but with a few differences: *v* is like the English *f* in *father*, *w* like the *v* in *vat*; *j* is the same as the initial sound of *yellow*; *ch* and *g* are like the hard sound in the Scottish *loch*; *ng* is as in *bring*, not *finger*, and *nj* as in *onion*. Otherwise double consonants keep their separate sounds – *kn* for example is never like the English *knight*. Vowels are lengthened by doubling the letter: *a* is like the English *cat*, *aa* like *cart*; *e* like *let*, *ee* late; *o* as in *pop*, *oo* in *pope*; *u* is like *wood*, *uu* the French *tu*; *au* and *ou* sound as in the English *ow*, *ei* and *ij* as in *fine*, *oe* as in *soon*; *eu* is like the French diphthong in *leur*.

Basic and greetings

Yes	Ja
No	Nee
Please/you're welcome	Alstublieft
No/thank you	Nee/dank u/bedankt
Sorry	Pardon
Hello/goodbye	Dag/tot ziens
Do you speak English?	Spreekt u Engels?
I don't understand	Ik begrijp . . . niet
How do I get to . . . ?	Hoe kom ik naar . . . ?
Where is?	Waar is?
How far to?	Hoe vaar naar?
Far/near	Ver/dichtbij
Left/Right/Straight on	Links/rechts/rechtuit gaan
Toilets	Toileten
Women/men	Dames/heren
When?	Waneer?
Why?	Waarom?
Post office	Postkantoor
Stamp(s)	Postzegel(en)
Bank	Bank
Exchange	Wisselkantoor
Cashier	Kassier
Ticket Office	Kaartjesloket

Asking for things

I want	Ik wil
I don't want	Ik wil niet . . . (verb) Ik wil geen . . . (noun)
How much is	Wat kost
It's too expensive	Het is te duur
Free	Vrij
Big/small	Groot/klein
Open/shut	Open/gesloten
Push/pull	Duwen/trekken
New, young/old	Nieuw, jong/oud

Good morning	Goeiemorgen
Good afternoon	Goeimiddag
Good evening	Goedenavond
Good night	Welterusten

Some signs

Bellen s.v.p	Please ring
Ingang	Entrance
Uitgant	Exit
Inlichtingen	Information
Toegang vrij	Free admission
Verboden te roken/niet roken	No smoking
Gevaar	Danger
Eenrichtings-verkeer	One way
Let op	Look out
Pas op	Beware
Rijwielpad	Bikes only
Fietspad	Cycle track
Toegang verboden	No entry

Monday	Maandag
Tuesday	Dinsdag
Wednesday	Woensdag
Thursday	Donderdag
Friday	Vrijdag
Saturday	Zaterdag
Sunday	Zondag

0 nul	12 twaalf	30 dertig
1 een	13 dertien	40 veertig
2 twee	14 veertien	50 vijftig
3 drie	15 vijftien	60 zestig
4 vier	16 zestien	70 zeventig
5 vijf	17 zeventien	80 tachtig
6 zes	18 achttien	90 negentig
7 zeven	19 negentien	100 honderd
8 acht	20 twintig	200 tweehonderd
9 negen	21 een en twintig	1000 duizend
10 tien	22 twee en twentig	
11 elf		

ONWARDS FROM HOLLAND

Travel onwards from the Netherlands means just about anywhere in Europe, and whether you're hitching, driving or training it, you're within reach of the warmer climes of Mediterranean Europe or more hostile environments further north.

Apart from the rest of the Low Countries, **WEST GERMANY** is the most obvious next step, though it offers little this far north and you'll most likely want to avoid the industrialised mess of the Ruhr conurbation. Still, there is **Cologne,** itself in part a bleak modern city, but not without its attractions, and definitely worth a visit on your way south. There are regular train connections from a number of Dutch cities and you can be there in a little over three hours from Amsterdam, set down in the shadow of the massive Cathedral, which towers graciously over the mostly post-war heart of the city – the grandiose Gothic produce of a number of different centuries. The city also has a diverse selection of museums and galleries, some very good, plus a fair bit of action at night in its more bohemian quarters. Deeper into Germany, trains run at least once a day from the Hook of Holland direct to **Berlin,** finishing up eventually in Warsaw and Moscow. You can pick them up in Rotterdam or Utrecht, and the journey takes around twelve hours.

From Groningen you can make your way slowly up to **DENMARK** via the seedy port-towns of Bremen and Hamburg. **Bremen** retains an explorable medieval centre and **Hamburg** a somewhat notorious combination of prestigious museums and what is probably the last word in European red-light districts. From there it's just five train/ferry hours to the equally vibrant enticements of **Copenhagen.** If you're in more of a hurry, two trains a day leave Amsterdam for Copenhagen, via Hamburg, and take about twelve hours.

You can reach the further parts of **SCANDINAVIA** either via Denmark or by a direct ferry connection from Amsterdam. *DFDS* run regular summer services – and offer 50 per cent reductions to InterRail travellers – to **Bergen,** Norway's second and more atmospheric city, within striking distance of some breathtaking fjord scenery a little further north. The same company sail up to **Gothenburg,** described by some guidebooks as 'gateway to northern Europe', and certainly an ideal first port of call if you're planning a thorough look at Scandinavia. From here you're well poised for a full assault on all the respective capitals of **Stockholm, Oslo** and **Copenhagen.**

Last, if you're heading on south for sun and sea, two major routes serve the purpose: for the south of France and Spain, Paris is the logical first stop; otherwise forge straight on down to Basle – trains leave Amsterdam something like three times a day, and are even more frequent from Brussels and Luxembourg. Those making for Yugoslavia, Greece or even Turkey, should go via Munich, which in itself isn't a bad place to stop over – trains run direct from Amsterdam twice daily. If you're hitching, you can follow roughly the same paths, but it's good advice – unless you're actually visiting it – to avoid France at all costs, since lifts can be few and far between. If you're thinking of thumbing it down to Italy, for instance, it's far better to pick up long lifts down the German autobahns than get stuck somewhere on the outskirts of Paris. If you *are* aiming for southern France or Spain, try going via Luxembourg and Dijon – the roads aren't as busy but you do avoid the capital.

INDEX

HELP US UPDATE

We've made a lot of effort to ensure that **The Rough Guide to Amsterdam and Holland** is thoroughly accurate. However, things do change from time to time, and if you think we've got something wrong, or you feel more should be said about a particular place, please write and tell us. We'll be revising the book before long and hope to make it better. We'd very much appreciate any views or accounts, and the best letters will be rewarded with a free copy of any one of the Rough Guide series. Send them along to:

The Rough Guides,
c/o Routledge & Kegan Paul,
14 Leicester Square,
London WC2H 7PH.